D0794366

AUTHOR AND PRINTER IN VICTORIAN ENGLAND

VICTORIAN LITERATURE AND CULTURE SERIES

Karen Chase, Jerome J. McGann, *and* Herbert Tucker, *General Editors*

———•••◄◆►•••———

DANIEL ALBRIGHT
> Tennyson: *The Muses' Tug-of-War*

DAVID G. RIEDE
> Matthew Arnold and the Betrayal of Language

ANTHONY WINNER
> Culture and Irony: *Studies in Joseph Conrad's Major Novels*

JAMES RICHARDSON
> Vanishing Lives: *Style and Self in Tennyson, D. G. Rossetti, Swinburne, and Yeats*

JEROME J. MCGANN, EDITOR
> Victorian Connections

ANTONY H. HARRISON
> Victorian Poets and Romantic Poems: *Intertextuality and Ideology*

E. WARWICK SLINN
> The Discourse of Self in Victorian Poetry

LINDA K. HUGHES and MICHAEL LUND
> The Victorian Serial

ANNA LEONOWENS
> The Romance of the Harem
> Edited and with an Introduction by Susan Morgan

ALAN FISCHLER
> Modified Rapture: *Comedy in W. S. Gilbert's Savoy Operas*

BARBARA TIMM GATES, EDITOR
> *Journal of Emily Shore,* with a new Introduction by the Editor

RICHARD MAXWELL
> The Mysteries of Paris and London

FELICIA BONAPARTE
> The Gypsy-Bachelor of Manchester: *The Life of Mrs. Gaskell's Demon*

PETER L. SHILLINGSBURG
> Pegasus in Harness: *Victorian Publishing and W. M. Thackeray*

ALLAN C. DOOLEY
> Author and Printer in Victorian England

AUTHOR
AND
PRINTER
IN
VICTORIAN
ENGLAND

Allan C. Dooley

UNIVERSITY PRESS OF VIRGINIA
Charlottesville and London

THE UNIVERSITY PRESS OF VIRGINIA
Copyright © 1992 by the Rector and Visitors
of the University of Virginia

First published 1992

Library of Congress Cataloging-in-Publication Data

Dooley, Allan C.
    Author and printer in Victorian England / Allan C. Dooley.
    p.   cm. — (Victorian literature and culture series)
    ISBN 0-8139-1401-9
    1. English literature—19th century—Criticism, Textual.
    2. Authors and publishers—England—History—19th century.
    3. Literature publishing—England—History—19th century.
    4. Printing—England—History—19th century.   I. Title.
    II. Series.
    PR468.T48D66   1992
    820.9'008—dc20   92–10420
                                                             CIP

Printed in the United States of America

To Susan, my wife, with deepest gratitude and affection this book is dedicated

Contents

Preface

I have been assisted during the writing of this book by many friends, colleagues, and institutions, all of whom deserve my sincere thanks. For access to research materials both published and unpublished, I am indebted to the curators and librarians at the Armstrong Browning Library, Baylor University; the Berg Collection, New York Public Library; the British Library; the Cleveland Public Library; the Henry E. Huntington Library and Art Gallery; the Department of Special Collections, Kent State University Library; the London College of Printing; the Morgan Library; the University of Virginia Library; the Wing Collection, Newberry Library; the St. Bride Printing Library; the Tinker Library and the Beinecke Library, Yale University.

My researches have been supported by grants in aid from the Bibliographical Society of America; the Newberry Library; the Research Council, the Office of Research and Sponsored Programs, and the College of Arts and Sciences, Kent State University; in less direct but no less essential ways I have been aided by the director and staff of the Institute for Bibliography and Editing at Kent State University.

Many of the letters of Matthew Arnold quoted in this study are cited from the forthcoming edition of Arnold's letters, with the generous permission of the editor, Cecil Y. Lang, and publisher, Harvard University Press. Grateful acknowledgement is also due to Herbert G. Smart, F.I.O.P., F.R.S.A., for permission to quote from his as yet unpublished account of stereotyping and electrotyping, deposited in the St. Bride Printing Library.

My deepest gratitude must go to those who have done what true scholars will always do for one another—the referring, sharing, recalling, reviewing, checking, rechecking, confirming, looking into, digging out, prompting, inquiring, and encouraging that constitute scholarly culture. I thank them all, with special warmth to Robert Bamberg, Nancy Birk, Betty Coley, Susan Crowl, Susan Dooley, James Edwards, Paul Gehl, Bruce Harkness, Jack Herring, W. Speed Hill, Rita Humphrey, Philip Kelley, Roma A. King, Cecil Y. Lang, John Maynard, James Mosley, Louis Paskoff, Sidney W. Reid, and James M. Wells.

At the University Press of Virginia, Cathie Brettschneider and Gerald Trett have repeatedly provided expert editorial guidance and assistance, for which I thank them.

A word about gender references: in the nineteenth century, the world of the printing trade was uniformly male; in the name of historical accuracy I use *he* / *him* / *his*, *man*, and *boy* when referring to the various workers in the printing house. The realm of Victorian authors, readers, and critics, however, was quite notably *not* exclusive by gender, and I have adjusted my forms of reference accordingly.

AUTHOR AND PRINTER IN VICTORIAN ENGLAND

Introduction

I think it would be better to send me every proof twice over. I should like the text to be as correct as possible. To be sure this proceeding would somewhat delay the publication, but I am in no hurry.

Tennyson to the publisher of his *Poems*, 1832

The strain of thought generally is no doubt much too doleful and monotonous. I had no notion of how monotonous till I had the volume printed before me. I thought too when the poems were in manuscript they would possess a more general attraction.

Arnold to a friend, upon first seeing *Empedocles on Etna*, 1852

THE CENTRAL PROPOSITION of this study is that printing technology shapes texts. To be more precise, I argue here that several technical advances employed by Victorian printers significantly influenced the texts of classic works of English literature as we read them today. The ways in which the tastes of the rapidly expanding Victorian reading public shaped the literature of the period have often been noticed and documented at length. Far less attention has been given to the potential literary influences of the series of technological improvements that constituted, by the end of the nineteenth century, a revolution in printing. This revolution touched every aspect of book production, from initial typesetting through reprinted editions, and the technological changes were powerful enough to affect both the writing of Victorian literature and our reading of it. To demonstrate as fully as possible the evidence for this view, most of this book is empirical and historical, devoting itself to the exploration and analysis of the practices and interactions of specific Victorian authors, printers, and publishers. The few more general and theoretical observations I have to offer about textual studies are confined to the final chapter.

The present work began with several specific problems which emerged from my study of the works of one author. While attempting to edit some of the poems of Robert Browning, I came to wonder why there are surviving manuscripts of all of his later works but so few of the earlier and much more famous ones. The sharp rise in Browning's reputation after his return to England in 1861, as well as the growth of book collecting and the trade in literary artifacts, might have been sufficient to prompt the author, publisher, or printer to preserve the later manuscripts, but where had the earlier ones gone? Why, for example, do we have the printer's copy for only one poem (the final one) from Browning's richest collection, *Men and Women*? From Philip Gaskell's account of printing during the period,[1] I inferred that unless Browning made special requests, his manuscript may never have been returned to him, either with his proofs or after his work was published. If Browning's poems were handled in the typical way, the printer's copy for *Men and Women* may have been discarded when typesetting was done; perhaps the survival of the manuscript of "One Word More" was a fluke. Browning himself made special arrangements to recover the manuscript of *The Ring and the Book* (1868–69), but in the 1870s and 1880s his manuscripts seem to have come back to him routinely. Had he issued a standing order, or had printers' practices changed?

Then there was the matter of Browning's close correction of proofs and his habit of making numerous small revisions at every opportunity. He gave extensive, minute attention to every detail of his individual and collected editions, often requiring multiple stages of proof. The numerous surviving proofs and the collation of the editions he supervised demonstrate Browning's success at getting his revisions incorporated into his texts, and in his last years he carefully prepared the printer's copy and closely scrutinized the proofs for every page of the massive *Poetical Works* of 1888–89. Was this idiosyncratic to him, and the witness to his renowned dedication to accuracy, or had changes in printing methods somehow made such meticulous control of the printed text more possible? As I tried to discover what patterns of behavior Browning might have been adhering to or departing from, it began to appear that his close involvement with the production of his volumes of poetry was typical, not eccentric. The Victorian authors I investigated—Dickens, Arnold, Eliot, Hardy, Trollope, and others—seemed to be strikingly knowledgeable about and active in the printing of their books, perhaps more so than authors before or since. Furthermore, they apparently understood immediately the significance of the technical advances and moved to exploit them.

Modern scholarly studies of Victorian printing technology, and indeed studies of the entire machine-press period, are few and brief. Nowhere could I find a detailed description of the progress of a typical book from manuscript through collected editions during the machine-press period. Gaskell's *From Writer to Reader* presents individual case studies on several Victorian authors, but cautions that generalization becomes difficult after printing machines came into wide use. Difficult it has sometimes been, but I have tried to establish, from the historical record of actual practice, the typical patterns of book production and textual change which textual scholars can expect to lie behind a given copy of a literary work produced in mid-Victorian England. The fact that major Victorian authors have in recent decades been receiving the attentions of scholarly editors for the first time made the need for such an effort more urgent, and I hope that this work will prompt further studies of the relationships between authorship and printing. I am convinced that the modern editor of a Victorian writer cannot confidently employ a traditional bibliographic approach, especially as regards revised, collected, and stereotyped editions. The revolution in printing technology during the nineteenth century changed the relations of authors to the printed texts of their works so significantly as to render inadequate some scholarly methods which were effective for earlier texts.

Some brief examples, all of which are illustrated and discussed at length in the ensuing chapters, will help to show how distinctly practices differed after the arrival of the machine-press period.

(1) The conventional wisdom asserts that before our century, a printer's compositors closely followed the author's manuscript as to its wording, but freely altered and regularized spelling, capitalization, and punctuation. In fact, though Victorian printers tried to continue this common practice of earlier eras, Victorian authors, even when they were neophytes, often demanded and achieved substantial control over the so-called accidentals of their printed works.

(2) The fact that Dickens revised extensively during the proof stages of his first editions, while Arnold revised heavily for his collected editions, could be attributed to differences in their personalities, circumstances, and writing habits. That different authors compose differently is true, but in the Victorian era this may not be a complete explanation. The state of printing technology at a given date determined whether an author could receive proofs in complete sets or piecemeal, and whether the manuscript or printed copy could be sent along with the proofs.

(3) Scholars have customarily assumed that stereotype printing, which became almost universal during the nineteenth century, so stabilized a printed text that reimpressions of an edition are of minor or no textual significance. While publishers and printers since the introduction of stereotyping promoted this supposed fixing of the printed text as a great

advantage of the process, there is plentiful evidence that stereo plates could be freely altered. Many authors knew this and sent their printers or publishers lists of changes intended to make each subsequent impression of an edition conform more exactly to the author's desires than the last. Running counter to this, stereotype plates were subject to an insidious typographical entropy through which textual changes that nobody intended could occur.

(4) Almost every aspect of the nineteenth-century revolution in printing was aimed at increasing the speed with which books—large numbers of books—could be produced. Though the historical record often supports the commonsense view that speed is an enemy of accuracy and a limitation on authorial control, some inventions actually aided the author's cause. The introduction of typefounding machines increased the supply of type and speeded up typesetting so that eventually whole sets of proofs could be delivered to the author. Later, high-speed printing machines and stereotyping made it customary to issue an edition in numerous small impressions, each of which presented an opportunity for revision and correction.

These examples of the changes wrought by printing technology point to changes in how and to what extent authors controlled the printed texts of their works. Nothing portrays the importance of the interaction of printing and authorship more clearly than the changes in how proofs were handled; advances in technology made it possible for an author to see an entire work in proof. The ability to view a long work as a whole, to have "the power of fitting the beginning of his work to the end," as Trollope put it, must have changed the nature of revision.[2] Consider the situation in the 1830s: the author of a book sent in a complete manuscript, but received from the printers only a few sheets of page proof at a time; these, the only proofs the author would see, had to be marked without the printer's copy and returned as quickly as possible with a minimum of alterations. Small wonder that the resulting edition often reflected neither what was in the manuscript nor what the author actually wanted. By contrast, an author in the 1880s was likely to receive, within a week or two of submitting a manuscript, a complete set of galley proofs with the printer's copy for comparison; publishers encouraged authors to make whatever changes they wanted, and revised proofs continued to be exchanged until the text gained the author's approval. Furthermore, each subsequent edition and impression of a work could incorporate any later revisions and corrections, enhancing the author's control still more.

The technology which provided so many new opportunities also placed new limits on authorial control. While each impression from stereo plates might present a chance to correct textual errors, publishers and printers discouraged a degree of revision which might require the casting of new plates. And when numerous small impressions were run from a set of plates in direct response to sales, the actual amount of time during which an author could ask for changes might be quite brief. Even more than in the hand-press period, authorial control was entwined with the processes of printing. Did authors seek to assert textual control by demanding multiple proofs? Their ability to get them was in part dependent on the available technologies. Do an author's printed texts show a history of textual alteration within a single edition? Such a pattern may represent compositors' mistakes, corrections by the printer's reader, unauthorized revisions, or the slow disintegration of the printing surface; but the changes could also include important authorial revisions, made feasible within an edition by the printer's ability to alter stereotype plates quickly and easily.

All authors try to control their texts, though their tenacity in seeking control and their success at achieving it vary according to their personalities, reputations, immediate circumstances, and the opportunities available within the constraints of custom and technology. It is also true that some authors dissemble about the matter, suggesting to everyone but their printers that they are not too particular about accurate printing, and can't be bothered with proofs or with rereading their work; while others claim to have worked over every last syllable of an edition, despite the persistence of howling errors throughout the "revised" text. To find out what was actually going on, I have drawn upon the careers of various nineteenth-century authors who worked with various publishers and in differing forms of literature, and examined a wide range of documents with, I hope, a suitable blend of imagination and skepticism. My purpose has been to make the historical record speak for itself about the interrelations of Victorian authors, printers, publishers, and the ingenious technology that served them.

No study of a subject and a period so vast can be exhaustive, and I have limited this study in several ways to maintain a focus on the most important technologies and their impact on well-known Victorian authors. First, I have for the most part restricted my investigation to the years between 1840 and 1890. These dates approximately mark two genuinely revolutionary events in printing history. Before the 1840s, high-speed printing machines were used almost exclusively for magazines and newspapers, and books were produced on traditional hand-operated presses or the early powered versions of them. By the 1890s, the introduction of the Linotype and later the Monotype composing machines drastically changed the way typesetting, proofing, and printing were done, and another chapter in printing history had begun.

Second, in my coverage of printing practices I have concentrated on bookwork, because for most Victorian literary works, publication in a magazine or newspaper was a step toward an impending appearance in volumes. I do not mean to minimize the great importance of magazine serialization or publication in individual parts, both of which I allude to repeatedly; but it is a fact that Victorian authors aimed at book publication, and it was with the technology of book production that they were most involved.

Finally, I have avoided as much as possible entering into the ongoing debates among textual critics and other specialists on matters of literary and critical theory. I have my own views on many subjects of current discussion, and have stated them strongly on occasion, but my intention in this book is to inform and explore, not to persuade or attack. Thus a great deal of very interesting subject matter, and a large number of very important books and papers, are simply not mentioned in this work. To take up one would create an obligation to treat all, and such an attempt (even were I capable of it) would soon overshadow my central historical purpose.

I

Composition

Ye authors list! we must a tale unfold,
Which, doubtless, some of you have oft been told;
You little dream how much poor Typo's *vex'd,*
When with bad copy *his mind's sore perplex'd;*
. . . . .
Reflect, when next you wield your potent quills,
And spare the printer all these dreaded ills:
Revise, transcribe, *and make your* copy *right,*
Thus save his labour and his precious sight!

Songs of the Press (1833)

TO UNDERSTAND one of the more subtle ways in which printing technology affected an author's control over the text of a work, we have to employ two meanings of the word *composition*. The interaction of author and printer becomes a material fact with the beginning of the composition of types from the author's manuscript. Throughout the history of printing, however, the struggle for control over a printed text began before a manuscript ever reached a typesetter's hands—in fact, before an author had composed a single line. Both actions signified by the term *composition*—the creation of a manuscript and the setting of types from it—are affected by the technology and conventions of printing.

In a broad social sense, printers, publishers, and booksellers have always been the most powerful force determining the content of what can be read. Unless like William Blake they compose, print, and publish by their own hands, authors work under restraints (both conscious or unconscious) on what they will write about and how they will express themselves. The history of literary and political tastes, of censorship imposed to enforce those tastes, and of self-limitations by authors serving those tastes, provides ample demonstrations of how a culture's professed values direct and permeate the efforts of its writers. The subjects and styles of a literary era are controlled by the social, moral, intellectual, and linguistic conventions of the time, and we recognize this when we call the writings of the mid-nineteenth century "Victorian."

In the much narrower sense I am concerned with here, nineteenth-century authors found their texts partially controlled by printers, who had to operate within the limitations of their technologies, who strongly preferred to uphold established linguistic practices, and who attempted to make their work easier and more profitable by bending the author to their own needs. It is easy enough to see why they would try to do so. The manuscript proudly handed over to the printer would often be written in too small a hand, on both sides of the leaves, and with numerous insertions, deletions, and revisions crowded in. It might well be spelled and punctuated oddly or inconsistently, or make extensive use of the writer's personal set of abbreviations. Before this mass of paper could be used as copy, it would need to be gone over carefully by the printer's reader, have its printed length estimated according to the number of lines per page, and be divided up into portions ("takes") for the compositors to work from. Throughout the nineteenth century, printers' manuals carry on a litany of complaint about the messiness and incomprehensibility of copy as submitted.

Printers' Manuals and Authors' Guides

Thomas Hansard's *Typographia* (1825), a comprehensive work from which several later manuals freely borrow without acknowledgment, was relatively mild: "In all cases, but particularly in those where the author has it not in his power to see the proof sheets, accuracy and distinctness of copy is peculiarly desirable."[1] C. H. Timperley, one of Hansard's debtors, observed in 1838 that it was "rare, indeed, to meet with a work sent properly prepared for the press; either the writing is illegible, the spelling incorrect, or the punctuation defective."[2] Time and advice, apparently, did not improve matters; in 1859 Henry Beadnell pungently stated: "It is very desirable that an author should write as nearly as possible what he would like to see in print. Let him, therefore, revise his copy thoroughly . . . and make the corrections . . . ; and if these are extensive, let him re-write the whole."[3]

In an effort to convince writers to present exactly what was desired, printers and publishers in the 1830s began to issue guides for authors. These ancestors of today's publishers' style manuals often went far beyond the request for tidy manuscripts, though this was a universal feature. The earlier examples, such as *The Author's Printing and Publishing Assistant* (1839), mainly confine themselves to attempts at controlling how the author sets pen to paper. The manuscript must be conformed to the necessities of typesetting: "There is another point of which Authors are frequently not aware—the necessity of their Manuscripts being written on one side only. . . . In the process of Printing, it may, if needful for speed or otherwise, be divided at any given point, without danger of mistake or confusion." To make the printer's work easier still, "when a Manuscript is therefore about to be written or copied for the Press, it would be desirable to have prepared a Quarto Book, Ruled, with a narrow margin, and lines across, and to have it Paged beforehand, on the right hand page only, on which page only the Manuscript should be written."[4] The English printer Edward Bull, who published his *Hints and Directions for Authors* in 1842, disparaged the second suggestion: "There are various modes of writing manuscripts intended for the press; the worst of them being, in our opinion, the fashion much cherished by ladies, of writing in pretty copy-books . . . which must be torn to pieces before they are put upon the compositors' cases."[5] The tedious labor required of an author to meet such prescriptions had at least one benefit: since there was no guarantee that the manuscript would ever be returned, the author would have the prior version at hand when proofs began to arrive.

If authors heard this advice, they did not universally follow it; the sole manuscript of many a Victorian masterpiece went off to the publisher or printer with no fair copy or complete draft as insurance. George Eliot seldom if ever made or kept copies, preferring to send her manuscripts to Blackwood by registered mail or to hand them directly to his manager Simpson. She expected confirmation of their arrival, and gently mocked herself for being anxious: "Of course, after the fashion of authors, I hold my manuscript to be among those precious things peculiarly liable to casualties in this perverse world."[6] Browning seems to have sent George Smith the only manuscript of *The Ring and the Book* for use as printer's copy, though he would have preferred not to. In 1862 he wrote to his old friend Isa Blagden that he would soon "begin on my murder-case [the subject of the poem]. I shall have no amanuensis however!" Later he lamented, "What I feel in not having you to help & copy!" Decades earlier, Browning's sister Sarianna had served as his amanuensis.[7] Tennyson was perhaps uniquely careless and indifferent toward his manuscripts, but in the case of *In Memoriam* he took some precautions. After absent-mindedly leaving the only manuscript in a rooming house, Tennyson got Coventry Patmore to retrieve it. Emily Andrews Patmore made a complete transcription of the poem, and it was this fair copy that went to the printers.[8] Hardy, with the aid of his wife Emma, often transcribed his manuscripts,

but in 1877 he asked Smith to send back the opening chapters of *The Return of the Native*: "I cannot well get on for want of it, as I have no exact copy."*
A few months earlier, Hardy had passed on some familiar advice to a novice: "It would be also a good thing if you were to write in a clear round hand in a first MS., though after you become known this does not matter so much."9

The authors' manuals wax vehemently eloquent on the subject of punctuation. There were several competing theories of punctuation in the first half of the nineteenth century, the main rivalry being between the "grammatical" and the "rhetorical" systems. Printers seem to have been almost uniformly of the "grammatical" school, while many authors, particularly poets and novelists, explored the subtle expressive potentials of unorthodox punctuation. The inevitable battle to decide who would govern punctuation was sharp and sustained. Traditionally, the printer's reader (or corrector, as he was called) and the compositors had taken a pretty free hand with the punctuation, no matter what they encountered in a manuscript. Hansard expresses the long-established view, which appoints printers as guardians of style and form while allowing for the demands of eccentric authors:

> It is certainly the author's province to see that his book be correctly published, either by delivering his copy very accurately and fairly written, or by carefully perusing the proof sheets: but the advantage is great in having the aid of a well-qualified Corrector, who may detect the inaccuracies in thought or language of the author. . . . If a printer be aware that the copy put into his hands is incorrectly written or badly digested, he should either refer it to the author for revisal, or, if the incorrectness be such as he may venture to rectify himself, it should be done before it is wanted by the compositor. . . . In all cases where he perceives an unusual spelling or use of words; a changing and thrusting in of points, capitals, or any thing else that is ill-judged and has nothing but fancy to warrant it, it is requisite for him to divest a work of all such pedantries. . . . [The corrector] is to spell and point according to the best authorities (though, after all, he will find himself continually called upon to vary his practice according to the opinion of the author, whose work is passing through his hands).10

---

*In 1881, while *A Laodicean* was being serialized, Hardy wrote to the publisher: "Parts VII and VIII are sent by book-post herewith. No copy kept—so perhaps they had better be printed as soon as possible" (*Letters*, 1:86).

Timperley went farther: "The late Dr. Hunter . . . advises authors to leave the pointing entirely to printers. . . . I am decidedly of this opinion; for unless the author will take the responsibility of the pointing entirely on himself, it will be to the advantage of the compositor . . . not to meet with a single point in his copy, unless to terminate a sentence." The vigor of Timperley's insistence actually constitutes a hint that practices were beginning to change. William Savage's *Dictionary of the Art of Printing* (1841) suggests that although compositors retained some freedom with punctuation, they must not make unauthorized "improvements" to a manuscript. In 1842 Bull essentially granted authors control of punctuation by recommending "particular care and *distinctness* in punctuating [their] manuscripts . . . ; moreover, if authors do not punctuate, printers are pretty sure to punctuate for them. . . . There seem to be various and conflicting theories of punctuation . . . , but, of all methods, that of the compositors, when left to themselves, appears to be about the worst."[11]

The early literary career of Robert Browning offers several illustrations of the gains authors made in controlling their texts during composition of the types. At the age of twenty-three, Browning was almost unknown as an author. With a very few literary insiders, he was notorious as the anonymous progenitor of *Pauline* (1833). By 1835 he was ready to try again; with the assistance of W. J. Fox (editor of the *Monthly Repository*) and the guarantee that his father would cover printing costs, the young poet presented the manuscript of *Paracelsus* to the publisher Effingham Wilson. What Wilson and his printer beheld must have elicited thoughts much like those of Hansard cited above, since Browning was much given to a "thrusting in of points."

Throughout his career, Browning's system of punctuation was rather like his theology, which has been described as defining a Christian sect of which the poet himself was the only member. *Paracelsus* is a good example of a rhetorical use of punctuation, in which the familiar marks cluster, disperse, and regroup in an attempt to reflect speech patterns, link up extended or multileveled parallelisms, and embed subordinations within subordinations. Typically, Browning overlays a relatively standard grammatical punctuation with elaborations which not only meant something to him but do indeed contribute to a reader's perception of the poetic discourse struggling toward the surface of the words. Commas, colons, semicolons, parentheses, periods, question marks, and exclamation points are used normally, but they also are followed at times by dashes (one, two, or even three of them). Browning differentiates among ellipses with two, three and up to six points. Though quite confusing at first sight, these oddities become comprehensible to most readers after a suitable period of immersion. The subtle shadings, separations, and junctures accomplished by Browning's substantive punctuation were part of a specifically poetical system; in his private correspondence he employed relatively orthodox pointing. A sizable portion of Browning's tricks with punctuation marks aim solely at the eye, not the ear, of the reader (it is unlikely that one can hear a discernible difference between a colon and a semicolon). Such an awareness of typographical appearances, and the employment of the visual effects of punctuation as a component of meaning, were artistic adjuncts to the detailed knowledge of printing and its techniques that became widespread among Victorian authors. Though some elements of typography had, since the earliest days of printing, reached back to condition authors' manuscripts, Browning's "visual-rhetorical" punctuation went far beyond the occasional striking effects of Herbert or Sterne.

It appears that several people working for Wilson and his printer tried to push Browning toward standard punctuation. The punctuation in parts of the *Paracelsus* manuscript has been regularized by someone other than the poet, and at various points there are revisions by Browning which follow the pattern laid down by the unknown corrector. The lesson did not take. The first edition of *Paracelsus* is punctuated very differently from the surviving manuscript (which was probably not used as copy during composition), and though it nods in the direction of regularity, it is hardly orthodox. Young and unknown though he was, Browning's determination (perhaps buttressed by his father's financing) and the growing willingness of compositors to defer to an author's choice of punctuation seem to have secured him the right to control most of this aspect of his text.

In a similar instance, albeit on a smaller scale, Matthew Arnold negotiated the control of punctuation in his "Stanzas from the Grande Chartreuse" when it first appeared in *Fraser's Magazine* in 1855. Arnold's response to the editor's queries is a model of insistence through patient explanation: "I think in the first stanza [i.e., the first suggestion, for the 10th stanza, lines 55–56] the comma will not do—for *mild* refers to *flowering*—not to *garden*—and to put in a comma would make it at least doubtful to which of the two it was meant to refer." To secure the one point, Arnold gives way on another by claiming it as essentially his own: "In the second case [i.e., lines 110–11] I think the comma will be an improvement. I had left it out because *last* agrees with *us* in the following line & is governed by *leave*. Still I think the comma is wanted." And with the suave presumption that a poet has as much right to make last-minute changes as an editor, he proceeds: "If it is not giving you too much trouble, will you substitute *boiling* for *black-worn* as an epithet for the cauldrons of the Guiers Mort, in the last line of the second stanza of the Poem. If it is now too late to make this change it does not matter."[12] Arnold prevailed, and the change was made.

Perhaps such struggles, which became more frequent, eventually wearied printers and editors. Probably the spread of literacy and the growth of a national school system tended over time to regularize the punctuational habits of most English writers. Certainly it was easier for printers to order compositors to follow their copy to the last comma than to impose uniformity on authors' unconscious idiosyncrasies and deliberate experimentation. For these and other reasons, among them the distinct rise in the social and economic status of professional authors which the romantic poets achieved for their successors, the printers lost the battle. By 1859 Beadnell could do no more than weakly offer a nostalgic alternative: "An author need not trouble himself much about punctuation. Let him mark the end of his sentences distinctly, and insert a few points where confusion is likely to arise, and he will generally find that the printer, if at all equal to his business, will point his book pretty satisfactorily. But if the author is unwilling to trust this matter to the printer, let him do the work thoroughly himself, and insert every point just as he wishes it to appear, — and then the compositor will thank him."[13]

The printers did not capitulate overnight, however. As late as 1876, Joseph Gould advised the novice compositor: "Always make enquiries as to measure, whether anything special is required to be observed in the punctuation. . . . In many cases, however, the compositor is allowed to use his own discretion as regards punctuation." Until, that is, the author saw proofs. The degree to which authors had come to assume that they would control the so-called accidentals of their works is revealed by the complaint of Richard Blackmore, author of *Lorna Doone* (1869). In 1864 Blackmore published his first novel, *Clara Vaughan*, with Macmillan. During the proofing, Blackmore wrote to the publisher: "Another thing—they won't keep to my pointing. Very likely they sometimes improve it, but more often they throw the whole sentence out of gear; for no compositor can know the writer's meaning so well as his pen does. . . . All I wish is that as a *general rule* they would observe my punctuation."[14]

On the evidence of other letters to Macmillan, Blackmore, even when an unknown, routinely and vehemently objected to any and all changes to his manuscripts.* But far more established and less demanding

---

*And not without just cause: the liberties taken with his works by editors and printers would have outraged the mildest of authors.

authors had to insist on their rights. When Matthew Arnold prepared a new preface for the 1873 edition of *Higher Schools and Universities in Germany* (a republication of part of his earlier *Schools and Universities on the Continent*), his travels for the education department made it impossible for him to receive and return proofs. Since the book was intended to contribute to a current debate, Arnold entrusted the proofreading of the preface to Macmillan: "I shall send a fair copy of it and I write (when I take pains) very plainly; only I will ask you to let some one go through the proofs carefully, and not to suffer the printers *to depart from my punctuation*." Even under more settled circumstances, when he could do his own proofing, Arnold submitted a manuscript to the *Contemporary Review* with a warning to the editor: "Do not let the printers change my stopping or put capitals where I do not."[15]

The printers did convince authors to hand in less troublesome manuscripts. According to a later guide in which a seasoned professional instructs the novice, "Nearly everybody knows now, that one side only of the paper must be written on, and obviously it is well that the sheets should be of uniform size. Lined paper and, if possible, small octavo size can be recommended, but many writers prefer foolscap. Let the young writer sedulously avoid all eccentricity or affectation in the preparation of his 'copy.' The more nearly he approaches to the character of a legal, or, let us say, a mercantile document the better." A bargain had been struck: authors would present clean copy (which was what the printers wanted most) in exchange for an exact following of it by the compositors. By 1869 the authority of the printer's reader was limited to making suggestions about "deviations from established usage in style and syntax as well as in orthography," but the *Comprehensive Guide to Printing and Publishing* could enforce no more than the plea to let the reader "put right what is wrong."[16]

It would be misleading to suggest that the nineteenth-century guides aimed only for this kind of limited success in directing the compositions of authors. For each page dealing with the proper construction and appearance of printer's copy, literary advisors offered entire chapters that spoke frankly of the subjects, content, forms, and styles that were likely to succeed with the public. Percy Russell's *The Literary Manual; or, A Complete Guide to Authorship* (1886) includes chapters on poetry, fiction, and drama (with subsections on "Errors to be avoided by young verse-writers," "The Way to Success in Fiction," and "Novel Writing reduced to an Art") and five succinct pages each on "The Imaginative or Creative Faculty" and "Constructing of Plots." Given some official standing as a publication of the London Literary Society, *The Literary Manual* is a mine of information for a history of authorship or popular taste. Much of its fascinating content is unfortunately beyond the scope of the present study, though it sheds light on a set of social forces (as distinct from technological ones) that worked to limit what authors wrote. Caught between a desire for success and the drive to tell the truth as he saw it, a George Eliot or a Thomas Hardy had made numerous adjustments and compromises to meet the expressed or imagined demands of publishers, publishers' readers, and the public, long before a neat manuscript in a "clear round hand" reached a printer. Perhaps a sense on the part of authors that they had already done enough to make a work acceptable caused some of their irritability upon finding that printers too would make changes to a text.

The Handling of Printer's Copy

Even the best-prepared manuscript had to undergo the severities of use as compositors' copy. Manuscripts were, after all, objects to be got beyond, articles of little significance once the text had ascended to the realm of print. Gaskell's thorough account of the division of a manuscript into small segments (called *takes*)* for each compositor,[17] makes the procedure sound a bit gentler than it sometimes was. If the author had stitched folded sheets together, or had composed or fair-copied a work in a bound-up blank book (among the famous, Tennyson and Browning sometimes did so), the manuscript had to be reduced to individual leaves, or "torn to pieces," as Bull put it. To achieve an equal sharing of the copy when the compositors were paid by the number of lines set, or to achieve greater speed by parceling out the copy to many hands, single leaves might also be cut up; the manuscript of Dickens's *Bleak House* was so divided.[18]

In bookwork, the compositor made up his typeset matter into page blocks for proofing, either tied up with cord as single pages or imposed in a chase as sheets (until late in the century, only newspapers and magazines were routinely proofed in galley). Lines beyond the end of his last full page, whether they were already set up or still in the copy, were passed to the man setting the following pages. The take of copy, except for any overrun, remained with the man who had set it until the proofs were

---

*The size of each take clearly would vary according to the nature of the copy and the skill of the individual compositor, but as an example, the average portion for the compositors of *Bleak House* (1853) was one to two manuscript pages (Dickens, *Bleak House*, 805).

brought to him. Meanwhile, the first compositor moved on to set a take from a later portion of the copy; when he received the proof of his earlier work, he gave it and the copy for it to the reader. When the marked-up proofs were sent back for correction in the type, only the copy for a sizable omission (an "out") would be returned to the compositor.[19] Of course this routine would be seriously disrupted or suspended if the author was sending in manuscript in successive batches, a fairly common circumstance.

Thus did pieces of the manuscript circulate in the composing room, coming to rest eventually with the reader. The composition of a book was orderly and systematic, but it could not be continuous or sequential, because of the necessity of keeping the compositors busy and the limited stock of type on hand. A substantial printing firm would have its compositors working on multiple jobs simultaneously, and when the initial sheets for a work had been set and the in-house corrections made, the remainder of its manuscript was set aside until the return of the author's proof. Few, if any, printing firms owned enough of a single face of type to compose an entire book at once. Until the second half of the nineteenth century, printing type was made entirely by hand; it was very expensive, and the supply was limited. The cost of type alone constituted the largest single expense in setting up a printing house.[20]

The limits on compositors' time and the amount of type available had profound effects for authors on how they would read proof, when and how extensively they could revise, how many copies of a given edition could be printed—in short, on how fully they could control the texts of their works. The early authors' guides both explained and warned:

> It is the custom of printers to send out only two or three sheets at a time to the author, and not to send more until these are corrected and worked off. . . . In some of the largest printing-offices, there is indeed no difficulty in getting up six, or twelve, or even more sheets set up at a time; but, in the general run of establishments, the type employed for the first three or four sheets, is often wanted for the second three, and is taken to pieces and reset, or recomposed, as soon as the author's final corrections have been attended to.[21]

> It has sometimes been supposed that the Proof-sheets of an entire work may be furnished at once. This it will be seen could not be, in a work of any extent, as the quantity of Type required for each sheet renders it necessary that the Type should be liberated as speedily as convenient, in order to facilitate the progress and completion of the Printing.[22]

Composition, proofreading, revision, and printing went on concurrently, with the author, compositors, and printers leapfrogging from one phase of the text to another and back. The author did not always lead the race: G. H. Lewes noted that with George Eliot's *Felix Holt* (1866), "the printing has overtaken the writing." Subsequent chapters on proofing and revision will discuss the ways in which this basic routine and later improvements on it affected authorial control; it should be pointed out here that despite the limitations of the technology, the speed of composition was remarkable. Saunders in 1839 described a rate of four sheets (each containing sixteen pages, if octavo) per week as "tolerably good speed, allowing for the unavoidable impediments occasioned by the transmitting and correcting of Proofs, &c."[23] But large London houses could work faster; in 1822 Spottiswoode is said to have been capable of "10 or 12 sheets a week, or even more if necessary, if the proofs were regularly returned." And when all resources were applied to the task, the results were astonishing: according to Bull, "Lady Lytton Bulwer's novel of Cheveley [*Cheveley, or the Man of Honour* (1839), printed and published by Bull himself], which occupies three octavo volumes, or above a thousand pretty full pages, was completed in nine days, although every proof-sheet had to be forwarded to the author for correction, and to travel, to and fro, the distance of two hundred and sixteen miles." Earlier, Lady Rosina's husband, Edward Bulwer-Lytton, obtained the same speed: "Messrs. Saunders and Otley of London, had [the] volume printed in the astonishingly short space of three days. . . . The effort was rendered necessary in consequence of the arrangements made for the Foreign Editions."[24]

Such feats could be accomplished only when the printers had a readable and complete manuscript in hand, and this was not the case with many longer works, particularly novels. A new author's first book would have been composed, revised, and perhaps fair-copied long before it made the rounds of publishers, but established Victorian authors were free to send in manuscript as it got written. Thackeray, Trollope, and many others, including Dickens, who was notorious in the matter, read the proofs of early sheets while composing the next section of their latest work. The correspondence of George Eliot and Blackwood creates an impression of manuscript leaves, fresh proofs, proofs with corrections, and corrected revises, each of a different portion of the work in hand, whizzing from the Priory to London to Edinburgh and back again through the miraculous Victorian postal system. This practice was most common with novels that appeared serially in magazines or in monthly parts, but George Henry Lewes submitted *Sea-Side Studies* (1858) and *The Physiology of Common Life* (1858–59) to Blackwood as they were composed.[25]

Given the limitations of a technology which could produce only a few sheets of proof at a time, the approach had its advantages for authors. It could enhance opportunities to revise: Hardy circulated the opening chapters of *The Return of the Native* to various magazines, finishing it only after Chatto and Windus accepted it for *Belgravia*. In late August of 1877, he submitted the first two parts, to be published in January and February of the following year, adding "I forward the MS. thus early that there may be full time for early proofs"; on 8 November he sent off the manuscript of three more parts.[26] Furthermore, if a writer was composing well ahead of the printers' needs,* only one section of a work, the one currently being set in type, would be unavailable at any time; if duplicate proofs were requested, a set could be retained to cover what went before, and manuscript would still be on hand for what followed. If proofs came back without the manuscript, an author who had not retained a copy of it had at least the opportunity to check what was about to go in against what had just been set, revising as necessary to avoid blunders and inconsistencies in the next section. If the necessities, pace, and mechanics of printing restricted composition (in that no changes could be made to the portions of a work already printed off), they also provided authors with the option of adjusting or entirely recasting the latter parts of their work as they composed ahead of the typesetters.

The Fate of Manuscripts

With manuscripts created and handled in such ways, we should be more surprised when they survive than when they do not. After the last sheets of a first edition had been printed, the complete manuscript should have come to rest in one of three places. The routines of the composing room would lead to an accumulation of copy with the printer's reader; if the appropriate segments of copy had been sent out with the proofs, the author would have had all or most of the manuscript back; if the author could not for whatever reason read proofs, both proof sheets and manuscript may have been given to the publisher during printing or at its end. It is difficult to determine and document which of these fates was most likely at a given date, but it seems that many manuscripts which scholars and collectors would consider precious were simply discarded by printers. A

---

*As Trollope did, for instance. As he put it, "I have not once, through all my literary career, felt myself even in danger of being late with my task. I have known no anxiety as to 'copy.' The needed pages far ahead—very far ahead—have almost always been in the drawer beside me" (*Autobiography*, 110).

fresh manuscript may have been of supreme importance to author and printer alike, but once the types were set and proofing had begun, it was merely "dead copy." Being primarily intent on getting into print and into the marketplace, many Victorian authors seem not to have valued their manuscripts enough to make efforts to preserve them.

It may be that during the first half of the century the practices of some printers made the recovery of manuscripts impossible. Robert Browning carefully saved all of his poetic manuscripts from *Dramatis Personae* (1864) through *Asolando*, published on the day of his death in 1889; all of these show signs of use as printer's copy. Of the earlier works, however, very few manuscripts have been found, only one of which was printer's copy. Perhaps the manuscripts used by the compositors did survive and were later lost; perhaps the younger Browning was indifferent to their fate and never got them back. The crucial case is that of *Men and Women* (1855), arguably Browning's most important collection, and specifically of "One Word More." This, the last poem in the work, was of deep personal significance to the poet. "One Word More" is addressed to Elizabeth Barrett Browning, and in it Browning reflects on the other poems in *Men and Women*, how they came to be written, and Elizabeth's role in his life and work. The manuscript, used as printer's copy, is dated 22 September 1855; the chronology of the proofing of *Men and Women* strongly suggests that "One Word More" was added to the collection at the last minute. And accordingly, this manuscript is the one surviving bit of printer's copy for Browning's earlier poems. But what of the rest of *Men and Women*? The two volumes contain some of Browning's greatest work, and he knew it; he had succeeded in getting back the manuscript of "One Word More," which admittedly had special standing; why did he not retrieve and save the other poems? My speculation is that whether he tried or not, it was too late. The copy for the earlier poems had been set in type months before; proofing was well advanced by August, and the bulk of the manuscript had probably been discarded.

With Matthew Arnold, the situation is more extreme: only a very few of his manuscripts, whether draft, fair copy, or printer's copy, have been preserved. The editors of his poems lament: "Our search . . . for such manuscripts has been almost entirely fruitless. It seems incredible that more should not have survived."[27] Arnold's distaste for the romantic cult of personality was so strong (he published his first volumes of poetry anonymously and wanted no biography written of him) that he may have quite deliberately placed no value at all on his own holographs. Furthermore, his dual careers as school official and man of letters gave him neither time nor inclination to fetch back his manuscripts from the dozens of publishers and printers who served him. And since his volumes of poetry were mainly the work of the 1840s and 1850s, the practices of the composing room and the reader's office may have made it unlikely that he could have kept his manuscripts even had he wanted to. The lack of documents in his hand is indeed discouraging, but not incredible.

The means by which many of George Eliot's manuscripts were saved indicates that unless special arrangements were made, manuscripts would disappear: G. H. Lewes wrote emphatically to Blackwood in 1860, "Yesterday I consigned . . . volume 1 of the Mill. The second will come when you have advanced some way with the printing. *Please keep the m.s. for yours truly!*" Seven years later he made a point of asking the publisher to "keep the m.s. of the poem [*The Spanish Gypsy*] for me to have it bound like the others when complete." By the time *Middlemarch* was published (1872), Lewes apparently had established standing instructions, since he made an additional request to Blackwood's Mr. Simpson: "When you have the m.s. of Middlemarch bound for us will you kindly give directions to have the top edges gilt—sides uncut, and order the russia to be of a rich dark color."[28] The correspondence about *Middlemarch* gives no sign that manuscript had accompanied the proofs, so presumably it had been gathered up by Simpson as it was set in type.* But though it was not her habit, George Eliot probably could have had much larger batches of proof and the accompanying manuscript by this time. Since the *Comprehensive Guide* told authors that "the *copy* need not be returned [to the printer] . . . unless for some special reason,"[29] sending back manuscript with proof sheets must have become fairly customary by 1869.

Technological Changes

These changes in practice—forwarding more proof pages at one time and returning manuscript copy—have great consequences in matters of revision and control. They occurred not because authors demanded them, but because the capabilities of the composing room had rapidly increased. The 1860s saw a major advance in the long revolution in nineteenth-century printing technology: the development of machines to make type. The first truly successful mechanical typecaster was perfected in America in the late

---

*Blackwood continued the practice; in 1879, Eliot wrote to William Blackwood, "The M.S. of Theophrastus [*Impressions of Theophrastus Such*, her last work] came yesterday afternoon in its beautiful fragrant binding which corresponds with the Deronda and Middlemarch" (*Letters*, 7:228).

1830s, and within twenty-five years improved versions of the machine were common in England. A mechanized foundry could produce five times as much type per day as the old hand-casting methods, and prices fell accordingly. Even the large and wealthy printing houses gained from the improvements, for ample supplies of type in any face were now assured. Neither compositors nor pressmen would run out of work for the lack of types to set and print. No longer would one publication be delayed because another had tied up the necessary types, as had happened with *Adam Bede* when Bulwer-Lytton's *What Will He Do with It?* kept a ton and a half of type standing idle.[30] Given enough type, copy, machines, and workmen, the Victorian printer could now compose and print books as fast as proofs were returned.

The increased speed of the initial stage of printing may be seen as detrimental to an author's control over a text, since haste and accuracy seldom travel together. As the interval between submission of copy and the arrival of author's proofs shrank from weeks to days, the pressure on the author to correct and return proofs increased. Previously, the printer needed to free up his types; now he wanted to free up his men and machines for the next job. No compositor ever liked to make corrections (for which he would not always be paid) or work in authors' revisions, but with plenty of type awaiting his hand he might understandably rush the work more than he had in the old days.

Yet the ready availability of type could also work to an author's advantage, if publisher and printer were so disposed. Large quantities of a work could be set up in type and left standing without hampering business, and an author could be allowed to revise at leisure without significant loss to anyone. Such a practice was highly inconvenient and expensive when types were handmade, but it did occasionally occur. Tennyson, for example, frequently required his publishers to have his poems printed in "trial editions" of a handful of copies which he "circulated . . . some months before publication and gave . . . prolonged study." Even early in his career he successfully forced this arrangement on Edward Moxon, who found himself stalled for over a month with the whole of the 1832 *Poems* standing in type.[31] The burden of setting up and holding back a volume for weeks or months while the poet solicited his friends' reactions, revised his texts, and reconsidered matters of design and appearance would become easier to bear after the mechanical caster came in. In later years, Tennyson's unrivaled position and reputation enabled him to continue this means of artistic control with several successive publishers.

Other major authors, when sufficiently established with agreeable publishers, made similar use of the increased capacities of the composing room. George Eliot, struggling with *The Spanish Gypsy*, agreed to Blackwood's suggestion that the 3,000 lines she had drafted be set up and printed to aid her in revision: "It would be good for Mr. Lewes to have them before him in print when he sets to work to read them critically. Defects reveal themselves more fully in type, and emendations might be more conveniently made on proofs, since I have given up the idea of copying the M.S. as a whole." The proofs were sent in less than a month, and Eliot took six months thereafter to complete and revise the poem.[32] Similarly, in 1883 Matthew Arnold asked that the entire forty chapters of biblical text he had prepared for *Isaiah of Jerusalem* be printed and sent to him before he finished the edition. He assured Macmillan that the work was "ready for the printer, except the short notes which I shall add when I have the printed and re-arranged text before me." The publisher offered to "have the text set up in a fortnight," but Arnold, habitually optimistic about meeting his deadlines, needed four more months to write his preface and notes.[33]

Until the last decade of the century, when the arrival of Linotype and Monotype machines changed the very nature of the composing room, the composition of types for the printing of books went on as it had since Gutenberg's day. What changed significantly were the speed of the work and, even more importantly, the attitudes of compositors and printers' readers, and the result was a net gain for authors in their attempts to control their printed texts. The technology provided a few more opportunities for revision, and increasingly knowledgeable professional writers put an end to printers' wholesale alterations to spelling, punctuation, and wording. By the 1880s, the formes of pages laid into a proof press represented, as far as the compositors and correctors could manage, what the author had submitted as copy. Though there was no guarantee that an author would be able to confirm this by comparison of proofs with manuscript, the next stage in book production—proofreading and correcting—constituted the best chance to assert textual control and accomplish artistic intention.

II

Proofing

"The Poet's
Anathema.
On a
Printer
Who Had
Displeased
Him."
*Songs of the
Press* (1833)

May all your columns *fall in* pie,
Each chase *be gnawed by rust;*
Weak, weak as water be your lye,
Your cases *filled with dust.*

A PASSING OBSERVATION by Lionel Stevenson on the working habits of Victorian novelists neatly summarizes a commonplace of modern scholarship. Of Thackeray in particular he writes: "Even more than most of them, he was a careless and hasty worker, submitting his manuscript to the printer at the last moment and evading the rigors of proof-reading." Though to an extent this may be true of Thackeray, such a generalization will not hold for nineteenth-century writers as a group. With all the emphasis typography could afford, *The Perils of Authorship* (c. 1840) pressed on the author "the necessity of his *remaining in town, and in the printing office* ALL NIGHT rather than let a single sheet of his work go to press, without being thoroughly revised, *even to a letter.*" And Dickens, for one, seems to have done just that, according to the historian of one of his printers; he "used to come to [Clowes' printing house in] Duke Street to correct the proofs of each [serial] part as they were composed." Nineteenth-century printers generally felt that authors gave proofs not too little attention but too much: "Some authors seem to look upon first proofs as a sort of fair copy to be altered to any extent at [their] pleasure," complains an authors' guide from 1876.[1] The present chapter traces how proofs were produced and employed by Victorian printers and authors, whose aims in the proofing process were often in conflict. Changes in both the technology of and attitudes toward proofing ultimately enhanced authorial control, but only by shifting some of the drudgery from the composing room to the writer's study.

Proof Stages and Proofing Routines

Despite the eternal complaints of authors about misreadings, inaccuracies, unauthorized alterations, and other blunders by compositors, the commitment of nineteenth-century printing houses to textual accuracy is demonstrated in their established proof routines. Considerably more proofreading and correction than are common today were done in-house, before an author saw a proof. Simply listing the normal stages of proofing is instructive; through most of the century, when typeset matter was tied up into pages and imposed as sheets immediately, a typical sequence was

first proof
first revise
author's proof
author's revise
press proof
press revise

After the introduction of galley proofs into bookwork, the stages multiplied to

rough galley
fair galley
galley revise
author's galley
author's galley revise
page proof
forme proof
author's page proof
author's revise
press proof
press revise

And if the work was to be printed from stereotype plates, at least two more stages, foundry proofs and plate proofs, were added.[2]

Before considering the kinds of proofs and their varying importance for an author's control over a text, it should be noted that some of these proof stages were repeatable (in-house revises and author's revises, for example), and that they represent discrete steps in the development of a printed text. Each listed proof was produced from a printing surface (types or plates) which was expected to be and often was different from its precursor. Since changing any aspect of the printing surface but its margins and registration required its removal from the press or printing machine, most of these proof stages could actually be construed (though they are not) as separate impressions, in the modern definition. Henry Beadnell used this particular term: "A second author's proof is pulled if required; if not, the next impression is called the *Press Proof*."[3] Though in the realm of the printer's ideal all proofs would be typographically identical, the purpose of a sequence of proofs is after all to incorporate and confirm changes. And though the aim of the process is to drive out errors, it is a fact of the mechanics of printing that deliberately altering a printing surface in order to correct it admits several occasions for mistakes. The following discussion attempts to characterize the stages of proofing under the two systems outlined above. Examples of how the participants viewed and exploited the process will be treated later in this chapter.

PROOFS IN SHEETS

First Proof. When a compositor reached the end of his take of copy, he divided the typeset matter on his galley into page-length blocks. He then imposed the pages into their correct order for folding and locked the forme up in a chase, which was fixed in the bed of a standard hand press. This was often an outdated or troublesome device that had been moved to the composing room after the end of its useful life as a production press. Well into the era of printing machines, proofs were pulled for compositors on the same kind of equipment which had been used for generations.[4] The resulting proofs in fully printed sheets had the same arrangement and appearance as would the finished product sent to the gathering room and bindery.

The pressman struck off a single proof on cheap, thin paper and returned it (and the forme of type) to the compositor, who delivered this first proof and the copy for it to the reader or corrector. After comparing the two, correcting literal errors, marking faults of layout and appearance (such as errors in page length, line spacing, justification, type height, etc.), accepting or overriding the compositor's deliberate changes to the text and adding his own if custom allowed, the reader sent the proof back to the compositor for correction "in the metal." While the reader had been marking his proof, the compositor had been setting fresh type or correcting that which had been proofed and marked earlier, and the pressman had returned the current forme to the compositor and gone on to other work. Following the marked proof (and any copy he had omitted, if more than a few words), the compositor incorporated the requisite changes. To do this, the forme had to be loosened enough for the compositor to lift out and insert letters and spaces with his awl-like bodkin. New errors might be introduced by inserting wrong types, or as the result of disturbing areas adjacent to corrections, or during the resetting of previously faultless type that shifted or suffered dropouts when unlocked or untied. If an entire forme "fell to pie" when loosened, the imposition pattern of proofs being taken in sheets could go wrong when the whole was recomposed.

First Revise. Locking up the corrected type again, the compositor took his forme to the pressman, who again pulled a single proof copy, the "revise." The typeset matter was removed from the proof press and taken back to the compositor, who gave the first revise and the marked proof from which he had worked to the reader again. If errors persisted or new problems appeared (or if the author had persuaded the publisher or printer to make changes before proofs were sent out), the compositor went back to work and one or more further revises would be taken. If on comparison of the two proofs the revise was deemed successful, the reader retained it and discarded the first proof.

Author's Proof. When the last revise was approved, the forme went back into the proof press for the pulling of "clean" proofs. These were printed on thin paper of a slightly better grade, with a harder finish than, say, newsprint. At least three copies were normally struck off—one each for printer, publisher, and author—but more were often called for. After checking the imposition and carefully reading the clean sheet against the preceding revise, the printer's reader discarded the latter and sent clean proofs to the publisher and the author. The remarkable fact that the manuscript or other copy was not necessarily forwarded to the author with proofs is discussed later in this chapter. If the reader discovered minor errors at this time, he had the option to delay their correction until the return of the author's proof rather than call for yet another revise. Publishers might at this point become indirect agents of textual change, since they commonly urged or even ordered authors to revise in proof. Even without such direction, as one commentator observed, "it is rarely that the most practised author does not feel it necessary to make considerable alterations."[5] Knowing that his choice was either to accede to all the author's changes or do battle over most of them, the printer also had to endure the sight of a quantity of standing type awaiting further, and possibly extensive, correction. The number of sheets the author received varied through the period, depending on the printer's stock of type, the availability of compositors, the nature of the work itself, the author's preference, and whether the copy arrived in batches or all at once. In the 1840s the norm was two or three sheets. Mechanical typefounding made it easy to send out more, and when stereotyping made possible the release of type and the printing of all the sheets of a book in sequence, complete sets of proofs could be produced. But as late as 1875, according to Southward, "in printing regular volumes, one sheet is usually corrected at a time."[6]

Author's Revise. Having made alterations great and small, the author sent the proofs back, either directly to the printer or through the publisher. If copy had accompanied proof, the author normally kept it: "The *copy* need not be returned with [marked proof] unless for some special reason"; but practices varied, and Neill's *Guide to Authors* recommended sending back copy and proof.[7] If duplicate proofs had been provided, the author would retain them, perhaps copying on them the changes requested. The printer's reader examined the marked sheets and handed them to the compositor, if the changes were acceptable and legible, or transferred the alterations to the in-house copy of the clean proofs, adding to them in either case any further corrections discovered since the author's proofs had been sent.

This combined set of changes was then worked into the type by the compositor, with the same possibilities of erroneous correction and accidental alteration of surrounding text mentioned under *First Proof.* Particular difficulties arose when the author had canceled or added entire lines or passages; beyond a very limited amount that could be accomplished by inserting and removing spaces, several pages before and after a major alteration could be affected. The corrected forme was once more placed in a proof press and the author's revise was printed. The reader compared this with the marked preceding proof to ensure that the required changes had been made, repeating the process as necessary, but what happened next was inconsistent. According to the *Comprehensive Guide,* "A 'revise,' or second (corrected) proof, is rarely sent to an author, unless his 'corrections' are numerous or *peculiarly* technical"; but Southward's statement that the reader "if satisfied sends out the second A. P. [author's proof] with the first A. P. to the author" is confirmed by other authorities and by plentiful testimony from nineteenth-century writers.[8] It appears that often two or three copies of the author's revise were printed, and the author was allowed to compare this proof with the previously marked sheets, make additional changes, and see further revises.

When a revise proved satisfactory to the author, "he [wrote] the word 'Press' upon it . . . which is the order for Printing,"[9] and normally returned it to the printer.* If duplicate revises had been provided, the author would retain these as well as the preceding set of marked-up proofs. Southward summarizes what occurred at the printing house: "This second author's proof has been returned with an intimation that the author is satisfied and the sheet may go to press. This proof will be made the 'Press Proof,' and will be preserved in the office as evidence that the author's directions have been carried out." Apparently it was not uncommon for authors to put "press" on a revise that still required some changes, trusting that these would be made and saving the time and trouble of another revise. The author's revise sometimes received attention that the printer should have given earlier, as Southward indicates: "Now, from the speed with which works are hurried through the press, the proofs are frequently sent out with but one reading, the careful press reading being reserved until the author's revise is returned."[10]

Press Proof. When the author's revise marked "press" required no further work, it was simply declared the press proof. If last-minute alterations had been requested, these had to be worked in and a clean press proof pulled for the reader. Errors could of course appear in the process, which was beyond authorial scrutiny, and there are instances of deliberate textual changes made by the printer's reader after the author's last revise. At a minimum, the press proof was read carefully once again for any errors overlooked (or created) in the earlier proofing stages.

Press Revise. Last-minute authorial changes, remaining errors, and any further alterations to the types were attended to, and another proof, the press revise, was taken for the reader. Although the press revise was sometimes called the final proof, this was accurate only when it had been pulled on the press to be used for printing the sheets of the book. All but the smallest nineteenth-century printing houses used separate proof presses, and after the press revise was approved the formes of type were moved to the printing department and fixed in the bed of a press or printing machine. With machines, since some aspects of the folding format and imposition scheme could not have been checked earlier, one more proof was necessary: "As a final precaution, in most large offices there is a

---

*In one case, however, Tennyson assumed that a forthcoming revise would do, gave permission to print, and added, "Should this last revise be already on its way to me it will be better for me to retain it, and if there be any other mistake . . . I will give you notice by letter" (*Letters*, 1:84).

'Machine Reviser,' who, last of all, after one copy has been worked at the machine, compares it with the author's press proof [or the press revise] to see that every imperfection has been rectified. He marks this proof as a machine revise, and it is put away on a file."[11] Some methods of stereotyping also necessitated a further proof from either hand press or machine (see *Foundry Proof* below). Press proofs and revises would be taken again any time the formes had been lifted from the bed—when, for example, they were damaged during printing and had to be repaired, or when a new impression was to be printed.

PROOFS IN GALLEY

Through the first two-thirds of the nineteenth century, taking proofs from types in galleys (prior to making up and imposing pages) was universal in the printing of newspapers and magazines but almost unknown in bookwork. In the 1870s, according to Southward, the specialized slip-galley was "usually used for bookwork, such matter being invariably made up into pages, and imposed, previous to the first proof being pulled." The standard view is that galley-proofing of books did not become common, even for compositors' first proofs, until the 1880s, but there is evidence of the practice considerably earlier than this. A remark of Beadnell's suggests that at least the first proofs of bookwork might be done from galleys by 1861: "*Galley Proofs*, on newspapers and periodicals, are pulled by the compositor; but, on bookwork, generally by the pressman."[12] And in 1868 both George Eliot and Robert Browning received author's proof in galley form (see discussion below).

Beadnell's reference to proofs being pulled by the compositor brings to attention a key technological change that altered proofing practices for printers and authors alike: the introduction of specialized galley presses. Using a full-sized press to pull galley proofs could be troublesome and a waste of time. Since types could not be as firmly fixed in the galley as in the chase surrounding a forme, there was greater risk of derangement when a galley was laid into or taken from the bed of the press; the press itself could eventually suffer damage from having the force of its large platen concentrated on a single column of type. When printing machines, especially the rotary presses of the 1860s, came to be used for newspapers and magazines, proofing in the galley stage became a necessity. The simplest method involved applying ink to the type in the galley with a brush or roller, laying on a long slip of paper, and running a dry, soft-faced roller over it. This was fast, but the proof could be of poor quality due to movement of the slip and uneven pressure from the hand roller. A simple press in which a cylinder rolled on guides over a bed designed to hold a galley was later developed. From at least the early 1860s, printers could buy a small lever-operated press with a galley-sized platen which, when used on improved galleys that could be locked up, produced excellent slip proofs.[13] We may infer from Beadnell that newspaper compositors pulled their own proofs to save time and that there must have been several galley presses available in the composing room.

Gradually these devices spread from newspaper and magazine printing to bookwork, and by the 1870s they were "found in all newspaper offices, and in most bookwork houses."[14] The proofing routines that consequently became practicable made correction of the types easier in the early stages and afforded authors two distinct periods of involvement and control. It should be remembered that however common the use of galley proofs became inside the printing houses, authors did not necessarily receive them as a matter of course.

Rough Galley. This initial proof was not the direct equivalent of the first proof in the system of proofing in sheets; it was in a sense a prior stage. The copy was divided and distributed, and working from his take the compositor set types until his galley was relatively full. But since no exact number of lines was required, he could break off at the end of a page of copy, ignoring the restrictions of the page length to be printed. Thus it was less likely that a page of manuscript would have to be cut up or passed around among compositors. When the galley was set, a rough galley proof was taken (presumably on the cheapest paper available) solely to detect large outs and gross defects of appearance, spacing, etc. The compositor himself compared this proof with his copy and immediately made his corrections in the types. Since the matter had not been paged and imposed as a forme, time was saved, the risks of releasing and resecuring the types were reduced, and problems of overrunning or filling out pages did not occur. The rough galley stage could of course be repeated, but this would have been necessary only for an extremely incompetent compositor. Upon completion of his corrections in the metal, the compositor discarded the rough galley proof.

Fair Galley. The corrected galley of types was taken to a pressman, who pulled the fair galley proof on the special press described above. The type and proof went back to the compositor, who then delivered proof and copy to the reader. As with first proof when proofing in sheets, the text now received its first thorough reading and comparison with the copy.

Since any substantial outs should have been rectified in rough galley, the copy stayed with the reader. When he had marked the errors in the proof, it was returned to the compositor, who performed his corrections to the type in the galley.

Galley Revise. Retaining the marked fair galley proof, the compositor called for a proof of his corrected type; this galley revise and the preceding fair galley went to the reader for comparison. Further revises might be required to incorporate the reader's demands and rectify new errors arising during the process of correction; when the last revise conformed to the marked fair galley, the latter and any intermediate revises were discarded.

Author's Galley. If the author was to get galley proofs, the type that produced the last galley revise was placed in the galley proof press again, and multiple copies were pulled on medium-quality thin paper with a hard finish. Direct references by nineteenth-century authors and the survival among their papers of galley proofs containing manuscript trial revisions suggest that issuing duplicates to the author was common. Proofing in galleys did not in itself affect how much proof was sent at one time; this was subject to the same conditions mentioned under *Author's Proof* in the preceding discussion of proofing in sheets. And though the move to galley proofing coincided historically with an increasing likelihood that manu-script copy would be sent to the author with the proofs, there is no necessary causal relation between the two practices. With or without copy in hand, the author made revisions and corrections on the galley slips, perhaps (for writers who knew that type in galleys was easily altered) rather more freely than with proofs in sheets of pages.

Author's Galley Revise. Upon the return of the author's marked galleys, the printer's reader directed the compositor's incorporation of authorial changes, adding to them the corrections of any errors overlooked in earlier readings. The perennial contest of wills about the nature and extent of alteration to be permitted probably tilted slightly in favor of authors, who could cite the ease of working with types in galleys. When the agreed-upon changes and any further corrections had been accomplished in the metal, a revise was pulled and inspected by the reader. If few alterations had been called for, the author would see them in page proof; if the changes had been numerous, the galley revise would be sent back to the author with the preceding marked galley proofs. Several author's galley revises might be required before the text was divided into pages.

Page Proof. Some nineteenth-century printers' manuals suggest that the revised matter in galleys was occasionally divided into pages, complete with running heads and page numbers, and proofed again before imposition. This could be done on a galley press, but how common the practice was and how such proofs were used are difficult questions. It appears from Southward that this intermediate step between galley and forme was unusual, but one reference to sending out proofs of unimposed pages has been found.[15] For specimen pages, or in regular printing when a sheet at the beginning or end of a volume contained only a few pages of text, it would be quicker and easier to pull proofs in single pages. If proofing this way was intended to eliminate unlocking the forme and making alterations after imposition, all final authorial changes would have to be made on page proofs, and revises would presumably have been taken.

Forme Proof. After the pages were imposed, a proof of the entire sheet was pulled on a standard hand press. A reader checked the imposition, margins, registration, and other details of format; if errors were discovered, the forme was removed and corrections were made in the metal. Barring disaster during correction, the forme proof could be quickly discarded and a revise was probably not taken, since any persistent or new faults could be rectified when the author's final changes were worked in.

Author's Page Proof. After any required correction, several clean proofs in sheets were pulled on good paper with the proof press. The author's page proofs (perhaps in duplicate) were sent out, accompanied by the last galley revise, which incorporated all or most of the changes called for on previous galleys. Probably seeing the text in pages for the first time, the author now had another chance to revise and the obligation to search again for compositors' errors. The page proof, bearing further requests for alterations, or marked "press" if all was well, was returned to the printer; the author would retain the last galley revise.

Author's Revise. This proof was identical in function and form to the *Author's Revise* when proofing in sheets; see the discussion above. As in printing and publishing today, it would have been hoped that the author's galleys had allowed for major revisions and that only minor changes if any would be required at this point. A revise would be pulled on the proof press and sent to the author with the preceding (marked) page proof. A satisfactory revise was to be marked "press" and returned, though the author might give approval by letter and keep the last revise, as well as the marked page proof.

Press Proof and Press Revise. These proofs also were identical to the stages so named when proofing in sheets. Since proofing in galleys did not become commonplace for bookwork until well after printing machines (as opposed to hand-operated presses) were universally employed, these two proofs existed primarily to assure the reader and the machine operator that imposition, registration, and margins had been correctly established when the formes were fixed in the bed of the machine.

Foundry Proof. The nature, manufacture, and use of stereotype plates is treated at length in the subsequent chapter on printing, but the effect of plating on proofing patterns should be mentioned here. The foundry proof stood in place of the press revise, and it was sent to the stereotyper with the types from which plates were to be made. The handling of the formes and the consequent purposes of foundry proofs varied according to the printing equipment in use and the techniques of stereotyping. For stereotype printing, Southward recorded, "instead of one revise being pulled to be marked 'for press,' two are pulled; one is marked 'foundry,' and kept in the establishment, the other being given to the stereotyper."[16] In the plaster-mold process (common in bookwork through the 1860s), an individual stereo plate was cast for each page of a work; with the later papier-mâché method, plates could be made of entire formes.

Thus for plaster-mold stereos the forme that had produced the proofs the author had approved was unlocked in the composing room (with the usual attendant risks to the types), and each page was placed in its own chase. After casting, the stereotyper used his own small proof press to take individual *plate proofs*, and read them against the foundry proofs "for errors that may have escaped former readings, or for defects that may subsequently have happened."[17] If errors in the type were revealed by the plate proof, they were corrected in the plate if possible; if not, the page would be returned to the composing room for unlocking and correction. Upon repair or recasting, another plate proof was pulled, and when the proofreader was satisfied, the foundry proofs and plate proofs could safely be discarded. After the plates were returned to the printer and placed in the bed of a press or machine, another proof had to be pulled and compared with the press revise to recheck imposition, margins, and registration.

By the early 1870s, paper molds were employed for bookwork, enabling the casting of a correctly arranged forme of pages as one plate; the imposition and the interior margins were not disturbed by stereotyping. Barring newly discovered errors in the type or faults caused by the molding and casting processes themselves, the plate proof matched the foundry proof (and press revise) in every respect. (On the other hand, correcting or recasting involved the whole forme, rather than one page.) The stereotyping of entire formes postdated the widespread use of printing machines in bookwork, and thus a machine revise for registration and appearance would be compared with the press revise following the mounting of plates for printing.

The Uses of Proofs

One purpose of pulling proofs and reading them is obvious and straightforward: the detection and correction of textual errors. But to say only this, given the number of people involved in the process, the variety of their responsibilities, the differences in their notions of the erroneous, and the divergence of their aims, is to beg several questions. What is a textual error, and what does "correction" mean? Who is entitled to define the one and perform the other, and according to what discernible standard? The first pair of questions are considered in a later, more theoretical chapter of this work. As for the second pair of questions, the multiplicity of agencies, both human and mechanical, that had effects on a text during composition and proofing precludes a simple answer of "the author, according to his or her own lights"; history will not support that. As Jerome McGann and others have pointed out, writing and publishing books is a subtly collaborative effort, and few parts of that endeavor are more visibly collaborative than proofing.

Yet this stage of authorship and publication is also of paramount importance to the author in the quest for control over the text: when you have read proofs carefully and revised to your own satisfaction, when you have won the important points and compromised on the lesser ones, when you have endured attentively through the last revise and written the word *press* in proud confidence, you have done all in your power to make the printed text read as you want it to. In one version of an ideal case, a perfect fair-copy manuscript saying exactly what the author intends is faultlessly composed into correct formes; the author has no second thoughts, and all the proofs are typographically identical with the printed edition. Sketching one of the many worse cases, we might imagine an ill-written draft manuscript that arrives in fragments and is set by semiliterate compositors who freely alter their copy; the author rewrites extensively on abominable proofs, hastily inspects one revise, and leaves further correction to the reader, who inserts and deletes whole passages without informing anyone. The resulting edition satisfies no one, and the surviving documents show thousands of differences between one stage of the text and another.

Since the first textual situation would be uninteresting and the second insoluble, it is fortunate that with nineteenth-century literary works, the reality seldom approaches either extreme. Then as now, authors, publishers, and printers worked in consort more often than in opposition, and instances of their utter incompetence are rare. Still, the study of the history of texts is a search for differences, and textual differences occurred during proofing for several reasons. Focusing on the changing technology of proofing, I have grouped examples in the following discussion to illustrate how Victorian authors worked with proofs and, where possible, why they revised and corrected as they did.

PRINTERS' VIEWS OF PROOFS

Despite their wide variance on many matters, the nineteenth-century printing manuals are unanimous about author's proofs: the printers wanted them returned instantly and revised as little as possible. Had they been able, printers would have enforced on authors the same orders given to compositors: "Immediately on receiving his proof, the Compositor should begin to correct the matter, as the delaying it may occasion him to stand still for want of a return of letter [i.e., types]; or be the means of keeping a press idle."[18] But since moral suasion was all a printer could employ while the proofs were out of his hands, much of the commentary attempts to shame authors into cooperation.

> *The proof having been properly read and corrected, is then to be sent to the author, or person authorized by him . . . either of whom, if they understand the nature of printing, will not defer reading the sheet, but return it with as few alterations as possible, to be got ready for the press. But authors who give much consideration to these circumstances, are very rarely met with.*[19]

> *But because such good authors are very scarce, compositors are discouraged every time they send a proof away, as not knowing when or how it may be returned, and how many times more it will be wanted to be seen again, before the author is tired, or rather ashamed, of altering.*[20]

> *Authors are very apt to make alterations, and to correct and amend the style or arguments of their works when they first see them in print. This is certainly the worst time for this labour.*[21]

> *[Authors behave] in some instances, as if they actually considered that they could not satisfactorily Correct their Work, until they saw it in Print.*[22]

Some authors . . . have been known to complain that they could never properly correct their own proof-sheets, particularly if the matter had been but recently written; for then the mind and the memory went faster than the eye, and overran mistakes which the eye ought to have detected.[23]

In addition to urgings and contumely, one practical alternative was offered: "If desirable, arrangements may be made for having the proof sheets corrected and revised by an experienced hand, in a careful and accurate manner, without any trouble to the author."[24] This method does not seem to have been much adopted, but one manual places a rather surprising stricture on it: "[Proofing and correcting] should invariably, when possible, be done by the Author; . . . where this cannot be done, and the task must be deputed, the Manuscript should, in all cases, be considered the Authority, and no departure be made from it, except as may have been directed, or in extreme cases."[25]

PRODUCTION RATES

The rate at which proofing went on, both before mechanical typecasting and after, was distinctly brisk. In magazine work, the interval between the arrival of manuscript and the issuance of author's proofs ranged from a week to as few as two days, and revises were produced in one day or less. Blackwood delivered proofs of the magazine version of George Eliot's "Mr. Gilfil's Love-Story" (1857) within three days of receiving the manuscript; there are hints in the correspondence that these were proofs in sheets. Some years later, Matthew Arnold accompanied the final portion of manuscript for "My Countrymen" (eventually part of *Friendship's Garland* [1871]) with several requests and promises to George Smith, the proprietor of the *Cornhill*, where the essay first appeared. "I am very nearly, if not quite up to time. If possible let me have the proofs tomorrow night (Saturday) in Chester Square . . . if I have them in Chester Square on Saturday night, I will break the Sabbath, and you shall have them back on Monday morning."[26] That Smith presided over a major and progressive publishing house which had its own printing works increases the probability these were galley proofs.

In bookwork, the pace was generally more relaxed, though the incomparable Blackwood mailed George Eliot the proofs of the penultimate chapter of *The Mill on the Floss* (1860) by the end of the same day on which he received the manuscript. Eliot then sent her conclusion, followed it with a letter asking for three further revisions, got back proofs, returned them, and left the country—all in two days.★ At a more normal rate, Eliot was sent a total of twenty sheets (of sixteen pages each) of *The Mill* over twenty-four days. Much earlier in the century, Tennyson sent the manuscripts for his 1832 *Poems* to Edward Moxon in two batches, and on both occasions Moxon began to send sheets of proof in a week. Often the process was slower; Macmillan began to send Arnold proofs of his *New Poems* around 24 May 1867, and by 31 May four sheets (totaling sixty-four pages) were in proof, though Arnold had received only the second. After this quick start, it took over six weeks to complete the remaining twelve sheets of the volume, though some of the delay may have been due to Arnold, not the printers. About the same time, Dante Gabriel Rossetti urged Macmillan to work quickly on Christina Rossetti's *The Prince's Progress and Other Poems* (1866). He wrote on 4 April 1866: "With this I post to you . . . the MS. . . . She may be going to Italy in May and would like to see all the proofs [216 pages] before then."[27] Whether this schedule was met is not recorded.

Sometimes even the best-equipped, most cooperative publishers and printers ran up against the limits of a technology they ordinarily manipulated so adroitly and found they could not issue a swift and regular flow of proof sheets. On 16 November 1858 George Eliot submitted the last pages of *Adam Bede* to Blackwood; he sent the proofs of two sheets of the first volume to her a week later. But by the end of the month, she had received only four sheets in all, and no more arrived during the first week of December. This delay was particularly worrisome because rumors had begun to circulate about the identity of George Eliot, and both she and Lewes feared adverse critical and commercial consequences if the mystery were revealed. Blackwood may have had the same fears, but there was little he could do to accelerate his printing works. Bulwer-Lytton's *What Will He Do with It?*, which had been serialized in *Blackwood's*, was being issued in volume form using the same types as *Adam Bede*, and there was not enough type on hand to compose both works. Finally, Blackwood announced on 9 December that the type was liberated, promising that all of Eliot's novel would be set up by the end of the year; still Eliot complained on 22 December about "a stingy allowance of proofs the last five

---

★The flurry of correspondence and indistinctness of some references make this matter confusing, but it is indisputable that Blackwood had read the very end of the novel when he wrote a letter accompanying "proof of the conclusion" on 22 March 1860 (*Letters*, 3:275–79, 285n.).

days." Blackwood sighed, "It was one of those unexpected fixes which will arise in the best regulated establishments."[28]

Despite the anxieties on all sides, this constitutes a rather refreshing instance in which an author pressed the printers for speed, rather than vice versa. With this should be recorded a demand by Matthew Arnold, who throughout his career had to work toward short deadlines and plead for extensions. On an occasion when he happened to be well ahead of the printers, he wrote to Macmillan: "Do fire another shot at that bundle of dawdles, Messrs. E. Pickard Hall & Co. I have had *one* sheet since I saw you—and Monday, Tuesday and today, *nothing. . . .* The thing will drag on in this fashion till I leave London."[29]

PROOFREADING WITHOUT COPY

In Edward Bull's deprecation of authors who "could never properly correct their own proof-sheets" because in reading proof "the mind and the memory went faster than the eye, and overran mistakes," a single word—*memory*—points to one of the most astonishing facts of Victorian printing and publishing: authors frequently corrected from memory, reading their proofs without access to the manuscript they had submitted. More accurately, an author working on proofs without the printer's copy (or an exact facsimile) is not "correcting" in the modern sense of making a typesetting conform to its manuscript; what is happening under such circumstances, beyond the level of marking literal errors or remedying inconsistencies such as getting a place-name wrong, is revision. Modern scholars' conclusions about the origin, nature, and significance of textual differences between surviving manuscripts and proofs, as well as of authors' alterations to proofs, may be faulty if they depend too much on a unified comparison of a complete manuscript with a complete set of proofs—a comparison the author may well have been unable to conduct. Certainly it is unwise to presume that any particular Victorian author got back the manuscript of a particular work as a matter of course during the proofing process.

The printers' manuals and authors' guides of the period offer inconclusive evidence on this matter for two reasons: first, they manifest the varying practices of different times and kinds of printing; second, the question of whether copy was sent to the author with proof is so elementary, and was so thoroughly governed by widely understood conventions, that anyone who would read a professional manual could be presumed to know what was done. Thus even the most basic treatments of authorship and printing give little more than passing notice to the subject. Hansard is inconsistent; in the discussion of proofing in *Typographia* (1825), he says only: "The first proof having been corrected, another is pulled to be put into the hands of the reader, or sent to the author for examination." But in the later section on the printer's reader, which Hansard acknowledges as coming directly from Stower's *The Printer's Grammar* (1808), we find this: "When a proof-sheet has undergone the regular process [of correction] . . . , the next thing is, to forward it, along with the copy, to the author or editor of the work." An anonymously revised and updated version of *Typographia* published under Hansard's name in 1851 casually remarks: "The proof is then sent, generally with the copy, to the author for his perusal." Saunders, writing for authors in 1839, allows an inference about what normal practice was: "When the Type has been made to correspond with the Manuscript, the first Corrected Proof is struck off, and transmitted to the Author. Should the Author not have occasion to make many alterations . . . he writes the word 'Press' upon it."[30] Saunders's primer gives such a detailed, even pedestrian, account of book production that one would expect him to specify whether authors will or will not receive copy. He does not, but his phrasing suggests that the role of the author at this stage is not to ensure that the proofs agree with the manuscript, but to make "alterations."

Thirty years later, the anonymous *Comprehensive Guide* indicates that authors did get copy with their proofs. When the necessary alterations are completed, this manual advises, the author should "send the proof in an envelope by the ordinary letter-post. The *copy* need not be returned with it unless for some special reason." That practices were changing is confirmed by another guide, this one from near the end of the century, which gave authors the opposite advice about returning proofs: "See that copy and proof are carefully wrapped up and properly addressed [for return to the printer]." The seeming indecisiveness in several of Southward's works also illustrates that the likelihood of an author's receiving both copy and proof was increasing in the last third of the century. In 1875 things had changed little enough that Southward's *Dictionary* simply repeats Hansard: "The proof is then sent, generally with the copy, to the author." In *Authorship and Publication* (1884), the same qualification appears: "If . . . the proof is accurate, or, to use the language of the printing-office, 'clean,' it is sent, generally along with the original manuscript, or the "copy,'to the author." But in the 1884 edition of his influential textbook, Southward is definite: "The proof and the copy for it . . . are now despatched to the author through the proper channel."[31]

More specific evidence about this crucial aspect of proofing can be found in records and studies of the careers of individual Victorian authors. Although there was no uniform rule in practice, it seems that more often than not they had to revise and correct their proofs with only their memories to guide them. When George Eliot was informed that her corrected sheets of the final pages of *Silas Marner* had not reached the printer, she wrote to Blackwood with what alterations she could remember. It is plain from her letter of 19 March 1861 that she is recalling both her manuscript and what she found in the proofs, and has no written record of the changes she made. Similarly, the apparent inconsistency about the first name of Mr. Tulliver in *The Mill on the Floss* (he calls himself Edward in chapter 29, but he had "felt somehow a familiarity" with Jeremy Taylor "because his name was Jeremy" in chapter 3) may also reflect the difficulty of working with neither copy nor duplicate proofs at hand. And during the long process of proofing *The Spanish Gypsy* (1868), Eliot wrote to Blackwood: "Now I have no copy (beyond fragments) of the M.S. in your hands."[32]

Of course the fact that a printer's-copy manuscript happened to survive, as that of *The Spanish Gypsy* did, does not establish that the author used it during proofing; a printer or publisher may have collected and preserved a manuscript but not returned it to the author until long after the work was published. Such may have been the case with *Vanity Fair* (1847–48), for which a partial manuscript, marked for use as copy, has survived. Though the existence of two manuscript versions of one chapter might indicate otherwise, Thackeray's repeated references in his letters to writing frantically against deadlines strongly suggest that he had no time to make a copy. His failure to sort out his own inconsistent use of names, and the nature and extent of his revisions, hint that no manuscript was at hand to aid (or restrain) him during proofing. And the famous misplacement of two paragraphs in chapter 59 of *Vanity Fair*, which persisted through all editions during Thackeray's lifetime, may have originated in the composing room as a result of the handling of takes of manuscript by the compositors. Of course it can be objected that Thackeray should have noticed and corrected this mistake, but if, as seems very likely, he did not have his manuscript to compare with the proofs, his oversight is easier to understand. That he did not correct the arrangement in any of the later revised editions is less comprehensible.[33]

As mentioned at the beginning of this chapter, Charles Dickens is known to have read the proofs of the serial parts of his novels in the print shop itself. This might have allowed him to consult his manuscript, but the amount of revision he carried out in proof, at least in the case of *Bleak*

House (1853), suggests that he did not feel bound by it, no matter how accurate the typesetting. The modern editors of *Bleak House*, who closely examined a mountain of manuscripts and proofs, observe that toward the end of the novel "the compositional errors grow more numerous and escape correction more frequently, as if Dickens had failed to check the proofs against his own MS."[34] Given the practices of the day, and the rate at which Dickens's works were written and printed, that is very likely.

In at least one case, and an early one at that, manuscript copy was returned to the author with proofs. In *Tennyson and His Publishers*, June Steffensen Hagen reports that Tennyson copied the various manuscripts that were to make up his 1842 *Poems* into a large accountant's ledger (similar to the famous "butcher's book" in which *In Memoriam* was composed). He then tore the leaves out of the ledger and sent them to Moxon. Hagen continues: "After they came back with proofs and were checked, these manuscript pages were consigned to the fire, except for a few which Fitz [Edward FitzGerald] saved and later gave to Trinity College library." A letter of FitzGerald's confirms at least part of this account. Of course, Moxon was by that date accustomed to meeting Tennyson's notorious demands about proofs, and this instance should probably be taken as an illustration of an exception to the normal proceeding. But it also seems that Edward Moxon was rather careful about poets' manuscripts. Because he returned the manuscript of *Colombe's Birthday* to Browning (after publication in 1844, not during proofing), it has survived while most of Browning's early manuscripts are lost.[35]

PARTIAL AND COMPLETE PROOFS

When we examine a surviving set of proofs for a nineteenth-century literary work, we will almost inevitably imagine that the author originally beheld them and worked with them in their entirety, as we do now. This impression may be strengthened by the presence, throughout the whole, of corrections and revisions in the author's hand, done apparently at one sitting and with the same pen. Such markings appear, for example, in a set of proofs of Browning's *Men and Women* (1855) now at the Huntington Library, and in the proof copy of his *Dramatis Personae* (1864) in the Berg Collection at the New York Public Library, both discussed in a later chapter on surviving evidence. Yet it is a virtual certainty that for books printed before the 1870s, and for many produced later in the century, proofs came to the author not in complete sets but a few sheets at a time. This was true whether a complete manuscript was presented or whether the author sent in copy as it was written.

The primary cause of this practice, already discussed in chapter 1, was the limited amount of type available in even the largest Victorian printing houses. But well after the adoption of typecasting machines in the 1850s and 1860s, in bookwork printers continued to send out authors' proofs a few sheets at a time; established authors were accustomed to it, and though there was no requirement to set up an entire work, the printer would still prefer to tie up as little of his type as possible. As late as 1884, Southward urged authors to "return the proof without unnecessary delay. This is due to the printer, who does not want his type engaged longer than is necessary."[36] This at a time of nearly universal stereotyping or electrotyping, processes that freed the type immediately upon completion of proofing. In earlier times, sending partial proofs was inescapable; continuing to do so, even after advances in technology had obviated the necessity, was a matter of custom. It also served the printers' interests: since authors did not always share with printers a ruling passion for speed, the dispatch of a few more sheets each week acted as a goad upon the author to return the previous proofs. In the eyes of printers, the less time authors had to consider making wholesale changes in proofs, the better. For authors, however, rushing through several sheets of proof and turning immediately to the next batch constituted a limitation on both the quantity and quality of their revisions, and thus on their control of their printed texts.

Historical evidence of the persistence of this nearly universal practice is plentiful, and a few examples from individual authors and works will provide sufficient illustration. In the first two-thirds of the century, there was no possibility that proofs would be sent out in any form but sheets of pages. Thus Tennyson, about two weeks after Moxon began setting type for the 1832 *Poems*, wrote to the publisher: "You will have received by this time the first proofsheet corrected. I think it would be better to send me every proof twice over." In 1854, when George Eliot was publishing her translation of Ludwig Feuerbach's *Das Wesen des Christentums* (1841; English title: *The Essence of Christianity*), she wrote to a friend: "The printers have been so dilatory with Feuerbach, that I am only just going to correct what I think will be the last sheet but one." That two books of the 1860s, Eliot's *Mill on the Floss* and Arnold's *New Poems*, were proofed serially in sheets has already been alluded to, and the number of sheets sent out at one time had increased by then. Blackwood sent Eliot the first seven sheets of *Mill* at once, having inquired of her "whether you would like a good batch at a time or to have them sheet by sheet." Arnold complained to Macmillan: "The proof of the *first* sheet of my poems has never reached me. . . . Have it sent to me, as the second sheet has been"; four sheets were in fact composed at once.[37]

The new possibilities that resulted from the development of mechanical typefounding gradually become visible in the 1870s. When Macmillan republished parts of Arnold's *Schools and Universities on the Continent* (1868) under the new title *Higher Schools and Universities in Germany* (1873), a new typesetting was required. Arnold wished to see proofs before he took his family to the Continent, but there was a delay. Macmillan wrote: "I am sorry I have not been able to send you the whole of the proof of your book on German Schools & Universities. We have two sheets only . . . but I don't suppose you would care to have it in bits." Apparently he did not, since a few days later Macmillan sent the entire set. This was still an exceptional proceeding, made easier in this case because composition was much faster and more accurate with printed, rather than manuscript, copy. Exchanging proofs serially as Arnold moved around in France and Italy would have been awkward and risky, and the new preface he was to provide would be easier to write with the complete revised text before him. Finally, Arnold was exhausted after reworking *Literature and Dogma* for publication in book form and wanted to get *Higher Schools* off his mind at a stroke. Just a year earlier, in settled circumstances, he had worked through the proofs of *A Bible-Reading for Schools* over a three-month period in the customary way, as individual sheets.[38]

Blackwood and Sons, a large, well-equipped firm, was able in the 1870s to set up a great many sheets of a book at once, and did so for George Eliot's *Impressions of Theophrastus Such*. There were again special circumstances; the complete manuscript of the work had reached Blackwood on 22 November 1878, six days before George Henry Lewes died. In a grief which "has broken my life," Eliot had no interest at all in writing or publishing anything, but on his own initiative her publisher carried on as loyally as ever. He wrote to Lewes's son Charles: "The M. S. is not long so that its standing in type will not matter and I propose setting it so as to be ready when she is able to turn her thoughts that way." Blackwood's intuition that work would eventually be therapeutic for Eliot was in time proved accurate, though she touchingly reopened the subject on 13 January 1879 with an expression of concern for his business: "I write now because I ought not to allow any disproportionate expense to be incurred about my printed sheets. To me now the writing seems all trivial stuff, but since he wished it to be printed, and you seem to concur, I will correct the sheets (if you will send me the remainder) gradually as I am able, and they can be struck off and laid by for a future time." Blackwood reassured her the next day: "Do not allow the proofs of 'Theophrastus Such' to concern you in the least, the type can wait your perfect convenience. I had it set up that the proofs might be ready to your hand when you were able to turn your thoughts that way. It is all in type now and I shall complete your set of proofs tomorrow."[39]

It is safe to say that by the 1880s the rapid assembly of a complete set of proofs was an ordinary option for publishers and authors. The increased availability of type, the existence of specialized proof presses, the simplicity and lowered cost of improved methods of stereotyping, and the printers' ability to convert large quantities of typeset matter swiftly into finished books all helped to make the proofing of an entire volume at once both practicable and profitable. Probably some authors and publishers still continued in the old way, as may be suggested by Thomas Hardy's remark in a letter of October 1895. At the time, a number of the Wessex novels were being republished as a set by Osgood, MacIlvaine; Hardy read proof on these, describing his work as "correcting a proof-sheet every day."[40] Unfortunately the correspondence contains no direct evidence as to whether Hardy's working on proofs one sheet at a time was caused by their being sent out sequentially.

SHEET PROOFS AND GALLEY PROOFS

The proofs that Hardy got in 1895, no matter how they reached him, were still in sheets of pages. He noted to Alexander Macmillan, who was bringing out the same set of novels for the colonial market: "I see that you page your edn at the top, while MacIlvaine pages his at the bottom." That these sheets of pages had not been preceded by galleys is indicated by Hardy's characterization of his revisions to the sheets: "I am making no alterations in the old stories, beyond the correction of a name, or a distance, here & there." Such changes would certainly have been made on galleys had Hardy got them. The complete set of proofs for *Theophrastus Such* that Blackwood sent Eliot consisted of sheets of pages, and if galley proofs were taken, they had not gone to the author; she spoke of the proofs as having come directly from her manuscript: "The printers seem to have been unusually at a loss with my handwriting in Theophrastus."[41] But some years before this, while writing *The Spanish Gypsy* and *Middlemarch*, Eliot had worked with galley proofs provided by Blackwood. Since the circumstances surrounding the two works were quite different, each requires its own explanation.

As was mentioned in an earlier chapter, Eliot lost confidence in *The Spanish Gypsy* after composing about three thousand lines of the poem. Blackwood suggested that putting the existing manuscript into type might assist her, and she agreed. It is likely that the first proofs Blackwood sent were galley slips, although the matter is clouded by overlapping references in the relevant correspondence to both "slips" and "sheets." Six copies reached Eliot by 12 December 1867, and at this early stage both Blackwood and Eliot refer to them simply as "proofs." Upon reading them, Eliot must have found numerous errors, since Blackwood apologized to her on 28 December: "The Printers set your Poem very badly and they had no excuse." It appears that when Eliot's revisions to these proofs were worked in, the types were paged and imposed, and a revise in sheets was sent to her. On 11 March 1868 she acknowledged receipt of a revise and specimen pages; her objection to "the printing off of these earlier sheets at present" may mean that when she received sheets of pages she assumed that printing had begun before she had finished revising. By this time she was already awaiting "the proof of the second batch of M. S." At the end of March, she sent back "all the printed sheets of the poem" [the "earlier sheets," presumably bearing further revisions], adding the request "that the revise [of the galley slips of the second batch of M. S.] be put into pages and sent to me for a second revisal." That she was working with both kinds of proof is confirmed by Blackwood's statement the next day that "the corrected sheets and slips of the great Poem arrived safely at the same time."[42]

Galley proofs were preferable to both Eliot and Blackwood on this occasion, not because they were rushing toward a deadline, but because large-scale revisions could be made with ease in types that had not been paged and imposed in a chase. This kind of situation, with an unfinished work going into type, was precisely what Southward envisioned as requiring an extra stage of revision: "In printing regular volumes, one sheet is usually corrected at a time; but where extensive alterations, omissions, or additions are likely to be made by writer or editor, it is more convenient to take the proofs on long slips before division into pages."[43] Even with the additional proof stage, however, one embarrassing mistake long escaped Eliot's notice; in late April she wrote: "It is a great bore that the name of my heroine is wrongly spelt [as *Fidalma*] in all the earlier sheets. . . . I would have confidently affirmed the name to be spelt Fedalma (as it ought to be) in my manuscript. Yet I suppose I should have affirmed falsely, for the *i* occurs in the slips constantly. As I shall not see these paged sheets again, will you charitably assure me that the alterations are safely made?" Blackwood responded on 30 April 1868: "The correction of the heroine's name to Fedalma will be carefully attended to. The bulk of the slips had already been turned into pages before your first correction of the error arrived."[44]

In the case of *Middlemarch*, galley slips were occasionally employed both for speed and ease of revision, but for at least part of the novel first author's proofs were sent as paged sheets. *Middlemarch* was first published as a serial, between December 1871 and December 1872; these were not the usual monthly parts, the eight parts of the novel being issued regularly over the twelve months. Such an arrangement might have been governed by the printing practices of magazines (with the first author's proof in galley slips),★ but the proofing process was as much a hybrid as the form of publication. When on 6 October 1871 Lewes provided proofs of the beginning of Book 1 to Osgood & Co., who were publishing the first American edition, he sent sixty-four pages in sheets and a galley proof of the Prelude: "The extra slip—Prelude—will of course *open* the part. The printer, treating it as a preface set it up last." The sheets could have been paged revises from previous galley proofs, but a later incident suggests that normally Eliot received her proofs in sheets. With the second book of *Middlemarch* partly written, Eliot discovered a problem in the structure of her narrative. Lewes's letter to William Blackwood on 7 December 1871 explains: "By this post I send you a batch of m.s. which we should like set up in *slips* AT ONCE. We think that the absence of Dodo and her husband from Part II will be felt injuriously and that the part would be greatly strengthened in interest if some of her story be introduced, and to make way for it some scenes must be transposed to Part III. The question of how much may be transposed can't be settled until we know how much what is now sent will make."

The fresh manuscript became eighty new pages for Book 2, and what had been chapters 19 through 22 became part of Book 3. Lewes's "*slips* AT ONCE" indicates how much work had to be done in a short time; the second installment was scheduled for early January of 1872, and Eliot appears to have wanted to stay well ahead of the printers—enough ahead that author's galleys would not be necessary. On 26 January, Blackwood acknowledged receipt of "your corrected sheets of Book Three"; it was published in March. The correspondence yields no further references to proofs in slips, and even in the rush to conclude the novel, Lewes wrote: "all is over except the comparatively easy pages of winding up, and I hope we shall send the final sheet on Thursday so as to be able to start for Homburg on Saturday." In the event, the final pages of *Middlemarch* were proofed on Monday, 16 September 1872.[45]

Another work for which both galley and sheet proofs were employed is Browning's *The Ring and the Book* (1868–69). This twelve-book epic

---

★This was the pattern, for instance, during the serial issue of *Vanity Fair* in 1847–48. See Thackeray, *Vanity Fair*, xviii, n. 14, and the essays by Shillingsburg cited in the Bibliography.

went through the printing process in such an exemplary fashion that it may serve as a paradigm of ordinary practice at the point when galley proofs began to augment page proofs in sheets. Browning's compositional manuscript, moderately reworked but by no means unreadable, served as printer's copy; the four volumes were published by Smith, Elder, who still operated their own printing works. The poem was essentially completed before typesetting began, and a relatively small number of compositors worked on it. The manuscript was not roughly handled and was preserved; Browning later had it bound for presentation to George Smith. Browning seems to have worked very closely with Smith in London during the proofing stages, and the published correspondence holds few clues as to when and in what forms the poet read proofs. However, a set of proofs of the first edition, now in the Beinecke Library at Yale, shows that galley slips were corrected by Browning, perhaps routinely. The Beinecke proofs combine various printed documents, probably assembled by a dealer or collector. Most of the first volume consists of proofs in sheets, now cut into pages; sixteen of the pages come from unbound sheets of the 1872 second edition of *The Ring and the Book*. Volume 2 is entirely proofs from sheets, but the third volume is made up of galley slips. Volume 4 begins in galley, then reverts to pages from sheets, the end of the poem (Book 12) being galley slips again. Disregarding the insertions from the later edition, it would seem highly likely that Browning received galley proof for all of *The Ring and the Book*, perhaps in large quantities at a time. The pattern of his revisions and corrections throughout the Beinecke proofs, however, reduces the certainty of this guess. If Browning got galley slips as first proof and pages in sheets as revises, we would naturally predict a higher incidence—and different kinds—of alterations in the first stage than in the second. Yet in the mixed set that survives, both the frequency and the nature of Browning's revisions are roughly the same in both slips and pages.

The mixed kinds of evidence provided by the proofs of *The Ring and the Book* may have muddied certain matters, but they demonstrate another quite clearly. By the late 1860s, newer technologies of type composition and proofing had found their way into the conservative realm of book-work, and authors quickly learned how to take advantage of them for artistic purposes. What Tennyson had accomplished—the accumulation of a great portion of his text in proof and multiple opportunities for extended revision—in the 1830s and 1840s by stubbornness and presumption became common options for authors and publishers a few decades later.

AUTHORS' USES OF PROOFS

If Victorian writers had done no more than follow the wishes of their printers, they would have read proof as an editor does, confining themselves to correcting literal errors and perhaps querying matters of appearance and layout. Some authors undoubtedly did little more than this; indeed, their ability to do more was somewhat hampered by proofing practices. If copy had not been returned with proofs, misreadings of the author's manuscript would be difficult to detect unless such mistakes gave rise to literal errors. And when authors had to read and return proofs piecemeal over a period of weeks or months, without manuscript copy or duplicate proofs on hand, they had to rely on their memory of what had gone before to prevent inconsistencies and blunders. Viewed from another angle, these seemingly unfavorable conditions call up a picture of an author in a rather pleasant position. Having only the initial printed version of a work to examine, a writer may be less inclined to let stand a correctly set reading which suddenly seems faulty; that the proof accurately presents what was written in the manuscript matters less if the writer cannot consult it. Furthermore, most authors find it difficult to restrict themselves to a simple process of correction; they have the exasperating habit of reading their own works in proof, and reading them with fresh eyesight. Despite their clear understanding that extensive revisions in proof made extra and burdensome work for compositors, despite the vehemence of publishers and printers, Victorian authors frequently treated their first proofs and subsequent revises as drafts to be improved; in some cases proofing became another stage in the compositional process.

We have already seen how Blackwood provided proofs to help George Eliot complete *The Spanish Gypsy*; years before, he had shown his understanding of how seeing a work in print could assist a writer in composition. After Eliot had submitted the first two-thirds of *Silas Marner*, Blackwood wrote: "In regard to the printing it will hardly be worth while to begin until the whole is finished or the end fairly in sight unless you wish to have the proofs by you." She was not the only author to find that "defects reveal themselves more fully in type," as she remarked in 1868: "I think I am less troublesome than I hear of other authors being with regard to proofs and alterations. . . . Mr. Lytton had a whole volume of poems in print by him to metamorphose as he chose, a long while before he published." Leisure alone was not always enough to carry out judicious revisions in proof; sometimes another set of eyes was called for. Lewes read all of George Eliot's works in manuscript and again in proof, and offered copious suggestions. Dickens, seeking to reduce the similarities between his character Harold Skimpole and Leigh Hunt, sent proofs of the second installment of *Bleak House* to John Forster: "I have gone over every part of it very carefully, and I think I have made it much less like. I have also changed Leonard to Harold. I have no right to give Hunt pain, and I am so bent upon not doing it that I wish you would look at all the proof once more, and indicate any particular place in which you feel it particularly like. Whereupon I will alter that place."[46]

Matthew Arnold, having submitted "The Function of Criticism at the Present Time" for its first publication in the *National Review*, anticipated a need to revise after he read the essay in print. He wrote to Lady de Rothschild on 24 October 1864: "I have said what must I fear give offence, but I am not sure whether my horrible cold and sore throat this last week have not left a *nuance* of asperity in my manner of saying it which need not have been there. I shall try and get rid of it, however, in correcting the proofs." Arnold noticed more than stylistic nuances when he viewed his proofs. Just before the publication of the first collected edition of his poems, he informed his mother that he had not arranged them in a satisfactory sequence: "On this final order I could not decide till I saw this collected edition. The next edition will have the final order."[47]

Additional composition and extensive revision during proof stages were raised to the status of planned ritual by Tennyson. June Steffensen Hagen has summarized his methods:

> In his first letter to Moxon about the 1832 Poems, . . . Tennyson had asked for more than one set of proofs. It was his life-long practice to have double sets of proofs sent to him twice [i.e., duplicates of first author's proofs and of revises]. . . . Each time, Tennyson would copy his revisions from the working proofs to the clean proofs, which he would then send back to his printer. Tennyson's custom in reading proof was not only to correct the printer's errors but also to adjust punctuation, to which he never paid much attention when writing out the poems in manuscript. . . . On his proof pages, moreover, Tennyson completely revised lines and even whole passages. . . . This habit of page-proof revision created problems for Tennyson's publishers no doubt, but, more importantly, helped eliminate aesthetic problems in the published poetry.[48]

Tennyson was anything but exceptional in using proofs to impose his own punctuation. Many writers seem to have regarded the alteration and insertion of thousands of punctuation marks as the last stage of composition, one which was best carried out after the printers had set up the manuscript, following copy in some cases and their own system of "point-ing" in others. The vast majority of Browning's proof corrections are to punctuation, often following a repeated pattern: the manuscript has one particular punctuation mark; the compositor or reader supplies a different one in the proof; Browning cancels this and inserts the punctuation that actually appears in the first edition. It is remarkable how often his proof corrections restore his original punctuation, considering that he did not always have his manuscript to consult. Arnold, we are informed by his editors, was "addicted" to altering his punctuation at every opportunity; that he was inconsistent in his practice is probably less important than that he insisted on the right to control it. But it was not only poets—though they were most interested in exploring the finer possibilities of punctua-tion—who finished this aspect of their texts after they were composed in type. Dickens did the same: "His punctuation was very incompletely shown on his MS, and he strove hard to establish it—according to his own idiosyncratic system—at the proof stage."[49]

Author's proofs served other purposes as well. Sometimes they served as a representation of copy that had already gone to the printers, allowing an author to look over the completed portion of a work in progress. George Eliot urged Blackwood to send proofs quickly for such use: "I shall certainly not linger unduly, and the sooner I can have the proof of the second batch of M.S. [of *The Spanish Gypsy*] . . . the better will be my advance, for when I see what I have done as a whole, I am helped to conclusive determinations. Now I have no copy (beyond fragments) of the M.S. in your hands." And Arnold, having prepared the biblical text for his edition of Isaiah 1–39, held it back from Macmillan until he got an answer to this question: "What I want to know is, how long will it take to print the text (about 40 chapters) so that I may have it before me for writing the notes, which are to come all together at the end?"[50]

Very frequently English authors used duplicate sets of proofs to gain a little profit and forestall piracies of their works. In the absence of interna-tional copyright laws, some American publishers made large sums by acquiring a copy of a popular English author's latest work and rushing out an edition of it; the author, of course, got nothing from such piracies. The more respectable American houses were willing to pay modest sums to English writers, but only when guaranteed a jump on their competitors. With the informal cooperation of the English publishers, or by rights established in their contracts, authors could negotiate to sell a set of proofs to an American firm for a flat fee. The resulting American first edition would have honorable legal status, and usually was described in advertisements and on the title page as "from the author's advance sheets." Boston's James T. Fields (of, at various times, Osgood & Co., Fields & Osgood, and Ticknor & Fields) preferred to work this way, and repeatedly gratified Browning, Arnold, and many others with payments for editions on which they might otherwise have made nothing. Duplicate proofs of a typesetting also might be used as authors' worksheets and even as printer's copy for later English editions; Browning certainly did this, thus throwing his textual history into some confusion, and it is possible that Tennyson did too. These and other instances are discussed in the chapter on reprinting.

One especially idiosyncratic use of proofs by an author deserves inclusion here. Matthew Arnold composed "On the Study of Celtic Literature" in 1865 for one of his lectures as Oxford Professor of Poetry. The lecture was scheduled for mid-March; in February, Arnold wrote to George Smith, publisher of the *Cornhill* (in which a version of the lecture was to appear), to ask what seems an extraordinary favor: "I mean to give my lecture on Celtic poetry and literature . . . about the 17th or 18th of March, so it will do for the April number of your Magazine, if you like. I dare say if I send you the MSS [*sic*] about the 10th of March you will kindly let me have a proof that I may read my lecture from; a great comfort to me, and it will ensure your having the paper ready in good time." The lecture was in fact postponed some months; Arnold wrote his mother that he had finished writing it on 4 December. There is no evidence that he had it in proof when he delivered it on 6 and 7 December; even Smith might have found this insufficient time. But a few years later he availed himself of the publisher's good nature in the same way. His essay "A Persian Passion Play" began as a lecture given at Birmingham in October 1871; he soon sent the text to Smith for its appearance as an article in the *Cornhill*. In November Arnold told his mother he had "finished correcting [it] for the press." Shortly thereafter he was asked to repeat the talk at Leamington, and he wrote to Smith: "I do not want another revise of this for correction, but I should like to have a proof of it, because the Leamington people, who have heard the fame of it at Birmingham, offer me money to read it to them at Leamington." Smith presumably complied. Years afterward, while Arnold was touring America, he got Charles Eliot Norton and the Harvard University Press to compose and print his lecture on Emerson, again to be used as a script. "You and the printers at Harvard have indeed done wonders. I return the corrected proof; if I can find the fresh revise at Mrs Fields's on Saturday, that will do beautifully. Then they might strike off 5 or 6 copies for me on Monday."[51]

Tennyson's elaboration of the proofing process into his famous "trial editions" is well known. For his 1832 *Poems*, Tennyson got his proofs in the usual way, sheet by sheet. At first he marked and returned each sheet in sequence, but his desire to see and reconsider the volume as a whole was so strong that he ceased sending back the revises, forcing the printers to let their type stand. He eventually compiled a complete set of proofs by accumulating sheets which were sent piecemeal, and only after deciding at last to withdraw "The Lover's Tale" from the book did he allow printing to proceed. The invective and hostility with which the 1832 volume was met by the literary establishment shocked Tennyson deeply. By the time he was induced to publish again, nearly ten years had passed. Once again, the metamorphosis of manuscript into print brought him anguish and doubt. While the 1842 *Poems* was being set in type, Edward FitzGerald reported: "Poor Tennyson has got home some of his proof sheets: and, now that his verses are in hard print, thinks them detestable . . . and wishes he had never been persuaded to print." As a precaution against recurrences of such unhappiness, Tennyson later went a step beyond merely holding back proofs; the trial editions of his subsequent works were planned in advance. Despite the limitations on available types, and despite every custom of the printing business of the day, he contrived to get a long look at each of his volumes as a printed whole before publication. Hagen describes "the usual pattern: (1) his friends heard him read the poems; (2) his publisher produced a trial edition so the poet could see the poems in print and spend the next year or so tinkering with them; (3) [his wife] Emily read the poems and called them good; (4) the poems were published."[52]

The trial editions were more than just a complete set of page proofs. They were authentic books in their own right, pondered as such by the poet, who gave copies to close friends for their reactions. Printed but not "published" in the normal sense of the word, these copies were not meant to circulate. Tennyson sent a copy of the trial edition of *In Memoriam* to Aubrey DeVere, but strictly "on the condition that when the book is published, this vaunt courier of it shall be either sent back to me, or die the death by fire. . . . I shall print about 25 copies and let them out among friends under the same condition." That these truly must be called editions, rather than proof copies or first impressions, is shown in Tennyson's orders to Moxon about *In Memoriam*: "You may print these and distribute the types. . . . Print 1/2 dozen copies and send me them. Give none away and retain none yourself."[53] The "first" edition of *In Memoriam*, released to the world in late May of 1850, was typographically, bibliographically, and historically the second edition of the poem.

The manner in which a given work by a specific Victorian author went through the process of proofing depends on many variables: the era, the form of publication, the printers and publishers involved, the time available, the skill of compositors, and the author's general habits and immediate circumstances. The stages may have been many or few, revisions elaborate or minimal. But in one regard proofing was always the same: it was transient, a labor to be endured by the participants until a final press or machine revise was approved, and printing could begin.

III

Printing

Oh! rare, Printing, the fam'd Art of Printing!   *Songs of the*
Long may it flourish, and never decay.   *Press* (1833)

As we have seen, Victorian authors' control over printed texts was enhanced during composition and proofing as a result of both technological advances and authors' demands of printers. When granted, these demands gave authors increased opportunities for revision along with a greater responsibility for textual accuracy. But when a set of revised proofs marked "for press" reached the printing house, the author's control over a text began to diminish. Despite an author's wish or belief that the printed copies of a work would present the text just as it had appeared in the final proofs, the printing process provided numerous occasions on which textual changes could occur. Some of these alterations were intentional, others accidental; some of them arose from human actions, while others were purely mechanical in origin. The present chapter investigates how texts are altered during printing and explores the effects of two major technological advances: the conversion from hand presses to printing machines and the adoption of stereotyping for the printing of books.

Overruling the Author

Deliberate deviations from an author's approved text were commonplace in the Victorian era, particularly in the magazines. Publishers, editors, and printers' readers felt sufficiently proprietary about their products to suggest revisions to authors at any time, for any number of reasons. If an author proved inadequately responsive to suggestion during composition and proofing, changes could be made in the gap between the return of the author's final revises and the beginning of printing. Thus Richard Blackmore, later famous as the author of *Lorna Doone* (1869), found in 1864 that the first magazine installment of his first novel, *Clara Vaughan*, had been "improved" after proofing: "They have had the cheek to make seventy-two alterations (every one of them for the worse) in their first number of C.V. . . . *Omit* [the editor] may (under his proviso), but *insert* he shall not."

George Eliot, when nearly as unknown as Blackmore, discovered and strongly objected to an unauthorized textual change in the first part of "Janet's Repentance." She wrote to Blackwood in 1857: "The printer's reader made a correction after I saw the proof, and though he may sometimes do so with advantage, . . . I in this case particularly object to his alteration, and I mention it in order to request that it may not occur again. He has everywhere substituted the form—'the Misses So and So' for 'the Miss So and So*s*'—a form which in England is confined to public announcements, to the backs of letters, and to the conversation of schoolmistresses."[1] Beyond the interesting social forces at work, two technical matters are involved here. First, since one purpose of proofs is to make alterations, they must be pulled from standing types, which can be freely changed after the author has returned a last revise. Second, when stereotype plates were employed (as they nearly always were for magazine printing by 1860), the author never saw a proof of the plates which would do the actual printing and thus had no final check on unauthorized changes to the types from which the plates were cast.

But authors knew—and this accounts to some extent for their acceptance, grudging though it often was, of unauthorized changes—that they would have an opportunity to restore and revise their texts, when works first published in magazines went into subsequent editions as books. For fiction in particular, but often with poems and essays as well, it was normal to project both forms of publication from the outset. The double-column, closely leaded format of the magazines would make unattractive volumes, so a new typesetting was usually undertaken, complete with fresh author's proofs and revises. Control over first book editions reverted to authors, and publishers often invited revision at this point. Both Blackmore and Eliot, in the cases mentioned above, reestablished in book publication the readings they had originally intended. Further discussion of authorial control in similar circumstances appears in ensuing chapters.

Stereotyping

Though the French printer Firmin Didot (1764–1836) coined the term *stereotype* in the 1790s, the process itself had been proposed, discussed, and attempted long before. In the early eighteenth century, William Ged not only succeeded in casting metal plates with plaster molds taken from individual types but produced workable plates for two prayer books and an edition of the works of Sallust. Ged was granted a patent on his casting method in 1725. British printers and compositors, convinced that this innovation would ruin their trades, unanimously and successfully opposed stereotyping for decades. Meanwhile, experimentation went forward in the hands of eccentrics and amateurs; in 1802 Charles Stanhope (who also advanced printing by inventing the iron hand press that bears his name) and Andrew Wilson (who had studied Ged's patents) improved the process sufficiently to make stereotyping practicable and commercially viable. By 1820, despite continued resistance from the printing trades, stereotyping was in regular if not widespread use, and within sixty years it had become the preferred technology for all but small or specialized printing jobs.[2]

The partisans of stereotyping cited three primary advantages to the new process: once a mold was made, the types from which it was taken were freed for other use; cast plates could be stored and reused for successive impressions over long periods, eliminating the expense of resetting a text and issuing a new edition each time demand warranted it; and the texts of stereotyped works were fixed, immune from the incursion of errors that were inevitable in resetting. Additional benefits were said to include reduced wear on types, smaller capital investment in inventories of type, the elimination of proofing and correction when reprinting from stereos, and the evenly inked, attractive impression made by plates. Most of these claims appealed to printers' purses, though a few relied on their traditional pride in their work; as time and experience proved to them that stereotyping paid off, it was gradually adopted. Compositors, of course, saw quite correctly that rendering the resetting of popular and standard works unnecessary would throw many of them out of work. The compositors' entrenched opposition to stereotyping waned slowly, and only because the printing business expanded so greatly and continuously that more, not fewer, typesetters were needed every year.

While many of the claims for stereotyping had merit, there were matching disadvantages, each of which was pointed out with relish and in prolix detail by enemies of the process. Chief among these was master printer Thomas Curson Hansard, who railed against stereotyping for years. In several books,[3] Hansard devoted dozens of pages to technical and economic analyses intended to counter the proponents of stereotyping on every point. The type was indeed released for other use after casting, Hansard admitted, but molding plaster often stuck to the types and had to be laboriously picked and washed off. Stereotyping fixed a text for future impressions, but "what work is there so perfect as not to require some alteration and amendment in a new edition, which, in stereotype, is practicable only to a limited extent?" Furthermore, the new process did not of itself guarantee greater profits:

*An extravagant notion prevails . . . of the exceeding economy of ster-
eotyping; . . . [but] the cost of stereotyping may be taken as the same as
that of composition, or even higher. It is quite clear, therefore, that if the
first edition of a work is stereotyped, the speculator at once incurs the
expense of* printing *two editions, minus the press-work. The consequence is, that if his untried book does not succeed, he very much increases
his loss, or at best he increases his chance of loss, because many books that
just get through a first edition never arrive at a second.*[4]

Plates were troublesome to print from: "These plates are not exempt
from the same accidents to which type formes are liable in their progress of
working. . . . Such accidents may totally interrupt the work, and require
the damaged plate to be sent to the foundry to be repaired." Losing time
just when printing was to begin was most serious: "Some defects are only
discovered when the form is properly made ready on the press or machine,
when the necessary repairs to the plates often cause long and unprofitable
delays." And when repaired, plates produced unsightly results:

*I mean most distinctly to assert this: I never saw a single letter inserted
into a plate, which could not be distinguished by any practised eye: and no
three or four letters together can possibly be introduced into the space of the
same letters cut out of a plate in consequence of an accidental batter, or a
failure in the casting, which is a very common occurrence. So that, even
barring the chance of a letter or two not lining exactly, or not standing
quite square with the other part, or any error being made in composition,
the part amended must destroy the much-praised beauty and immaculate-
ness of the stereotype work.*[5]

Much as the modern textual scholar or historian of printing would
like to attain such a "practiced eye," Hansard elsewhere suggests that it is
unnecessary: "Printing from plates never looks so well as that from type;
and even the most inexperienced eye may instantly detect the difference,
even in the first edition."[6]

Hansard's sustained flights of invective can be entertaining, but in the
end several of his arguments are factitious at best. In 1825, when Hansard
himself was experimenting with casting plates, his opposition had to be
taken seriously; but by 1851 he was flogging a dead horse and knew it:
"Nevertheless, in some cases stereotyping is of great advantage; but
chiefly in books of numbers. . . . There is no fear of alteration from the
error of compositors or carelessness of readers, but the book remains the
same forever." A report on the state of the compositors' trade in 1834
shows that by then books which could be expected to go through many

impressions without revision were routinely being stereotyped: "Where are the heavy standard works, which used to afford constant employment to some of the largest houses in the trade? They have been stereotyped, and are all gone from the Compositor's hand, while the capital which was employed by masters in the production and re-production of those works, is laid out by them in the purchase of machinery, and the fabrication of stereotype plates."[7]

Publishers, especially those who subcontracted their printing and did not have to bear directly the initial costs of making plates, spoke in unison in their authors' guides of the benefits of stereotyping; thus Saunders and Otley in 1839: "Stereotype Printing is thus a very valuable process, for works not liable to alteration, as Bibles, School Books, and other works of which large numbers are required, as it would be impossible to keep the moveable Types standing for such works, without a very great outlay of Capital."[8]

But at the same time, the independent voice of T. H., alert as always for real and imagined ways in which printers and publishers denied profits to authors, warned in *The Perils of Authorship*: "Stereotyping should never be resorted to, except on very particular occasions." Since stereotyping was first employed for standard works, a certain aura of achievement and profitability became attached to it in the minds of authors. A later guide glowingly speaks of the author "who has, at last, reached what is rightly held to be the crowning honour of being stereotyped," but as discussion later in this chapter will illustrate, authors' knowledge and opinions varied considerably. Extra profits as a result of cheaper subsequent impressions formed a pleasant prospect, but severe limitations on revision did not.[9]

Being in greater economic control than the other parties, the publishers won out. Despite Hansard's insistence that "the first edition of a work should never be stereotyped, unless indeed the work be of such a nature as to insure a general sale at a low price," stereotyping was well established in the book trade by the 1840s. A surviving agreement from 1844 between Leigh Hunt and the publisher Edward Moxon reveals that plating was not reserved for Bibles or logarithmic tables: "Mr. Moxon agrees to publish a new edition of Mr. Hunt's Poetical Works to consist of 2000 copies . . . the same to be printed, stereotyped, published, and advertised by and at the sole risk of Mr. Moxon. . . . That Mr. Moxon shall from time to time be at liberty to print and publish any further such edition or editions [i.e., impressions] of the said Poetical Works (to consist of 1000 copies) as by him shall be deemed advantageous."[10]

Here we may catch a glimpse of the kind of arrangement that prompted T. H.'s warning to authors. Before stereotyping, unless type were left standing, the exhaustion of the supply of an edition afforded an occasion for negotiations. An author might ask for a larger flat fee per edition, or settle for a smaller share on a larger press run; an author might wish to revise, or delay, or refuse entirely to approve a new edition. Stereotyping gave publishers the technical ability to respond to demand by producing, "from time to time," an undefined large number of copies of a work; this empowered them to establish from the beginning the terms of payment for all the copies of all the impressions that might be printed. The custom had always been to pay an author a single sum (or a set proportion of profits) for a single edition; if a further edition was called for, the author negotiated another lump-sum payment for it. The Moxon-Hunt contract, despite its plurals, governs only one edition, which will be produced in multiple impressions. Behind the imprecision of Moxon's terminology lies a firm and exact definition: the publisher was paying by the typesetting. Alert authors soon responded by demanding payment on the royalty system (they "held a lordship," in the Victorian phrase). Given an expanding reading public and the number of copies that could be printed from a set of stereo plates, it was better to be paid a small amount on each copy sold than a lump sum (no matter how generous) for an edition of unlimited size.

By mid-century, stereotyping was used in printing almost all of England's newspapers and magazines. Soon it was routine in the larger publishing houses to stereotype their books—if not for the first impression, certainly for later ones; and if not for poetry, certainly for popular fiction. In 1869 the *Comprehensive Guide* recommended stereotyping as cheap, accurate, reliable, and labor-saving; about the same time, James Spedding described a hypothetical but typical contemporary book: four hundred and eighty pages long (i.e., thirty sheets of octavo), with three hundred words in the page, and "carefully but not expensively printed (in stereotype)." And by 1877 Jackson Gaskill's handbook for printing managers put apprentices and journeymen on notice: "Stereotype printing has now become so universal that all machine men must be well up in everything connected with this."[11] However, the stereotyping learned by printers in 1877 was technologically quite different from what had been perfected by Earl Stanhope. The product—a metal plate which replaced a forme of type in printing—remained essentially the same, but the method of making it changed significantly.

The Plaster Method

From the time stereotyping became practical until the middle of the nineteenth century, plates were cast by pouring molten metal into a plaster mold taken from typeset matter.★ The decision to stereotype had to be made at the outset, because setting for stereotyping differed from ordinary composition. As the plaster applied to the types dried, it had a tendency to stick to the metal surface, making removal of the mold from the forme difficult. To counteract this, taller lead spaces were used between words and lines when composing for stereotyping, effectively bringing the spaces closer to the printing surface. The resulting typesetting could not itself be used for printing, because the reduction in the distance from the letters' faces down to the adjacent spaces allowed the spaces to contact the paper. A page printed from such a surface would be marred by blackened areas (or "monks"). The proofing and correction processes went on as usual, foul though the appearance of the proofs may have been. But after the final author's revise had been approved, the formes of type went off to the stereotype foundry for casting into plates. Thus all the copies of an edition stereotyped with the plaster method were printed exclusively from the plates; such was not the case later in the century, when new materials for molding were introduced.

There were other differences in composition attendant on stereotyping. The overall size of a cast plate was restricted for several reasons. Uneven rates of expansion and contraction of the metal during casting and cooling caused warping, a problem that became more serious with large plates. Second, large plates were more likely than small ones to flex and crack under the pressure of printing. Finally, there was a limit on how much accumulated weight of plaster molds, casting metal, and iron casting boxes workmen could handle. Thus in this earlier form of stereotyping, an individual plate was cast for each page of text, a practice that necessitated changes in composing room routines.

When a work was printed from types and proofed in sheets, the author's final revise represented the typesetting as it would be printed, barring unauthorized interventions like those mentioned at the beginning of this chapter. The same forme of typeset pages used to print the last proofs, correct in margin and imposition sequence, would be imposed in a press or machine for printing. But for stereotyping in single-page plates, after proofing the forme had to be unlocked and the pages lifted. Each page was then locked in a special one-page chase for molding. Beyond the usual risks to textual accuracy when a block of type is lifted, there was a further

---

★This account of the plaster process is drawn from numerous nineteenth-century sources, chiefly the works of Southward, Hansard, Partridge, Wilson, and Hodgson, supplemented by the manuscript memoirs of Herbert G. Smart in the St. Bride Printing Library, all cited in the Bibliography.

hazard; to minimize problems in making and releasing the plaster mold, the pages of type were not to be locked up as tightly in a stereotyping chase as they were in a printing chase. The chances of having a page falling to pie were also increased by the amount of handling it would receive in the foundry.

The plaster, often referred to by English stereotypers as gypsum, was ordinary processed plaster of paris. The powdered form was mixed with water to the consistency of heavy cream. The one-page forme of type was placed within a molding frame standing about a half-inch above the type, and the surface was brushed with a thin oil which acted as a releasing agent. The plaster of paris was poured over the type, worked into the surface with a brush or the hands, and leveled across the top of the frame. Sometimes two grades of plaster were used, a fine-grained one in a thin layer contacting the type faces, with a coarser grade following it to make the mold stronger. The plaster was allowed to set up for fifteen minutes or more, after which the half-cured female mold could be carefully lifted from the forme. Not uncommonly, the plaster stuck to the type or cracked during removal; before another attempt could be made, the forme had to be scrubbed and washed down with lye, then rinsed and dried. Once a mold was successfully taken, it was cured further in a low-temperature drying oven. The forme of type, now encrusted with bits of plaster and oily residue, either remained in the foundry until casting and proofing were completed, or went directly back to the composing room to be cleaned and distributed into the cases. Washing and picking clean type after plaster molding were tedious and unpleasant tasks added to a compositor's duties, sometimes without additional pay.

Little wonder, then, that the compositors had opposed stereotyping. As it became a general practice, they demanded changes in their working arrangements with printers. In an 1845 agreement, an extra charge was exacted specifically for composing for stereotyping, "because of the loss accruing to the compositor, by the imposition, the many formes he has to lock up, and the loss of time he sustains, from the work being stereo-typed." According to a similar contract two years later, there was a surcharge of about 5 percent for composition when stereotyping, and an additional fee of one shilling per sheet for locking up individual pages in small chases.[12] Over the years, expansion of the printing business, especially the enormous increase in the number of periodicals, most of them printed with plates, turned stereotyping from a bane to a boon for compositors, and by the last third of the century there were large specialized foundries in every city.

After baking the plaster mold for about half an hour, the stereotype founder placed it in an iron casting box and filled it with plate metal. This was similar to type metal, but the proportions of ingredients were altered to give a softer alloy. Every stereotyper seems to have had a secret recipe. Here is Hansard's own, to be used in lieu of commercially prepared ingots: "1. From five to eight parts lead, one of regulus [of semipurified antimony], one fiftieth of block-tin. 2. One seventh of pure regulus, six sevenths of lead. The best lead is that which comes from China, in the lining of tea-chests." Hansard adds, "The mixing of the lead is exceedingly injurious to the workman, and should be avoided whenever it is possible. The foundry should be thoroughly ventilated, as the fumes . . . are very noxious."[13]

Several casting box designs seem to have been tried. Though details are scarce, apparently one early type stood on end with plate molds held vertically inside; the hot metal must have been poured in and allowed either to overflow or to vent through holes on the sides.[14] This approach was abandoned, only to be revived much later, after molding with plaster had been superseded. To prevent voids in the casting, it was imperative that the metal drive out the air in the box completely. A different form of casting box, in use by 1820, was univerally adopted. In this design, the mold was laid face down in a deep, heavy pan with a loose-fitting lid; a floating iron plate below the mold rose as metal flowed in, expelling the air. Box, lid, mold, and iron plate, all preheated in an oven, were lowered as an assembly into a vat of molten metal for about fifteen minutes. The box was then lifted out with a crane and cooled in water until it could be handled. The lid was removed, the mold and plate lifted out, and the plaster broken away to free the casting. The plate that emerged was a solid metal replica of the types from which the mold had been taken. In this unfinished state it was about three-sixteenths of an inch thick, and if the proportions of the alloy were even slightly wrong, or if the heating and cooling stages were too abrupt, it would be brittle. Because the plaster mold shrank in the drying oven and the casting metal shrank as it was cooled, the printing surface of the plate was slightly smaller in every dimension than the types from which it was made. The overall shrinkage rate ranged from 1 to 3 percent.[15] This seemingly small difference is quite visible when it is possible to compare proofs pulled from types with pages printed by stereos from the same types.

A stereo plate fresh from the casting box was far from ready for printing. If gross defects or cracks were discovered at this point, the forme would have to be cleaned, a new mold of it made, and a fresh plate cast. If all seemed well, the rough plate was handed over for finishing. After any large metal flashings at the edges were cut away, the surface was checked for flatness; indentations, caused by uneven cooling of the metal, had to be "beaten up" to type height by gently hammering the back of the plate while the front was held against a cushioned flat surface. A specialized lathe was then used to turn the back of the plate until it was flat and parallel to the face; the finished thickness was one-eighth to one-sixth of an inch. Next the edges of the plate were trimmed for squareness and cut with a bevel to accommodate the mounting blocks and retaining catches that would secure the plate in the press. Finally, the plate went to the "picker," who examined it closely for minute imperfections of the printing surface. The picker used a narrow gouge and an engraving tool to deepen the white lines and larger white spaces; this was necessary because of the high spaces and leads used in composition for stereotyping. Fragments of plaster remaining within letters and any extraneous bits of metal ("picks"), which would show in printing, had to be delicately excised.

A finished plate was placed in a proof press in the foundry and an impression taken; this plate proof was read by a supervisor against the foundry proof which had accompanied the formes of type from the composing room. If the proof revealed serious faults in the plate, such as irregularities too thick to be remedied by beating up and replaning the back, a new casting would have to be made. The probability of such problems was great enough that unless a rush was on, formes were kept in the foundry until the plate proofs were satisfactory. Lesser defects, ranging from turned or erroneous letters to missing words and misplaced lines, could be corrected by altering the plate. This work was performed by an expert picker with special tools.

Errors involving single letters were cut from the plate with a small hollow punch; the hole was filed to a suitable size and shape, and the correct piece of ordinary type was pressed in place. The picker then soldered the type to the back of the plate and filed off the protruding stub (inevitable because types were taller than the thickness of the plate). This method was marginally effective for corrections of a single letter or word. When the repair consisted of several words or entire lines, the correct matter was set in type, molded, and cast just as a complete plate was. The erroneous part of the plate was cut away, and the cast slug inserted and soldered in place. The degree to which existing plates were altered was remarkable; the twentieth-century stereotyper Herbert Smart characterizes "the possibilities of alteration and correction" as "almost limitless."[16] Whole paragraphs, sometimes comprising more than half a page, could be replaced; extensive, skillful repairing and substitution made it possible to

continue using a set of plates after the types had been distributed. An-
thologies could be altered, reference books updated, and works of literature revised, by altering existing plates and running new impressions
instead of setting up fresh type for a new edition.

But plate repairs and alterations, whether large or small, caused
problems, and not just for bibliographers struggling to identify editions
and concealed impressions. Pieces of type soldered into a plate do, as
Hansard pronounced, mar the appearance of the printed page. The inserted types are often slightly higher or lower than exact type height, and
will print darker or lighter accordingly. They will usually be off-line,
incorrectly spaced, or slightly turned from vertical. The insertions are
inevitably larger than the surrounding letters, even when taken from the
same font as the original setting, because of the shrinkage of the plate
during molding and casting. Replaced blocks of text, even when cast in
plate metal, are often not exactly parallel with the unaltered lines. Furthermore, the force of punching out errors and the heat of the soldering torch
stress and embrittle each point of repair, making both the corrected
portions and the entire plate more subject to damage during printing.

Successful as the plaster method was, its drawbacks were significant.
Besides the increases in labor and costs attendant on the molding and
casting, plaster-mold stereotyping was a slow process. If something went
awry in the latter stages, hours of work were wasted, and further time lost
to the printing house, while the steps of molding, casting, and finishing
were repeated. The necessity of composing types in a form useless for
anything but plaster molding, as well as the difficulty of producing
replacements for plates damaged by the press or in storage, were problems
that did not occur when printing from types. British printers, compositors, and publishers, who had become not only acclimated to but dependent on stereotyping, eagerly adopted a new way of making molds from
type, the papier-mâché process developed in France.

THE PAPER METHOD

As with the plaster-mold process, a multiplicity of claimants for the title of
inventor renders the origins and early developments of the paper method
somewhat indistinct. Authorities on British printing agree that the French
had cast printing plates with paper molds from type formes by 1830. An
English patent was issued for such molds in 1839, but little commercial use
seems to have been made of them before 1846. In that year, a maker of
plaster copies of statues, identified by Wilson only as "Vanoni," demonstrated in England a way of molding with papier-mâché. At about the

same time, James Dellagana established a stereotype foundry in London to
make plates by the "new French process," as the English called it. Dellagana quickly found great success, winning a contract to produce all the
plates for the *Times*. The immediate spread of the paper process is indicated by a contract between master printers and compositors in 1847.
There it was agreed that the surcharges on stereotyping, exacted because
of the inconvenience and messiness of the plaster method, would be
dropped if any new, less troublesome means of stereotyping were generally adopted by the trade.[17]

By 1860, according to Southward, "the change from movable type to
stereo plates for newspaper printing had been accomplished," but as usual
book printers clung to the older method for some time. The reason was
that the fine details of a typeface were not reproduced in a stereo plate cast
from a paper mold. Even the strongest proponents of the new process had
to admit that "the plates thus produced [with plaster molds] are in all
respects superior to those obtained by the Paper process, being deeper and
sharper." The excellence of reproduction achieved with the plaster tech-
nique can be seen in Hodgson's early history of stereotyping, which
includes specimen pages printed from plaster-mold plates made (or ac-
quired) by Hodgson. The printing in these pages is beautiful, the impression perfectly even, and every letter sharp and clear. Hansard had insisted
that pages printed from plates were inferior in appearance to those printed
from type, and unquestionably the paper method yielded plates that could
not rival their predecessors. The quality of Hodgson's samples, especially
in comparison with a late nineteenth-century magazine or other typical
product of paper molding, illustrates what book printers were reluctant to
give up.[18]

In every other respect, casting plates with paper molds was superior,
being faster, cleaner, and easily repeatable. The improvements were visible in the composing room: because the paper mold when dried was
tough, flexible, and cohesive, it was easily removed from types set in the
ordinary fashion. No high spaces and leads were needed, and formes could
be (and were) used for printing after molds were taken from it. Though
the types were still oiled before molding, they came back from the
foundry much cleaner than with the plaster method. Paper molding
eliminated the risk of cracking a large plaster mold when releasing it from
the forme, and more than one page could be molded at a time. Such a
multipage mold might have to be cut up before casting, since the size of
stereo plates was still limited by the weight, softness, and thermal response of the metal. But by 1875 metallurgy had improved enough for

Southward to report that "pages of newspapers and bookwork formes are now cast entire."[19] The total time required, from beginning to mold through delivering a finished plate, dropped from around two hours (when using plaster) to fifteen minutes.

On their arrival at the foundry, larger formes of type would be subdivided and reimposed in smaller chases holding two or four pages (late in the century, up to eight pages were cast as a single plate). After the types were cleaned and oiled, a sheet of "flong" was laid on the forme. This soggy substance was not simple papier-mâché; it was composed of layers of soft paper, laminated together with water-based organic glues. Dampening the flong made it possible to force the paper fibers down into the type faces. This step was called "beating the forme" because it was initially done by repeatedly striking the flong with stiff brushes; around the turn of the century a molding press replaced the beating-brush. The beaten flong, either still on the forme or separated from it, was then dried at moderate heat in an oven. With thorough beating and a little care in removal and handling, an excellent female mold (or matrix) of the type was produced almost every time. Paper molds shrank far less in curing than plaster ones, allowing for more satisfactory repairs to finished plates.

Once the paper matrix was removed from the forme, the types could be distributed. The cured paper and glue were durable enough that a series of plates could be cast from them; if a fault occurred during the casting, no remolding was necessary. Paper matrices could be sent immediately to the foundry, or stored for later use. After a set of plates was made, the matrices could be set aside to produce fresh plates for later impressions. Duplicate matrices could be produced initially, to be sold and shipped to overseas printers for foreign editions. Though on some earlier occasions multiple molds had been made in plaster from one set of formes, the resulting duplicate plates being stored or sold off, the paper method made such dealings cheap and easy.

The casting of the plates proceeded along the same lines as with plaster molds. The composition of the metal did not change significantly, though the purity of the ingredients improved. The thinness of the paper matrix allowed the molten metal to flow more easily inside the casting box. This in turn became a smaller and lighter device, which could be stood on end and filled instead of having to be lowered into a vat. The most notable advance was the successful manufacture of curved plates for rotary presses. The flexible paper mold was mounted in a curved casting box, and the plate produced could be mounted directly onto the cylinder of the rotary machine. These plates and machines were used for newspapers and magazines; flat plates continued to be the rule for bookwork. The trimming, finishing, picking, and alteration of plates were unchanged by the paper method, though the accuracy of the casting process improved enough that less turning and truing were required. Book plates were made lighter by casting them with concave backs; only the thick rim had to be machined to achieve a flat mounting. From the experiments of Stanhope to the fast, efficient molding and casting of the 1880s, a slow revolution took place in British stereotyping. And beyond the improvements in speed and tidiness at the printing houses, the paper method had great impact on publishers, who were given a new set of choices about how to handle an author's work.

Until the arrival of the paper-mold method of stereotyping, and the mechanical typecaster, a book publisher was forced to make a shrewd guess as to the size of an edition. Since the type used for the early sheets was needed for later ones, all the copies of a sheet had to be printed at once; the formes would then be lifted from the press or machine and the types cleaned and distributed for immediate reuse. If an unduly optimistic publisher ordered too many copies, he would be left with unsold stock of an aging book. On the other hand, if a work proved more popular than he had anticipated, he either paid the cost of composing and printing the text in a new edition or had to pass up an opportunity for further profits. Publishers could hedge against the first case by keeping edition quantities small, especially for new authors or works on subjects of limited appeal. Sometimes this precaution was taken with established authors as well; the first edition of Browning's *Men and Women* (1855) was probably no larger than 750 or 1,000 copies, but Chapman and Hall still had copies of it in stock over eight years later. Since publishers believed that buyers resisted paying full price for "old" books, they sometimes attempted another strategy: the expectation of a slow sale over a period of years was one reason why some Victorian editions bear no date on their title pages.

The second possibility was more problematic, and a publisher's temperament and outlook (and financial situation) dictated how it would be met. John Blackwood wrote to George Eliot about the size of the first book edition of *Scenes of Clerical Life*: "I think it wisest to print a short number [he had proposed 750] but do not let that discourage you. No man can approach to anything like an accurate idea of the probable demand for a book when there are no previous data to go upon, and it is best to err upon the safe side. We shall also be able to keep a large portion of the Type standing so that we will be ready to meet an extended demand very quickly." This approach, though troublesome in terms of type supplies, gave some flexibility, and Blackwood in fact increased the run of the first edition of *Scenes* to 1,050.[20]

Plaster-mold stereotyping made such business decisions even more complex, by offering an option which could pay great dividends but closed off other avenues once it was taken. Large publishing houses with their own printing works could let a book stand in type while public demand developed. With the plaster process, however, the decision to stereotype had to be made before composition began, and there was no going back. Formes for plaster stereotyping had to be specially composed and were unsuitable for printing. But the paper method, which could use types composed for regular printing, allowed a publisher to have paper matrices made before printing a relatively small first edition from the type; when this was struck off, the type could be broken up and distributed. If later demand warranted it, he could then have plates cast from the molds and carry on with successive stereotype impressions. This was exactly what Macmillan chose to do in 1878 with Matthew Arnold's edition of selections from Samuel Johnson's *Lives of the Poets*. His statement of Arnold's account as of 21 November read: "*Johnson's Lives*—We printed 1500. . . . Should we need to reprint you would be paid at a higher rate—for we have taken an impression in paper of the type & we could make stereo-plates."[21]

ELECTROTYPES

While the paper method swept the printing business, developments were also occurring in electrotyping. Though this method of producing a printing surface was introduced in 1839, electrotypes were used so little in printing the texts of Victorian books that a brief treatment will suffice. The aims of electrotyping are the same as those of stereotyping: the liberation of types for reuse and the production of a fixed printing surface durable enough to last through thousands of impressions. The process itself also has parallels with the making of stereos.

The first step was the preparation of a large sheet of wax, molded into a shallow tray and coated with graphite. The forme of type—composed as for printing, with normal spaces and leads—was liberally dusted with graphite and pressed into the wax, which took the place of plaster or flong in the other methods of plating. The resultant female wax mold was then coated with conducting paste and placed in a tank of copper sulphate solution; electric current was passed through the bath by means of copper anodes, the graphite on the wax becoming the cathode. Electrolysis slowly deposited copper on the mold, creating a thin but tough "shell" that replicated the original types. This shell was peeled from the wax and coated with molten tin; stereo metal was then poured into the back of the shell to make a plate, which was trimmed and finished as in stereotyping.

Electrotyping produced a sharp, fine image, and was thus perfectly suited for reproducing illustrations, large display types, and other complex figures. The copper printing surface was much harder than stereotype alloy, and electros lasted up to ten times as long as stereos. This hardness had the corresponding disadvantage of making electroplates more difficult to alter or repair than stereo plates, and if an electro was damaged beyond repair, there was no paper matrix from which to make a duplicate. An electrotyping works was also a dangerous, unhealthy place, full of caustic chemicals and poisonous fumes. Southward points out: "It costs less to stereotype a given surface than to electrotype it, and the operation can be performed, especially by the papier mâché process, in a shorter time than electrotyping."[22] For all of these reasons, to which must be added the habitual conservatism of those involved in bookwork, the vast majority of Victorian books continued to be printed from stereotype plates, through the rest of the century. Electros were used for illustrations; a small electrotype might be soldered into the stereo of a page of text, or a page containing illustrations could be electrotyped as a whole. The difference in sharpness between the electrotyped text of a page with illustrations and an adjacent page printed from a stereotype plate is frequently very obvious.

Printing with Plates

The foregoing discussion emphasized the utility for printers of freeing up composed types as soon as plates were cast or molds taken. After the introduction of mechanical typecasters, however, this was of less crucial importance; and with the advent of the paper process, with its use of conventionally set types, printers took advantage of the two innovations to increase their rate of production. Instead of being distributed after molding, formes of type could be used for printing simultaneously with formes of plates cast from them, effectively doubling the typesetting. The simplest way to print twice as many copies in a given time would be to run a job in parallel, on two presses or machines, but often the patterns were much more complicated. Depending on the imposition scheme, the types and the plates of the same pages might have been in one press at the same time; or one side of a sheet may have been printed from types and the other side from plates. Of course none of this had been possible with plaster stereotyping, in which all the copies of an edition were printed from plates. As will be seen, the difference in performance between type and plates during printing created significant textual problems.

Finished plates came from the foundry about one-eighth of an inch thick. To bring them up near type height (which was variable, but hovered around fifteen-sixteenths of an inch), they were fixed onto hardwood blocks ("risers") with small nails along the beveled edges of the plates, or clamped onto metal blocks with brass latches that captured the edge of the bevel. Plates were sometimes mounted individually and the several blocks imposed by the compositors in a standard-sized chase; but entire formes of plates were also imposed and secured onto a single large riser. This step seems to have given some difficulty, because in 1845 the compositors complained of stereos: "The trouble of imposition, in fact, is increased, at least two-fold, by the large bevels that encircle the pages." Time and experience led to improvements, and by 1884, Southward tells us, in larger firms "formes of mounts of regular sizes are kept ready locked up, and only require to be unloosened, the plates laid down in their places, and re-fastened up again, when they are ready to be worked from."[23]

A forme of plates lay in the bed of the press or machine like a forme of types, but fine adjustments were required with stereos. Variations in the thicknesses of plates and risers made it a certainty that a bedful of them would never print well the first time. The exact height required for an even impression was attained by underlaying the plates with layers of heavy paper. The pressman took a first impression on waste paper to check the imposition pattern and evenness of color. Uneven types would have been leveled by planing (loosening the forme slightly on a flat surface and passing a roller over it) in the composing room, but uneven plates had to be lifted up for careful underlaying. The pressman expected to have to repeat the process, and the printers' manuals viewed making a press or machine ready to print as considerably more complicated and tedious with stereos than with types.[24]

On the other hand, printers liked the fact that plates could be readily shifted to ensure correct margins and gutters, without any risk to the typeset matter. This also enabled the pressman to make adjustments for correct registration of the front and back of a sheet. Publishers exploited a related advantage, one that frequently compounds problems of bibliographical identification: by altering margins and paper, the same plates could be used for separate issues and states of the same edition. Furthermore, single-page plates could be locked in the same chase with pages of type, and this was done as early as 1841.[25] Combining the two printing surfaces allowed the easy substitution of title pages for different issues, the insertion of different running heads, or updating of the advertisements often used to fill the unused pages in the last sheet of a volume; all could be done without the danger of accidental disruption of the text itself. Since it can be extremely difficult to determine by inspection alone whether a particular page was printed from type or a plate, it might seem that this matter is of only peripheral interest to textual scholarship. But the combining of types and plates to print an edition is indeed textually important, because these two printing surfaces behave quite differently under the stresses of printing. We have seen that making a deliberate textual change in a forme of types requires a particular set of actions and entails a particular set of risks to typographical accuracy. Altering a plate requires different actions and imposes other kinds of risks. There is a similar divergence in the realm of unintended changes, for during printing types and plates wear, decay, and alter themselves in differing ways.

The primary cause of the difference in performance is that plate metal is softer than type metal. This was the basis of one of Hansard's early objections to stereotyping: "Type-metal is too hard to cast plates from. It must be lowered; that is, softened by an addition of lead." If the correct proportions were not used, the alloy would be faulty: "If it be too hard the plates will be more liable to damage by the failure of delicate strokes in the face of the letters, which cannot be so easily rectified as where such defects happen to fusil [i.e., ordinary metal] types. If, on the contrary, it be too soft, the want of durability is a self-apparent consequence."[26] British founders and printers evidently leaned toward harder alloys, because "the failure of delicate strokes" is a very common sight in nineteenth-century stereotyped books. But these harder plates also outlasted type. Though exact figures are scarce, standard type was worn beyond use after about twenty-five thousand impressions, while stereos could yield about sixty thousand. After the turn of the century, stereo plates were faced with nickel, giving them a useful life of one hundred thousand impressions, and copper electrotypes were good for over half a million.*

Enhanced durability was of great importance in newspaper and magazine printing, but most books were not produced in such vast quantities.

---

*These estimates come from twentieth-century sources, but type-metal and ordinary stereo metal had not changed appreciably since Victorian times. See Bastien, *Practical Typography*, 57; Billing and Sons, *The Foundry*, 21; Partridge, *Stereotyping*, 52; Smart, "Electrotyping and Stereotyping," x.

For book publishers, the value of stereotyping lay in the ability to order successive small impressions of a work in response to changing demand. Preserving an initial typesetting by stereotyping meant that a book was "in print" as long as the plates lasted or their paper molds were kept, though there might not be even one printed copy on hand. The sheer scale of the storage facilities for plates impressed Victorian observers. George Dodd, visiting the huge Clowes printing works in the early 1840s, described a warehouse holding hundreds of thousands of stereos: "The plates are all wrapped separately in paper (each page of the book having a distinct plate), and then stored away in a warehouse, properly marked and labelled. The stereotype warehouse affords a most striking example of the value which metal acquires when mental and mechanical ingenuity has been bestowed upon it. In this one apartment are collected stereotype plates whose estimated value is not much less than *half a million sterling!*"[27]

Forty years later, Percy Russell toured an unnamed London printing house and rendered the sight in similar tones of awe: "One store house is a large chamber some thirty feet long, divided into five alleys, giving access to the sets of pigeon holes which reach from floor to ceiling—some fifteen feet—each of which contains one sheet, in stereotype or electrotype plates, of various works which have attained the distinguished honour of being stereotyped. . . . Of these pigeon holes there are reckoned to be seventy thousand."[28]

Year after year, impression after impression, plates were reused—and unquestionably overused, as a glance at a late impression of the *Dictionary of National Biography* or the Cabinet Edition of the works of George Eliot will show. A relatively durable printing surface did not confer any special immunity on plates, as Hansard pointed out early in the century: "These plates are not exempt from the same accidents to which type formes are liable in their progress of working." And though Hansard admitted the economic advantage to a publisher of reusing stereos rather than paying for the composition of a new edition, he decried the results: "Every edition from the plates must also get progressively worse and worse. . . . These plates are particularly liable to injury, from their weight and brittleness, from blows, from picks and batters, which will happen notwithstanding the greatest care, from fractures at the edges in placing on the blocks or raisers, and many other fortuitous circumstances. These it is difficult to remedy, and, when remedied, they present a most unsightly appearance."[29]

The fragility of the finer details of letters, caused by the brittle nature of the plate metal, led Alexander Macmillan to ask Matthew Arnold to rescind a change he requested for the 1879 stereotyped edition of his selections from Wordsworth: "The printers appeal to us about a correction you suggest in the type of the Wordsworth Selections. It is making the head lines & titles of the poems in italics. . . . It is impossible to work from italic head lines after a time—for being at the top of the page & standing alone they break & look rotten after one or two printings, & we hope for many editions from this book."[30]

Obviously, headlines and titles were not the only part of the text so affected. Stereotype plates were liable to weaken, sink, and break at their edges, a problem caused and exacerbated by the mounting nails and catches. As a consequence, letters and words at the margins occasionally printed faintly or disappeared altogether. More subtle textual changes resulted from the pervasive decay of the smaller features of the printing surface, particularly punctuation marks. Exclamation points and question marks decay to periods; double quotes become single; semicolons turn into commas; commas erode and read as periods. These changes, creating readings no one ever intended, are reductive, in that they result from lost printing details. But it was also possible (though rarely) for plate decay to create a reading by adding something to the printing surface. Because plate metal was soft, and the distance from the printing face down to the white areas rather shallow, broken bits of metal tended to stick to the plate. The tail of a comma, once broken free, might lodge between letters or on a white space; it could then take ink and print on the next sheet of paper. This happened over several impressions of Browning's collected edition of 1888–89, and when sufficient copies are examined side by side, the punctuation at the end of one line can be observed to change itself gradually from the original period and double quotation marks to an apparent colon and single quotation mark.

Types, while subject to many hazards during printing, do not fail in exactly this way. When types, or clumps of type, loosen and disappear during an impression, they do so instantaneously, between the striking off of one sheet and the next. Loosened type will commonly adhere to the sheet and lift up slightly; the force of the platen or cylinder pushes them back into place and printing proceeds normally until they are loose enough to come free completely. The hardness of type metal and the greater height from shoulder to face make it far less likely that a pick will adhere and print.

The textually significant decay of plates described above generally occurred gradually, though such faults were not solely dependent on the total number of impressions a plate had undergone. They happened to plates that had been molded and cast perfectly, with no alterations required before going to press. Plates that had been altered or repaired were still more subject to failures. It was difficult for a picker to solder letters into a plate at precisely the correct height; if they were low, corrections might print faintly or not at all. If the insertions were too high, the force of the platen or cylinder could break them loose or crack the plate; with hollow-backed plates, the inserted piece could be knocked into the cavity behind the printing surface, escaping notice as a fractured plate would not. A particularly illustrative instance of this set of problems occurs in the history of Browning's sixteen-volume *Poetical Works* of 1888–89.[31] For this edition, the last in his lifetime, Browning carefully revised copies of earlier editions for use as copy; he read proofs of the new edition with meticulous attention, and stereotype plates were cast immediately after proofing. The first impression appeared in two issues, a large-paper one (limited to 250 copies) and a standard trade issue. Initial demand was strong enough that a second impression of the earlier volumes of the trade issue was called for while the later volumes were still being printed in their first impression. Never one to abstain from an opportunity to touch up his text, Browning sent his publisher a list of corrections to be made in the second impression.

Browning's alterations, or most of them, were made in the plates; all were small enough to be done by inserting types. But the life span of the textual corrections was severely limited by the fragility of the insertions. As the edition went through impression after impression—it was listed in catalogues at least until 1916, the title page of the second and later impressions always bearing the date 1889—the corrections decayed and in many cases disappeared. Since this did not happen all at once or in any determined order, individual copies of this edition vary significantly in the degree to which they represent Browning's intentions about how his text should read. For example, at one point where the first trade impression had a period at the end of a line, Browning asked that an exclamation point be substituted in the second impression. A few copies of the second impression have the exclamation point, proving that it was indeed worked into the plate; but most have no punctuation at all in the space where the period had been. With various dating techniques, these volumes can be placed in the sequence in which they were printed, and when this is done it can be concluded that the stresses of printing either broke off the inserted piece of type or drove it downward until it would no longer print. Thus a typesetting on which author, publisher, and printer had labored in pursuit of the highest possible degree of accuracy was rendered inaccurate as a direct result of the limitations of printing technology.

This sort of textual variation could not have been easily detected during printing because it was happening on a small scale and was diffused throughout a set of plates. If a plate actually caved in or split, it would either have upset the running of the press or produced sheets sufficiently botched to be noticed immediately. During the days of plaster stereotyping, a plate that failed after printing was well under way and could not be mended was a disaster, unless the rare precaution of making duplicates had been taken. Resetting the type, molding in plaster, and casting a fresh plate brought about not only a long delay but also the likelihood of new textual errors. With paper molds, duplicate plates might well have been made initially, but if they had not, a fresh plate could be cast up quickly. A replacement plate cast from an existing paper matrix would print a text in the state of the original plate proof, reproducing the typesetting as it had been molded.

It would seem that this convenient, repeatable process eliminated any legitimate excuse for printers' continuing to use worn or much-repaired stereos. Yet demonstrable instances in which book plates were replaced, whether with duplicates cast initially or with recastings done during an impression, are difficult to find. The close examination of early and late copies of stereotyped editions known to have gone through many impressions reveals consistent patterns of developing scratches, batters, and signs of decay from beginning to end. Minute faults appear in earlier copies and persist through later ones, the impression surface never reverting to the fresh, undamaged condition that would characterize a replacement casting. We may take this as an indication that irremediable plate fractures were relatively unusual, and as testimony to the skill of those who repaired the damage that did occur. The reasons why plates were not regularly replaced when substantially worn down are unclear, but they presumably had more to do with economics than with a concern for the quality of the printed product.

Textual Consequences of Stereotyping

Besides giving rise to inaccuracies caused by the decaying of plates as described above, stereotyping affected authors' control of their texts in several ways. Some of these matters have to do with reprinting and authorial revisions for reprints, and will be treated in later chapters. But it is worthwhile here to establish what Victorian authors knew about stereotyping, how they viewed it, and how they worked with their texts when plates were to be made. We have seen that most book printers and publishers had wholeheartedly embraced the virtues of stereotyping by the later 1860s. While few authors seem to have agreed with T. H. that "stereotyping should never be resorted to," equally few appear to have endorsed Russell's characterization of it as a "crowning honour."[32]

Those writers who edited or served on the great Victorian periodicals, as Dickens, Thackeray, and Eliot did, quite naturally learned about stereotyping as it became the normal way of printing magazines. Without such direct instruction, Arnold, Browning, and Tennyson still came to know enough about stereotyping to feel its advantages and limitations. Eliot, for instance, understood the usefulness of plates when simultaneous issues in different formats were planned. Blackwood proposed in 1861 to republish her earlier works in a six-shilling edition. The new typesetting was to be stereotyped, and Eliot seems to have been considering this as an opportunity to make revisions that would stand for some time. On 23 March she wrote to Blackwood: "I suppose the types of the 6/. edition whenever it is printed will serve for all cheaper editions, by altering the paper and narrowing the edges."[33]

Other comments by Eliot show that in her eyes the primary consequence of stereotyping was its freezing of a text. In 1873, she wrote to Alexander Main about an error he had discovered in *Middlemarch*, which was printed with plates from the outset:

> *Thanks. You are quite right. The reading ought to be—"any more than vanity makes us witty" [rather than "vanity will help us to be witty"].*
>
> *But the book is stereotyped, and I fear that I cannot well make corrections for the next edition [i.e., impression]. I shall note the error which you have kindly pointed out. There are doubtless many others either of pen or type, and I have a great longing to make the text as correct as I can. But I am afraid of looking at it, until I can be free from the sense that every correction demands a new plate.*[34]

The limited understanding suggested by the last sentence is a pose; Eliot not only knew about plate correction, but had often been reassured by Blackwood that she could request revisions to existing stereos for later impressions. Main was an enthusiast who was given to sending Eliot lengthy observations on the minutiae of her works, and on this occasion he had written at an inopportune time. Eliot's exhausting labors on the novel had been rewarded with ever-increasing sales; a new impression had just been ordered; and here was Main with his quibble about the agreement of verb tenses. By hinting at supposed great difficulty and expense in making any change to plates, Eliot was able to give Main a genteel brush-off; she closed her letter with the request that he "note any other errors which present themselves and save the register for me." A later observation to Main shows her clear understanding that it was not the *text*, but the size and length of a work which plating fixed: "There is one disadvantage among the many advantages of stereotyping, that the form of book becomes irrevocable."[35]

From the first, stereotyping had been recommended to printers and publishers on three grounds: it freed up type, it lowered the cost of reprints, and it prevented the introduction of typesetting errors in reprints by preserving a text just after it was carefully proofed. The latter point had been made so well that authors, who saw that corrections and revisions were prevented to the same degree as new errors, became wary of stereotyping. Their thoughts might have echoed Hansard, who had asked in 1851, "What work is there so perfect as not to require some alteration and amendment in a new edition, which, in stereotype, is practicable only to a limited extent?" The fixity of a stereotyped text we have seen to be an illusion; the impression surface gradually disintegrated and altered itself during printing, and deliberate changes could be made freely. Printers made allowances for authorial revisions, because "frequently . . . the author wishes to make changes or corrections in the matter after the plates have been finished." To deal with this, Russell tells us, "there is a department where corrections are made in stereo plates, generally the result of the author's afterthought."[36]

Yet there were practical limits on the amount of revision authors were allowed. For every publisher's invitation to an author to send in requests for alterations to a plated typesetting, there was a reminder that things could not go too far. Alexander Macmillan wrote to Matthew Arnold about the "library edition" of *A Bible-Reading for Schools*, which would appear with additional matter and the new title *Isaiah XL-LXVI* in 1875: "Your appendix, & adequate instructions to the printer, have duly reached us. We have sent it on & they promise to get it done on time. Is this a sort of book you would allow to be stereotyped? There is a good deal of advantage in this, if you feel that you are not likely to make more than verbal changes in future editions."[37]

Arnold agreed to this, but a few years earlier his reluctance to allow stereotyping had reflected the same thoughts about form that Eliot expressed. He wrote to his mother in 1869 about Macmillan's forthcoming two-volume collection of his poems: "The order of arrangement in this edition is not quite the final one I shall adopt; on this final order I could not decide till I saw this collected edition. The next edition will have the final order, and then the book will be stereotyped."[38]

The prospect of stereotyping, then, prompted Victorian authors to think deeply about the state a text was in. If a work had been revised, either before or after its first appearance, to a point where major rewriting was no longer likely, the casting of plates promised the elimination or substantial reduction of proofreading for subsequent printings; furthermore, the author's profits on later impressions would be greater, and a book need never be unavailable as long as the plates or paper matrices were kept. Conversely, only small (though potentially numerous) revisions would be possible after stereotyping, even though the opportunities for such changes would be multiplied by the practice of running numerous small impressions in response to demand. A Victorian author's revisions for a stereotyped edition may deserve a privileged textual status, on the grounds that the author had powerful incentives to make this typesetting represent as fully as possible his or her considered intentions.

Printing Machines

During the nineteenth century, the British printing industry converted from the printing press to the printing machine. In the vocabulary of Victorian printers, the term *press* was restricted to hand-operated printing presses; any printing device, of whatever configuration, which ran on steam or other power was called a *printing machine*. The rigor of this distinction (which was ignored only in established idioms like "going to press" and "in the press") is important to the interpretation of nineteenth-century documents, because it allows us to know exactly what was used at various stages of proofing and printing. So that source material may be clearly understood in its context, the following discussion, though concerned almost entirely with powered machines, will maintain Victorian terminology.

Detailed histories of the development of printing presses and machines are plentiful, and it would be redundant to repeat or give digests of them here. The best brief treatment is that of Philip Gaskell,[39] which reproduces useful illustrations of various machines. The present investigation of the ways in which changing printing technology affected the transmission of texts (and thus the representation of authors' intentions toward their texts) will focus on just two aspects of machines: their speed and those features of their operation which inhibited the detection of textual faults. There were many kinds of machines, most of ingenious and intricate design, and it is usually impossible to determine precisely which kind produced a given Victorian book. Yet educated guesses about this can be useful, since machines and the manner of their working had demonstrable effects on textual accuracy.

An early Victorian book is very much a handmade thing. Though it may have come from a press made of iron rather than wood, its text had been composed by hand with individual types; its sheets had been printed from those types with hand presses run by two or three people, in an edition of a few hundred or a thousand copies, each of which was folded, gathered, stitched, and bound by hand. And though the processes of printing, binding, and eventually even composition were mechanized during the nineteenth century, the hand press did not disappear. It was cheap, durable, simple to operate, and easy on the forme; it was thus perfect for pulling proofs, and Albion iron hand presses continued to be used for proofing in the British printing business through the 1920s. Toward the end of the last century, the English arts and crafts movement, the social and literary experiments of William Morris, and the infant industry in fine, limited, ornamental, and other special editions spurred a different kind of interest in the old-fashioned printing press. Nor was the hand press quickly replaced in ordinary book production. A pamphlet from 1856 entitled *The Search for a Publisher* solicits authors to submit their manuscripts to the firm of F. and W. Cash, who would print and publish books on the half-profits scheme. Besides sample pages and lists of works already published, the Cash brothers included an illustration of their London printing office, showing several rows of iron hand presses, but no machines. Since not every literary work we now call a classic found a major publisher in its day, it is likely that the first editions of some very famous late Victorian books were produced by hand, in the midst of the age of the machine.

But from the 1850s onward, the texts of successful authors appeared in numerous editions, thousands of copies at a time, printed from stereotype plates on advanced machines. The printing machine was a high-speed, mass-production tool; in comparison with a hand press it was complicated, tricky to set up correctly, and expensive to run, but it more than made up for this in efficiency and sheer speed. As daunting as contemporary diagrams and plans of them may look, the machines achieved their high rates of production by improving existing concepts, not introducing new ones. The design principles of nineteenth-century printing machines were fundamentally straightforward: a machine either imitated the action of a press by pushing together a flat platen and a flat impression surface, or relied on the turning of a cylinder to bring paper and impression surface into contact. The execution of these principles in practice, however, led to some wondrously complex engineering, in which intricate subsystems must combine perfectly to accomplish a relatively simple overall objective.

THE PLATEN MACHINE

Powered machines which duplicated the vertical motion of the platen of a hand press were first manufactured in Britain in the 1830s. These achieved an immediate increase in output, being capable of 600 to 1,000 impressions per hour as compared to the 250 to 400 per hour of the hand press.* Furthermore, the power of these machines was sufficient to operate a larger platen, and this in turn allowed the use of imposition patterns which increased the number of pages produced per hour. Inking and paper handling were mechanized as well as the operation of the platen itself, but the early machines had problems with uneven inking and jamming of the paper feeds. By 1846 David Napier's version of the machine had solved most of these difficulties and was in very wide use. The Napier double-platen (the "double" referred to the use of two formes in the reciprocating bed; there was only one platen, in the middle of the machine) became the standard for bookwork through most of the nineteenth century. Despite frequent attempts by proponents of the cylinder machines to sound their death knell, the platen machines had, as Napier's advertisements put it, "nae peer" when printers sought the finest results with delicate typefaces or complex engravings.

THE CYLINDER MACHINE

Though applying power to the vertical action of the hand press might seem the simplest approach, machines using the cylinder principle were developed in Britain before the powered platens. Various designs were developed for newspaper and magazine printing, where speed was more important than appearance and quality of the product. Cylinder machines printed from a flat type-table just as a press or a platen machine did; a cylinder rolling across the formes in the bed replaced the flat platen in pressing the sheet against the inked printing surface. The typical machine had its revolving cylinder geared to a reciprocating table which carried the forme back and forth beneath it. This single-cylinder type of machine was known as the Wharfedale, after the district in Yorkshire where several manufacturers made them from the 1850s through the end of the century. Like the platen, the Wharfedale gave about 1,000 impressions per hour, printing only one side of the sheet at a time, but it could achieve double the output because it took much larger paper. Perfecting machines, which

---

*These figures are approximate, representing a rough average of the differing figures given by several authorities.

printed first one side and then the other in a continuous operation, used two cylinders and two flat formes to produce up to 1,500 finished sheets per hour; the history of their development is preserved in the nickname "Anglo-French."[40] True rotary presses, printing from cylindrical rather than flat surfaces, were developed successfully only after wet-flong stereotyping made possible the multiple casting of curved plates; these extremely fast machines were not used to print books in the nineteenth century.

The two-cylinder perfector was regularly used for bookwork, though it was not capable of high-class work; in the late 1840s, the huge London printers Clowes and Company had the following equipment: "Nineteen of Applegarth and Cowper's [perfecting] machines. . . . Twenty-three hand presses and five hydraulic presses [i.e., power-platens]."[41] But several things stood against the Anglo-French machines: they were expensive, fiendishly complicated, and cost-effective only for large runs. Furthermore, to prevent smearing (the ink being fresh on both sides of the paper), set-off paper had to be interleaved with the printed sheets as they came off the machine.* This required two more apprentices, bringing the number of people needed to operate a perfector to five. The single-cylinder Wharfedale, in contrast, could be run by one machine minder and one or two apprentices. Simple, reliable, cheap to buy and operate, the Wharfedale design competed directly with the Napier platen in the printing of books; but it was some years before the cylinder's product could rival the platen's in quality.

The early cylinder machines, according to DeVinne, were very hard on type: "Pressmen stigmatized the cylinders as the 'type smashers,' and those I saw in 1849 [in New York] . . . fairly deserved the name." Given the expense of type and the fragility of stereotype plates at the time, most book printers would have strongly preferred the platen. By the 1860s, however, Wharfedales had improved enough to stand alongside platens in better firms. The manager of Blackwood's printing works wrote of the first edition of George Eliot's *Mill on the Floss*: "We are going to press immediately with another 2000. . . . Fortunately we have got the new cylinder machine working beautifully as well as another Platen within the last month, otherwise we should have been in a fix." Further improvements led to the eventual triumph of the cylinder machines; by the 1880s

---

*Whatever suitable waste paper the printer had on hand might be used for set-off sheets; in one case, 400 copies of the finished sheets of the first and most expensive edition of Eliot's *Silas Marner* were used as waste after a cheaper edition had been issued (*Letters*, 3:395).

the platens had "gradually but surely given way to the speedy and not less accurate machine of the Wharfedale type. The best book-work, at first confined to the hand-press and later on to the platen, can now be accomplished with equal nicety . . . upon machines of which the Wharfedale was the progenitor."[42]

Still, the platen set the mark: "Book-work, equal to the best platen work, may now be obtained from any of the improved single-cylinder machines," wrote Noble, and in 1888 Wilson and Grey observed the same standard:

> *While not disputing for one moment the distinct merits and capabilities of the platen, we would say that for the best class of cut book-work the Wharfedale will be found preferable. . . . But although we in no way wish to depreciate the capabilities of the platen machine, which prior to the present make of the Wharfedale, was employed in almost every first-class London house for cut and superfine book-work, . . . the single cylinder is capable . . . of doing superior work, besides being quicker and more economical in its working.*[43]

Obviously even this late in the century, printers needed some convincing. The initial superiority of the platen machine had derived from the limitations of nineteenth-century machine-tool technology. It was considerably easier to cast and finish a flat, sturdy platen and type-bed than to manufacture a cylinder with a true surface along its entire length and a precisely concentric bore for its support shaft. Furthermore, the operation of the platen produced equal, self-aligning forces across its surface, while the cylinder was subjected to bending loads that resulted in unequal downward pressure and a tendency to go out of adjustment. It was the risk of an uneven impression that led to two practices which hurt the quality of the cylinder machines' product: the use of soft blankets and excessive pressures. The platen machine required a lot of power to run, since it applied its force to a large area at once; but because of the accuracy of its components, the platen was capable of very fine adjustment. When properly set up, this machine delivered a delicate "kiss" so precise that only a parchment facing was used on the platen itself.

The cylinder of the Wharfedale, on the other hand, had to be wrapped with a cloth blanket to overcome irregularities, both in the type and of the finish and alignment of the cylinder; to get good "color," the cylinder then had to be forced against the printing surface hard enough to make firm contact across the sheet. High cylinder pressures could be accomplished with less power than a platen required, because the impression was delivered at any given instant across only a narrow band of the cylinder and printing surface. The combination of soft blankets and high impression force on the cylinder, without which the printing would be uneven and slurred, was what made these machines type smashers. As machine manufacture improved and new practices were introduced from America, British printers learned that careful underlaying allowed the elimination of the blanket and the lowering of cylinder pressure; with a "hard-packed" cylinder and careful makeready, the later Wharfedales and their derivatives achieved a very high standard of quality and a fast rate of production.[44] They were still in use in many British printing houses into the 1940s.

TEXTUAL CONSEQUENCES OF PRINTING MACHINES

Speed was what British printers and publishers wanted from the machines, and speed they got. From the days of the hand press, when only a sizable house could produce as many as ten octavo sheets a week in an edition of 1,000 copies,[45] printers had doubled their pace and more. Blackwood, for example, got the following report from his clerk in 1866 about the progress of printing Eliot's *Felix Holt*: "Vol. I is gathering. Vol. II is on the Machines up to Sig. K. [nine sheets, exactly half of the volume] and the whole of it will be on to-morrow. Vol. III one half of it will be printed by Saturday afternoon." This was less than three weeks after Eliot had received proof of the first volume and submitted the manuscript of the first part of the third volume; proofs had been sent out within days of Blackwood's receipt of copy, and Eliot and Lewes customarily read and returned them in two or three days. Remarkably swift and efficient as this may have been, it put pressure on Eliot to compose faster. To some degree at least, the new high-speed technology of printing was creating new demands on the writer. Lewes noted in a letter at the time of the above-mentioned report to Blackwood: "The proofs of volume 3 having come Mrs. Lewes is getting fidgetty lest the printers should have to wait for copy." In his diary he records: "Yesterday Polly finished *Felix Holt*. The sense of relief was very great. . . . To-day read the last proof of *Felix Holt*—which has been at press during the composition of the last volume (written in 6 weeks) and latterly the printing has overtaken the writing."[46] Authors writing for serial publication had often struggled to finish their writing as a magazine deadline neared; now any leisure enjoyed by the writer whose works would appear in volumes was gone as well. Perhaps the only remedy was Trollope's: write far enough ahead of publication to have one or more future works in manuscript while the current one was being printed.

Authors rushing to satisfy demands for more copy may have felt that high-speed printing caused works to be issued in an unfinished or imperfect state; certainly typographical imperfections and developing textual faults were more likely to escape detection as printing speeded up. The faster the machine, the less likely it will be that type batters, plate fractures, and other damage to the printing surface will be promptly observed; thus it became more possible for faulty sheets (which came off all the book machines with the freshly printed side down) to go by unnoticed. With a hand press, as Southward points out in his minutely detailed description of bookwork, the pressman had not only the time but the obligation to watch for and correct any faults in the printing surface, registration, impression, and appearance.[47] But even the most scrupulous machine-minder would find himself unable to see small imperfections when sheets went by at the rate of one every two or three seconds.

The problems of inspection and quality control were compounded by certain aspects of the machines themselves. In the Napier platen machine, the formes of type or plates were in a bed which during its reciprocation was obscured from view by either the paper-feed table or the platen itself; a swift, comprehensive inspection from above was impossible. The Anglo-French perfecting machines were even worse in this regard, while the Wharfedale was rather better, as Wilson and Grey observe:

> Both inner and outer formes [on a perfector] have to be inspected continually, and thus trifles are apt to escape notice that do not in the case of the man who has simply one forme to attend to. . . . The cylinders and formes of this machine are far more difficult to reach than in the case of the Wharfedale, and a slight defect which with little trouble or effort could be remedied on the latter machine, is sometimes allowed to go in the case of the Anglo-French; not that it should be allowed to pass, but it is frequently intentionally overlooked. When it is desired to attend to the outer forme, . . . this occasions a serious delay . . . ; whereas in the Wharfedale the forme can be exposed in a moment.[48]

Even more seriously, as far as textual transmission is concerned, the spread of machine printing and the multiplication of workers in the printing house coincided with an apparent diffusion of responsibility for the accuracy of the text when something went wrong. Many of the machine-printing manuals allude to the circumstances—picks and batters, inking problems, plate breakage, and so forth—under which erroneous readings might be created; occasionally it is mentioned that one or another of the machine's tenders was to call for repairs when a fault was noticed. But nowhere is it clear just who was entrusted with the custody of the text itself. If a machine damaged a plate, and if the operator observed this and called for repairs, who determined what the correct reading of the now-faulty portion of the text was? Who looked up the correct readings, what did he consult, and who (if anyone) inspected the results when printing was resumed?

An author may have had complete control over every detail of a text right up to the moment printing began, but once the machines began to turn, faulty readings could appear and slip through without detection, or be noticed and erroneously repaired. The situation drifts toward a depressingly familiar modern condition: no one intentionally caused textual errors, but nobody was responsible for remedying them either. The main textual consequences of the coming of printing machines, then, lie in the realm of textual corruption. Erroneous readings could be created by the greater force machines exerted, and the designs of the machines in some cases increased the difficulty of both detecting and correcting errors.

Textual changes that occur during the printing of a single continuous impression are completely beyond an author's control, and usually beyond an author's awareness. Whether intended or accidental, readings that originate in the composing room after the final author's revise, or in the stereotype foundry, or in the printing works, cannot reflect authorial intention. The fact that such changes did occur is one main reason—the other one being the possibility of authorial revisions—why reprinting assumes great importance both for Victorian authors and scholars who study their texts. A survey of the field reveals numerous instances in which authors accepted or approved first editions that did not fully represent their artistic intentions, secure in the knowledge that they would be able to reexert textual control when revising and proofreading a subsequent impression or edition.

IV

Reprinting

George
Eliot to
John Black-
wood, re-
garding the
second edi-
tion of *Mid-
dlemarch*

*I am not fond of reading proofs, but I am anxious
to correct the sheets of this edition, both in relation
to mistakes already standing, and to prevent the
accumulation of others in the reprinting.*

ELIOT'S STATEMENT OF INTENTION in the above epigraph establishes in a few
words what this chapter will demonstrate: Victorian authors conferred
importance on sequential editions and impressions of their works by
exploiting each reprinting as an opportunity to revise, correct, and control
their texts. They saw that a linked chain of editions constituted a developing text which could be so managed as to reverse the usual pattern of
textual corruption: repeated iterations of a text could accumulate revisions
and drive out errors, rendering each reprint better, not worse, than its
predecessor in representing the author's intention. A history of the technology and practices employed in nineteenth-century reprinting will
show that from the point of view of modern textual scholarship, later
reprints and collected editions of Victorian authors are of great significance—greater, in many cases, than that of first editions.

Editions, Impressions, and Reprints

I have so far used the imprecise words *reprint* and *reprinting* because of the
variety of operations subsumed under this term by nineteenth-century
printers, publishers, and authors. "To reprint" may mean to strike off an
impression of an existing typesetting (using either standing type or plates);
Macmillan used the word this way in 1878 about the *Selected Poems* of
Matthew Arnold: "We ordered the reprint as soon as we saw we were
getting low in stock. . . . It contains the changes you made." A few months
before, Arnold had made his alterations in a copy of the book and sent it to

Macmillan: "I think I may say that if this corrected copy is faithfully followed, no further change whatever will be required in the stereotype." But as has been previously noted, the Victorians frequently used the term *edition* for this same process and product. Macmillan reported to Arnold in 1885 that "we have printed another edition of the small paper Selected Poems (1000 copies)," when what had been produced was actually an impression from the existing stereotype plates.[1]

But when John Blackwood gave George Eliot the opportunity in 1857 to make changes in *Scenes of Clerical Life*, he used "reprint" as a bibliographer would use "edition." When he posted the proof for the *Blackwood's Magazine* version of the conclusion of "Janet's Repentance," he wrote: "Along with this I send you a copy of all the parts of the Clerical Scenes in order that you may make any corrections you wish for the reprint." That is, the magazine text was to serve as copy for the book form of the *Scenes*, which of course required a new typesetting. Eliot, knowledgeable about printing from her days at the *Westminster Review*, saw that she could save herself a double task: "By the way," she replied, "the sheets of the 'Clerical Scenes' are not come, but I shall not want to make any other than verbal and literal corrections, so that it will hardly be necessary for me to go through the sheets *and* the proofs, which I must of course see."[2]

In yet another case, a publisher used "edition" accurately, but attempted to make the product look like an impression. Chapman and Hall called Robert Browning's *Poetical Works* of 1865 the "Fourth Edition" on its title pages. This was quite the correct term for the substantial number of the poems that were appearing in their fourth typesetting: the first editions (or first appearances in magazines) plus the collected editions of 1849, 1863, and 1865. Yet Chapman made every effort to make the 1865 edition identical in appearance with the 1863 *Poetical Works*, which had been openly labeled "Third Edition." The contents of each volume were the same, no new poems being added; the same typefaces, line spacing, and pagination were used; even the binding was replicated. This obscured for many years the fact that the 1865 edition was a completely new setting, containing hundreds of changes ordered by the poet. Chapman, accustomed to being burdened with unsold copies of Browning's books, had ordered only one impression (of perhaps 1,000 copies) of the 1863 *Poetical Works*; these were printed by Clowes from types, which were immediately distributed.[3]

When Browning's reputation and popularity suddenly rose through 1863–64, demand for his collected works unexpectedly increased. Chapman and Browning planned the new edition as stocks of the 1863 *Poetical*

Works were being exhausted. Perhaps still skeptical of a lasting success for Browning's works, Chapman not only failed to stereotype the new edition, but again had it printed in relatively small numbers from types; it is today one of the rarest of Browning's publications. The publisher's motives in making the 1865 edition as much like its predecessor as possible can only be guessed at. Considering how much work Browning did on his text in preparation for it, the 1865 *Poetical Works* could have been advertised as "a new edition, revised by the author." But perhaps Chapman felt this would offend those who had recently bought the 1863 edition. Also, if we take as accurate Browning's frequent characterization of Chapman as stingy and slow with payments, the publisher may have been trying to avoid paying the poet a larger fee for his works. For an obviously new edition, thoroughly revised, issued in response to public demand, and incorporating all of his recent work, Browning could reasonably have expected a greater sum than for a "reprint" that appeared to be merely an extension of a previous edition.

Chapman was ambivalent about the weight and meaning of the term *edition*; though he was not ready to support any more than a typographical replica of the previous edition, he wanted the advertising value of the phrase "Fourth Edition." And indeed he and his poet did produce a genuine new edition in 1865. G. H. Lewes's suggestion to Blackwood about the commercial worth of labelling new impressions of George Eliot's poem *The Spanish Gypsy* (1868) as "editions" reflects the more common situation in Victorian publishing terminology. On 15 December 1868, Lewes wrote: "As from all appearance the poem is likely to go on selling don't you think it would be polite and fair to call every 1,000 a new edition? Absurd as the motive is people *are* influenced in their desires to possess a work by the knowledge that a great many other people possess it, and I often hear the number of editions referred to as proof of excellence."[4]

At this date, the book was in fact still in its first edition typesetting, of which three impressions had been run. The first impression (May 1868) consisted of about 2,100 copies printed from types; the second (August 1868), which included some revisions by George Eliot, comprised 252 copies printed from the types; the third impression of 1,055 copies (October–November 1868) incorporated further revisions by the author. These were the last copies printed with the types, stereo plates having been made after the third impression was struck off. When Blackwood wrote to Eliot on 29 December 1868, he heartily endorsed Lewes's notion: "We quite agree in what he says of calling each thousand an edition or even giving that title to a smaller number, and although our first edition was 2000, the second being so small brings the proportion very near. Of the third edition (7/6) we have already disposed of over 800, which I hope this season will clear out of the hands of the trade so as to let us go on quietly printing a fourth edition."[5]

This fourth impression, printed from the stereos, comprised another 1,055 copies.[6] These plates were used for many further impressions, and *The Spanish Gypsy* seems not to have entered a true second edition until the typesetting for the Cabinet Edition of 1878–79.

If one were to attempt any generalization about these several commutable terms, it would be that the word *edition* was used by Victorian publishers and authors to signify any identifiably separate group of copies of a title. Thus the "Large Paper Editions" and "Limited Editions" commonly referred to in the later nineteenth century turn out to have been printed from the same types or plates as the ordinary commercial copies of the work. Modern bibliographers would identify these as special issues or states, depending on the amount of distinction possible between each and the common trade copies. One also comes across references to "foreign editions" and "colonial edition"; in the age of paper-mold stereotyping, such are often separate impressions, not true editions; earlier in the century, however, separate typesettings may have been used. The example of Browning's collected edition of 1865 should remind us that while many a reimpression has been called an edition, some editions look very much like reimpressions. The situation has been baffling enough that many scholars outside the fields of bibliography, textual criticism, and the history of printing (and, alas, some scholars within them) to have recourse to phrases like "first printing," "word-for-word reprint," and "issued in numerous reprintings."

Authors and Reprints

A lack of precision in, or the outright misuse of, bibliographical terminology was of little concern to Victorian authors. What mattered to them was the reiteration of a text, and the attendant possibilities for revision and correction. In a letter of 1865, Matthew Arnold displays his awareness of publishers' options and gives us an author's perspective on reprinting. Sometime earlier, Arnold had been contacted by Moncure Daniel Conway, that peripatetic American friend to British authors. Conway, who sometimes acted as an unofficial agent for the Boston publishing house of Ticknor and Fields, was trying to arrange an American edition of some of Arnold's works. Arnold wrote to him on 29 November 1865: "I don't know how Messrs Ticknor & Field [*sic*] proceed—whether by printing batches, or by printing regular editions: in any case, when they are going to press again I should like the opportunity of making some corrections[,] extirpations and insertions." By "batches" Arnold presumably meant numerous impressions of a few hundred copies each, printed as often as demand warranted; "regular editions" would signify larger and less frequent impressions of, say, several thousand copies. But this distinction is of no interest to Arnold; he scents some sort of opportunity to alter his text for a reprint, and he wants to take advantage of it.

New editions and multiple impressions mean popularity for an author, and popularity means profits; this alone would make reprints as important to authors as to publishers. But fresh typesettings or reimpressions of existing ones represent more than the likelihood of income: to an author they offer an opportunity to revise and correct. Particularly when it occurs after sufficient time for reflection and reconsideration, reprinting enhances authorial control. Printers may have scorned the writer who could not revise thoroughly until a text was in type, but there can be no doubt that authors saw and read their own works in a new light when they were printed. They recognized faults far beyond literal errors and took them very seriously indeed. To take Arnold again as our example, within a month of the publication of *Empedocles on Etna, and Other Poems* (1852) he wrote despairingly to a friend: "The strain of thought generally is no doubt much too doleful and monotonous. I had no notion of *how* monotonous till I had the volume printed before me. I thought too when the poems were in manuscript they would possess a more general attraction."[7]

Dissatisfaction of this sort is not at all unusual when authors first see their works in print; Tennyson, George Eliot, and numerous other Victorian writers repeatedly expressed such feelings, sometimes during proofing and sometimes after a first edition had been published. On occasion an author has felt so strong a revulsion, or been so stung by criticism, that a work has been withdrawn from the market. As the histories of Browning's *Pauline*, Arnold's "Empedocles on Etna," and Tennyson's "The Lover's Tale" show, these attempts never quite clear the record, and withdrawn works have a way of reappearing, sometimes decades after their first embarrassing publication. The other approach to resolving artistic dissatisfaction with a work is to attempt a thorough revision, and here again reprints—whether in new editions or in revised impressions of existing typesettings—assume great importance. When an author's revisions are so extensive as to create a true second version of a work, the textual critic confronts a challenging problem: which version represents most fully the author's intentions? Before proposing an answer, the scholar must face several even more basic questions: what *were* the author's intentions? What evidence demonstrates them? Were they always the same toward the work under study? The texts themselves provide the largest and most important body of primary evidence on these matters: the alterations, revisions, corrections, and restorations demonstrably made by authors over a series of editions and impressions.

Even when the accumulated textual changes did not result in different versions of a work, second and later editions or impressions could be very important to Victorian authors and thus should be to modern scholars. Authorial control over first editions was often limited, and reprints provided opportunities for revisions that may have been denied, overlooked, or impossible during the printing of the first edition. An unknown author hoping to make a career was in no position to demand ample time and multiple revises during proofing; the same writer, after sufficient successes, would find publishers not only interested in reissuing earlier works, but also willing to grant and guarantee complete textual control. The forces affecting authorial control in such situations are social, having to do with manners and commerce; but until the 1860s, technology denied even successful established writers some chances to revise during the printing of an edition. Before mechanical typecasting made the supply of type abundant, proofs came a few sheets at a time, and all the copies of a sheet had to be printed off as soon as possible after proofing was completed. Only when the types were liberated—that is, after the early sheets were struck off—could the composition of later sheets go forward. As was shown in earlier chapters, the author was pressed to make revisions as fast as possible and to keep them to a minimum.

Perhaps even more severely limiting the author's ability to revise consistently and completely, a work could not be viewed as a whole until the very end of the proofing process, by which time no changes could be made in earlier pages: the sheets were already printed off. When a book was to be reprinted, whether from a new typesetting or a modification of an existing one, the author usually revised by working over a copy of a previous edition. Thus for the first time since submitting the work in manuscript, an author was free to consider and alter a text as a whole, at one time. In most cases, the largest portion of the text would have been successfully printed as the author intended it to read; revisions, restorations, and other alterations might now be tried and judged with some leisure and with a good chance they could be incorporated without objection.

Some aspects of the changing technology of Victorian printing imposed limits on revisions for reprints, while others multiplied the chances authors got to alter their texts. To observe what enhanced and what diminished authorial control, we must trace briefly the history of reprinting in the Victorian era.

The Technology of Reprinting

The technology used for printing books in the earlier nineteenth century—employing handmade types, hand-operated presses, and plaster-mold stereotyping—provided no cheap, easy, and risk-free way to prepare for the possibility of a need to reprint. George Dodd, contemplating the storage rooms at Clowes and Company in the early 1840s, laid out the options:

> There are three modes of arranging for a reprint of any given work: to keep the metal types standing in "forms" or collected pages; to prepare stereotype plates or copies, which can be used instead of the original type; or to re-compose the type just as in the first instance. . . . Such a vast capital is lying dead, if the type for a book be kept in 'form' or undisturbed, that it is rarely done. One of the exceptions relates to certain parliamentary papers for which there may be a sudden demand, and which are kept in "form." Another exception is where the printer agrees with the publisher that he will keep the type of a new book in 'form' for a certain period, during which the publisher may be enabled to make a guess as to the probable sale of his book. . . . As such an arrangement as this is advantageous to the publisher, and entails a heavy stagnation of capital on the part of the printer, a stipulated price is paid for it. Some of the warerooms of the establishment are loaded with many tons of type kept in this undisturbed state.

Dodd points out that if stereotype plates were made at the outset and stored after printing the first edition, they could be retrieved for reprinting at any time; but if plates had not been cast, then "for each successive edition of a book (if more than one be required), the type has to be set up anew. This is the most usual system."[8]

Before paper-mold stereotyping was widely used in bookwork, the "usual system" of reprinting meant that when a work succeeded, the author would probably get the chance to revise freely, since a new typesetting would be called for. The commercial definition of success, as well as the frequency, extent, and timing of new editions, depended to a considerable degree on the size of the first edition; this was quite variable, and differed according to the mode of first publication. Students of Victorian fiction are accustomed to the enormous numbers—thirty to fifty thousand copies—of monthly parts sold by Dickens or Bulwer-Lytton, but these quantities (almost always printed with stereo plates) were unusual even for serial publications. *Middlemarch*, stereotyped from the beginning and presumed by both Eliot and Blackwood before its publication to be a guaranteed huge success, was printed in about 5,000 copies per installment. For works which initially appeared in book form, much smaller first editions, printed from types, were the norm. J. A. Sutherland's *Victorian Novelists and Publishers* cites numerous cases in which the first editions of well-known authors consisted of 1,000 or 1,500 copies. In his days with Chapman and Hall, only one of Browning's books reached a second edition on its own, though the first editions were usually 500 copies; and even after he was thoroughly established, his first editions with Smith, Elder were usually printed in no more than 2,000 copies. Arnold, not expecting any great success for his 1853 *Poems*, set the size of the first (and only) edition at 750 copies.[9]

If there was cause for hope about the sale of a work, or if publisher and printer could afford it, type was kept standing, even before mechanical typecasting machines assured an adequate supply. The first edition of *In Memoriam* (1850), which was eagerly awaited by a substantial public, was printed in numerous impressions from standing type. The first impression of 1,500 copies was issued in May; another 1,500 were struck off in July. As sales increased in Autumn, Moxon ordered a third impression of 2,000, and for the expected rush at Christmas he had a fourth impression of 3,000 copies printed. It appears that this typesetting was kept standing at least through 1851, another 5,000 copies being printed that year. Although Moxon had stereotyped many works in the past, this first edition of *In Memoriam* had not been plated; his letters to Tennyson about these impressions (called, inevitably, "editions") specifically describe them as being "reprinted from standing type."[10] Perhaps Moxon felt that Tennyson's reputation, while growing, was not yet great enough to warrant the higher initial costs that plaster stereotyping entailed; certainly he had ample experience to anticipate that Tennyson would soon insist on revisions that might be extensive enough to render a set of stereo plates worthless; furthermore, the speed and efficiency of printing machines, which large London printers were using by this time, offset to some degree the cost of keeping the types together.

When a steady sale and thus a sustained demand for reprints could be reasonably expected, the prospect of long-term profitability justified the expense and trouble of stereotyping, even in the days of the plaster process. A contract between Moxon and Leigh Hunt from 1844 includes the following specifications:

> *Mr. Moxon agrees to publish a new edition of Mr. Hunt's Poetical Works*
> *to consist of 2000 copies . . . , the same to be printed, stereotyped,*
> *published, and advertised by and at the sole risk of Mr. Moxon. That the*
> *profits . . . shall be equally divided between Mr. Hunt and Mr. Moxon.*
> *That Mr. Moxon shall from time to time be at liberty to print and publish*
> *any further such edition or editions [i.e., impressions] of the said Poetical*
> *Works (to consist of 1000 copies) as by him shall be deemed advantageous,*
> *the profits of such future edition or editions being divided as aforesaid.*[11]

But for the vast majority of books published in Britain before the 1860s, deciding to reprint a work meant that there was an expectation of sufficient demand to exceed the cost of recomposing the text in a new typesetting. Indeed, a genuine second edition was guaranteed for most serialized works, when they came out in volume form after the last magazine installment or monthly part had appeared. Successful authors who regularly published their works initially as serials knew they would have a chance to revise their entire texts, and could plan accordingly. Thackeray, Dickens, Eliot, Arnold, Trollope, and Hardy, for example, all at various times submitted work for serial publication already knowing that they would make changes for subsequent publication in book form.

The introduction of the papier-mâché method of molding and casting stereotype plates made the entire business of reprinting much easier. A work could be printed from type in a first edition of a few hundred or a thousand copies; if initial demand suggested that it would continue to sell, paper matrices could be taken without difficulty and at little cost, before the types were distributed. Plates could be cast as necessary at a later date. "By the paper process," Southward notes, "a series of plates may be cast from one matrix. . . . The paper matrices may be preserved for future use."[12] If a work could be expected to sell well from the beginning, paper molds could be made just after composition, and plates cast immediately; the types could be distributed and the plates used to print all copies of all impressions, or the types could be kept composed long enough to print special issues or fancy "editions." If a work promised to be in demand for many years, the paper molds might be stored away, or duplicate plates could be cast at once. And since a reasonably good papier-mâché matrix could be made from an existing plate as easily as from types, the life of a typesetting could be extended through hundreds of thousands of reprinted copies. Furthermore, the skill of the printers at altering plates and mixing types and plates in the same forme meant that the peripheral pages of a text, such as half titles and other preliminary leaves or the advertisements that filled up unused pages of the last sheet, could be changed with ease while the text within continued to be printed from old plates. Formats could change, illustrations could be added, title pages could be altered, allowing the marketing of a work in varied forms without the expense of composing fresh type.

Making a precautionary set of paper molds made it unnecessary to tie up composed types while sales were tested, but publishers and printers continued to leave type standing long after paper-mold stereotyping came in. Ironically, mechanical typefounding machines were perfected not long after the introduction of the new method of stereotyping; the increased availability and lower cost of type made holding formes of composed type less burdensome. And when demand could not be clearly forecast, or when revisions were expected, printing from type and keeping it standing may have been more economical than making plates, even if paper matrices had been taken at the beginning. This was the approach taken by Blackwood in 1868 with Eliot's *Spanish Gypsy* and by Smith, Elder with Arnold's *Literature and Dogma* in 1873 (both discussed in chapter 5). From the printers' point of view, however, standing type was still anathema: "In a large office, . . . a great number of works, or portions of works, are nevertheless kept in type, or 'standing' [despite the cost]; but the circumstances are peculiar, and special arrangements have to be made in such cases. The general rule is to get the work printed and the type distributed as soon as possible."[13]

From the 1860s onward, reprinting conformed to a consistent pattern. Stereotyping was so cheap and easy, and the capacities of machine-equipped printing house so great, that publishers were able to minimize the risk of overestimating demand. Even for a new book, paper molds would be taken immediately. Plates might be cast and put to use right away, or the first impression might be printed from the types before they were distributed. In either case, the first impression would be kept small—perhaps 750 or 1,000 copies—but its price would be set high enough to cover the costs of composition and stereotyping. If sales continued strong, whenever the supply of copies on hand dwindled, the publisher could order another small impression from the plates. These impressions might or might not be identified as "editions" or bear new dates on their title pages. And once the first impression was sold, profit margins went up. A new impression cost only the price of paper, printing, and binding; the plates were already paid for. By using smaller margins, inexpensive paper and binding materials, the cost of these later impressions could be reduced still further, and it became apparent to many publishers that the real money was to be made in cheap reprints.

Blackwood took this kind of approach with the early works of George Eliot after her reputation was established. Following the rapid successes of *Adam Bede* (1859), *The Mill on the Floss* (1860), and *Silas Marner* (1861), Blackwood and Eliot prepared a three-volume collection of her works, to be sold for the relatively low price of 6 shillings a volume. The attention generated by *Romola*, serialized in the *Cornhill* in 1862–63, promised to boost the sales of Eliot's earlier books, and Blackwood wrote to her in January of 1863: "This edition is stereotyped, so that if there is a run on the three volumes when published together we will be ready to meet it."[14] Arnold's inquiry to Conway about the printing practices at Ticknor and Fields, cited above, shows that he knew the American reprints might be produced in this way. Macmillan handled Arnold's *A Bible-Reading for Schools* in the same fashion; he reported on 26 September 1872, just over four months after the work had appeared:

> *The first edition of 2000 is now out of print & we are printing another 1000, which I have no doubt we shall soon sell. I think that on the whole it will be best to let the book go as it is for a time and we will be better able to see whether it might not be worth while making two distinct editions, one dearer & finer in type and print for general readers, and a quite cheap one without the preface for schools. In the mean time we have the plates & may as well use them as long as we have a sale in the present form.*[15]

The new typesetting, bearing the title *Isaiah XL-LXVI* and many additions to the original work, was not composed until 1875.

Further (though indirect) light on how book publishers took advantage of the printing technologies now available to them is shed by a letter of 1867 from Arnold to George Lillie Craik of Macmillan. Arnold felt some disappointment that "between 400 and 500" copies of his *New Poems* had been sold in their first month, even though Craik described this as "doing well." Arnold wrote: "I expected the Poems would have been better subscribed for *in the first instance*; but any surprise on this score has disappeared since I heard from Mr. George Smith that the trade subscribed for not more than *800* copies of Prince Albert's Life. How very unforeseeing they must be!"[16]

Arnold's rueful surprise stemmed, I believe, from his misunderstanding of publishers' tactics and the nature of subscription sales. First of all, though he saw 800 copies as a small subscription, this was probably a quite satisfactory number. For comparison, we may cite the example of Bulwer-

Lytton's immensely successful *The Last Days of Pompeii* (1834), which sold 729 copies on subscription, a figure that was taken as a very good sale.[17] By 1867, in response to a much wider reading public, edition quantities had increased enough that 800 copies, particularly for a book about the late Prince Consort, may have seemed paltry to Arnold. But subscription sales were no longer the key indicator they had once been. In the 1830s it was crucial to guess as exactly as possible how many copies of a first edition to print, especially if the types were being rapidly distributed as was usual. A good subscription not only guaranteed that a known percentage of the initial costs would be covered, it also allowed the publisher to make a more informed estimate of sales to come. But the new reprinting technology made prepublication sales far less decisive for publishers or booksellers. The "unforeseeing" book trade, as Arnold deprecated it, was engaging to buy *in advance* no more than 800 copies, but it probably had every confidence that a life of Prince Albert was going to sell very well. Why, given the publishers' and printers' ability to produce copies on demand, should a bookseller or agent for a circulating library commit funds to a large stock before a new work was even published? Like the publisher, the bookseller had no need for a sizable inventory; he could wait to gauge public demand, because a small impression of fresh copies could be produced in a day or two with stereo plates in a fast printing machine.

Authorial Control and the Accuracy of Reprints

For Victorian books, numerous small impressions became the rule, and whether printed from types or stereos, any impression might contain authorial revisions or new textual errors. The degree to which reprints (whether simply new impressions or actual new editions) were under authors' control, and thus the extent to which reprints accurately reflect authorial intentions, must be considered in light of several related questions. The answers to these questions often depend on prevailing customs, available technologies, the practices of individual publishers, and the habits, temperaments, and reputations of individual authors.

First, *could* a nineteenth-century author control a given reprint? When authors sold a work outright for a single sum (a common arrangement adopted by Thackeray and Trollope, among many others), they customarily lost any right to supervise later editions or impressions.* A scrupulous publisher (or one who wanted to put "with the author's latest correc-

---

*As Browning put it to Edward Chapman in 1866, "Once paid for an edition, I have no further money-interest in the copies on hand." Browning retained a jealous nonmonetary interest in his texts, however (*New Letters*, 173).

tions" on a title page) might occasionally invite an author to revise, but was not required to do so. Of course piracies, domestic or foreign, were beyond any author's control, and generally so were more legitimate foreign editions. A few British publishers produced and sold their own foreign editions, but with no international copyright law in force, it was customary for authors to make their own arrangements with foreign publishers. The names that appear repeatedly in the correspondence of Victorian authors are Harper Brothers and Ticknor and Fields (later Fields and Osgood) in America, and Tauchnitz in Germany; these firms offered only moderate fees for the right to reprint, but something from them was better than the nothing that the pirates paid authors. In their fundamental textual heritage, these sanctioned foreign editions were no more under an author's control than a piracy was: both were set up in fresh types from a published British edition. I have found no evidence that a Victorian author ever read proof on a foreign reprint. However, a British author might impose some control by sending the foreign publisher a marked set of proofs or corrected first edition to be used as printer's copy, as Browning did with Fields, or by asking for the chance to make specific "corrections[,] extirpations and insertions" as Arnold did in the letter to Moncure Conway cited earlier.

When a British author or publisher sold stereotype molds or plates to a foreign publisher, and no fresh type had to be set, the reprints produced were in fact not an edition at all, but simply another impression of the typesetting. Since no new compositorial errors could occur, copies printed in this way would be more accurate than those from a new typesetting which the author had not proofed or corrected, but the author still could not exert direct and active control of foreign impressions.

Since authors cannot control the texts of reprints whose existence is unknown to them, a similar situation sometimes prevailed within the British isles. The contract between Leigh Hunt and Moxon, quoted above, gave the publisher the right to churn out 1,000-copy batches forever from the plates of Hunt's *Poetical Works*, without notification of the author. And when changing publishers, unless an author (or the new publisher) managed to buy back the original publisher's ownership of works which had been sold outright, he or she might be plagued by reprints which could not be revised and which yielded no payments.

Because these circumstances make possible any number of unreliable editions and impressions, and because the technology of reprinting changed significantly during the nineteenth century, meticulous bibliographical identification and a full grasp of the available biographical and historical facts are especially important to the study of Victorian authors and their texts. A parent set of plates or molds may have generated five or six varieties of descendent texts, most of them beyond any semblance of authorial control. Yet stereotyping technology did usually preserve a replica (perhaps a degraded one) of a typesetting which had at some time been proofed, revised, and corrected by the author; such reimpressions are better texts than, say, a contemporary fancy edition from a completely unauthorized new typesetting. In his autobiography, Trollope, describing his conviction that short novels ought not to be typographically inflated into three-deckers, tells us how his own publisher produced an unauthorized edition: "On one occasion, and on one occasion only, a publisher got the better of me in a matter of volumes. He had a two-volume novel of mine running through a certain magazine, and had it printed complete in three volumes before I knew where I was,—before I had seen a sheet of the letterpress. I stormed for a while, but I had not the heart to make him break up the type."[18]

However, despite this and all the other ways in which reprints could slip away from an author's control, the custom with the major Victorian publishers was to offer their authors—indeed, sometimes to press upon their authors—repeated opportunities to make textual changes for forthcoming reprints. As later examples will make evident, the answer to the question "Could Victorian authors control the texts of reprints of their works?" is usually "Yes, if they wanted to."

This in turn poses the question of how regularly, and how intently, nineteenth-century British authors did exercise textual control of reprints. Here the answers must be as varied as the artistic intentions, personalities, and circumstances of individual authors, but it is certainly wrong to hypothesize that as a group they were generally indifferent to reprints except as sources of income. Many Victorian authors seem to have taken a perfectabilitarian view of their texts, looking forward from the time of first publication to a series of editions and impressions, each affording an occasion to reduce errors, correct misstatements, add clarifications, or revise in response to criticism. Arnold, Browning, and Eliot all expected to be informed of forthcoming reprints, treating them as opportunities to make changes, polishing, refining, and correcting their texts over the years. Tennyson took great pains with every detail of his reprints; in 1852, at the time of the 8th "edition" of the 1842 *Poems* (some of these truly were editions, created when the poet added works to the collection), Tennyson wrote to Moxon asking for a correction, adding "I wish this to be as near as may be a perfect edition." Even the oft-maligned Thackeray sometimes paid attention to reprints: more than five years after *Vanity Fair* appeared in monthly parts, he went through the novel carefully, revising for the "cheap edition" of 1853. Though Thackeray may have failed to relocate two paragraphs in chapter 59 to their rightful place, his rereading was, as his editors put it, "critical and reasonably careful," and his revisions and corrections were extensive if not drastic.[19]

The same characterization—extensive but not extreme—could be applied to the revisions in a great many Victorian works that went through several editions controlled by their authors. Perhaps there was no definable cause for this pattern, beyond the zeitgeist; perhaps it must simply be called a common aspect of nineteenth-century authorship. But there were limits on revision imposed by printing technology, particularly by stereotyping, electrotyping, and high-speed printing machines. Previous chapters have exposed the contradictory claims about stereotyping; plating supposedly fixed a text and prevented errors, but stereo plates could be altered as necessary. In practice, although it was possible to substitute or replace large chunks of text within a single stereo plate without casting a new one,[20] alterations were commonly restricted to a few words or less in one location. With this level of modification the publishers, printers, and authors all seem to have been contented. George Lillie Craik's invitations to Arnold to request changes in Macmillan's *Poems of Wordsworth*, edited by Arnold in 1879, are typical: "You can make any verbal alterations you like in the plates before we print again. It might be well to send us at once anything that you see should be corrected [so] that the printer may alter the stereotype plates in readiness for a reprint"; and again, two days later: "if you send me everything else you see wrong the printer shall put the plates right for the reprint." And authors, in turn, typically promise that they will limit themselves to small-scale revisions. George Eliot assured Blackwood about the second edition of *Scenes of Clerical Life*: "I shall not want to make any other than verbal and literal corrections."[21]

All the parties to reprints were sensitive to a serious practical limit on revisions to stereotyped editions: pagination. If an author's additions or deletions were large enough, the text would either overrun the existing page or leave an unsightly gap; to correct this meant recasting several pages worth of plates. Tennyson was aware of the difficulties caused to printers when pagination was disturbed, as shown in a warning he sent to his publisher Moxon while revising *The Princess* for its fourth edition (1851; first edition, 1847): "With respect to the Princess you shall have her in a day or two but as I have inserted two or three passages which . . . alter the paging it may be as well for you to delay printing the remainder till you get the first sheets back."[22]

Whether or not *The Princess*, which went through twelve announced "editions" by 1865, had been stereotyped by this time is not clear (indeed, a clear and exact history of the editions and impressions of most of Tennyson's works has yet to appear), but that is not central at this point. What is interesting is that Tennyson, who throughout his career was given to making large-scale changes to his works, particularly to stanza structures and to the sequence of poems within a collection, plainly knew that changing the length of a text for a reprint could be troublesome. When the poet laureate signed on with Charles Kegan Paul in 1879, the publisher tried to control these tendencies by insisting on a contract provision that simultaneously established and limited Tennyson's right to change his text at will:

> *Before publishing any future edition of any of the works to which this Agreement relates [i.e., most of Tennyson's previous publications] the said C. Kegan Paul & Co. shall give notice of such intended publication to the said Alfred Tennyson who shall be at liberty at any time within one calendar month after receiving such notice to make any corrections or alterations . . . provided that no existing poem shall be withdrawn and that if such new Edition shall be printed from the existing stereotype plates the paging of the present edition shall not be interfered with.*[23]

Such were the restrictions of stereotyping; the technology (and those who paid for it) directly shaped the texts as we see them by allowing some revision, but not wholesale rewriting. With electrotype plates, which were far more difficult to alter, almost any revision would have required the making of a new plate. Reprints from types, however, whether new impressions from type left standing or editions from fresh typesettings, could be altered much more freely. A series of small impressions from types, when this approach was possible, enabled a publisher to adjust printing orders according to demand and an author to respond to readers, and Victorian authors seldom bypassed an opportunity to make at least a few changes for subsequent impressions.

When a new typesetting was employed, authorial control was asserted in two primary ways. First, the author would prepare the printer's copy for the new edition, commonly working any revisions into a copy of the latest existing version of the text. This, for example, is how Browning carried out his revisions for the second edition of *Dramatis Personae* (1864); his marked copy of the first edition is preserved at Yale University. Eliot, Arnold, Tennyson, and Hardy all prepared later individual and collected editions in this way, and the frequency of the practice suggests strongly that it was the norm. Because it has been so often ignored by even seasoned scholarly editors, the importance of this matter of the printer's copy for reprints must be emphasized. Scholarship grants without hesitation the significance of the author's manuscript from which a first edition was composed, but equivalent recognition has not been accorded to, for example, copies of first and later editions marked by the author for use as copy in setting up a multivolume collected edition. Once we grant the importance of reprints that were supervised, revised, and corrected by the author, the copy used to set up each reprint becomes as important as—and from the textual critic's standpoint sometimes more important than—the original compositional manuscript. And this is true not just for the last edition supervised by an author—the text often chosen as copy-text for modern critical editions of Victorian writers—but for every edition that formed a step along the path from first edition to the last.

A printed text with the author's manuscript alterations inserted could be set by compositors with a high degree of accuracy, and the very fact that a work was popular enough to warrant reprinting would give extra force to the author's desires for changes. The control achieved by preparing the printer's copy for a new edition could be reinforced by reading proofs of the new typesetting. While not every stage in a long series of editions and impressions got careful attention in proof, there are plentiful instances in which Victorian authors did go through the proofing process for reprints. As developing technology made proofing faster and easier and multiplied the available stages of proof, the monitoring of textual changes in new editions became easier for authors.

On the other hand, all the copies of a small impression from existing types or plates could be printed on a machine very quickly—so quickly as to prevent the insertion of an author's alteration that would have been made as a "stop-press correction" in earlier times. Cases of this frustration of an author's intent to control a text can be documented in the careers of Tennyson, Arnold, and Browning, and were probably relatively common occurrences; on the available evidence, such changes were often, but not always, made in subsequent impressions or editions.

It would be pleasant to conclude that in Victorian times, a series of editions and impressions at some point not only reached a high degree of typographical accuracy and a close conformity with the author's intentions, but also, because of stereotyping, suffered no further alterations or incursions of errors after this near-perfection had been achieved. That, indeed, is what many Victorian authors and publishers, and more than a few modern scholars, have chosen to believe. (Some years ago, for example, a well-known critic actually proposed that a photocopy of Browning's last collected edition would automatically present a better text than a scholarly edition could.) The claim that stereotyped texts could not go wrong was made so often in the nineteenth century that even specialists came to endorse it; here is the eminent printing historian John Southward in 1884:

> *Variations from the original text are effectively prevented; for the copies of the new edition, whenever printed, are absolutely fac-similes of the preceding one.*
>
> *On the other hand, if there are alterations likely to be required in new editions, stereotyping is not advantageous. . . . But for all books of which mere reproductions with but slight alterations are called for, stereotyping offers substantial advantages.*[24]

We have seen that this is true of the grosser features of a text—layout, pagination, and sequence of the major divisions of a work—but not of the finer aspects—individual words and punctuation marks—that occupy so much of the textual scholar's time and thought. Every time a new impression was called for, every time the plates come out of storage, the author had an opportunity to request changes (which might be small in nature but great in number) in the plates. And every time the plates went through the processes of storage, retrieval, reimposition, printing, removal, and return to storage, they were exposed to numerous opportunities for damage. Inserted corrections of previous errors were particularly vulnerable, so that the very processes which allowed a stereotyped text to be made more accurate also rendered it more subject to going awry on its own. That textual inaccuracies resulting from plate decay were inevitable had been recognized from the early days of stereotyping, and Hansard had warned that "every edition from the plates must get progressively worse and worse." Yet it appears—as much from the lack of comment as from direct evidence—that so much trust was placed in stereotyping that not much attention was given to monitoring or rectifying problems of plate decay. In one of the few observations on this matter, Jackson Gaskill's *Printing-Machine Manager's Complete Practical Handbook* (1877) tells the pressman that as a step in making ready a printing machine he is to "pull a revise, and send it to the press reader for his final approval."[25] But whether the reader performed a meticulous reading or a casual inspection, and what (if anything) was read against the proof, are unspecified.

Within the technical and conventional limits of correction and revision, and for at least some part of their history of reimpression, stereotyped texts could be made truly accurate reflections of authorial intentions. In a proper condition, before they suffered textually significant disintegration or accidental damage, plates included corrections but preserved the unaltered portions of a text from the fresh compositorial errors that would inevitably appear if a new typesetting were required for reprinting. But when plates continued to be used for impression after impression, long beyond their reasonable life span, corrections could be lost and new errors appear. More than anyone else, an author had to be the custodian of a work when it went into repeated reprints; no one at the printing works or the publishing house seems to have been customarily in charge of maintaining the hard-won accuracy of the text.

V

Some Victorian Authors
and Their Reprints

How judge if thy hand worked thy will?
   By reviewing,
Revising again and again, piece by piece.

Browning,
"Fust and
His
Friends"

THE VALIDITY of the observations offered in the preceding chapter can best
be demonstrated by considering the practices of a few representative
Victorian authors who modified and managed the texts of their works
when they were reprinted. The writers treated here represent what established, successful authors could achieve with their publishers and printers.
About the careers of the thousands of less famous authors we can know
very little, since their lives are unchronicled, their correspondence un-
collected, and their works never reprinted. As the authors discussed in this
chapter grew in fame, they dealt with different aspects of reprinting at
various times, and thus their habits, intentions, and understanding of
printing will show both the mean and the extremes of authorial involvement in reprinting during the Victorian era.

Robert Browning

The curious case of Browning's 1863 and 1865 *Poetical Works*, in which an
edition was made to look like a reimpression, has already been described in
some detail in chapter 4. Chapman and Hall had the bad luck to print only
one small impression of the 1863 volumes just before Browning's reputation began to rise.* Within eight months of its issue, this edition was

---

*John Blackwood, unhappy with the sales of George Eliot's *The Spanish Gypsy*, seems to
have felt that Browning's newfound popularity in the 1860s was unjustifiably eclipsing
Eliot's poem. He wrote to her in 1868: "The newspaper critics have I see got it into their heads
that it looks intellectual to admire or rather to praise Browning. . . . The words are as
laudatory as possible, but it is obvious that the creatures had the utmost difficulty in reading
the words of their idol. . . . I confess that I am a heretic as to Browning" (Eliot, *Letters*, 4:497).

selling out, and a new one was planned. For reasons of his own, Chapman aimed to make the new typesetting as much like its predecessor as possible, and for many years the 1865 *Poetical Works* was taken by Browning scholars as a second impression of the 1863 edition. Though one bibliography describes the 1865 edition as a stereotype reprint, Chapman had not, to his undoubted unhappiness, had plates made; he had to bear the expense of recomposing the three volumes. Browning seized this opportunity to revise his text, probably working his changes into a copy of the 1863 edition. Enough of the literal errors in the earlier typesetting persist in its successor to prove that the 1863 edition was used as printer's copy for the 1865. Revised though it was, the 1865 *Poetical Works* was produced with pagination, gatherings, paper, and bindings identical with the 1863 edition.

This history provides one of the clearest illustrations of how printing technology and authorial control are both reinforcingly and reciprocally connected. Had Chapman ordered the 1863 typesetting stereotyped, he could have cited the need for haste in printing more copies and the expense of altering plates, and allowed Browning few or no alterations to his texts. The poet's control over the edition would have been continued because of the stereotyping, but further control (through revision) would have been quite limited. With fresh types being set, new errors would inevitably be introduced; Browning had to prepare accurate printer's copy and read complete proofs carefully to achieve textual control. His additional work would normally have earned him the right to revise freely, but in this case he must have been restrained by Chapman's plan to duplicate the 1863 edition in arrangement and appearance. Nowhere in 1865, despite his close attention to every poem, did Browning go so far as to add or delete a stanza or even an entire line; to have done so might have affected pagination and layout sufficiently to undermine Chapman's intention to make 1865 as much like 1863 as possible. Yet Browning did manage to change scores of individual words, and he altered punctuation and capitalization in hundreds of places. Though the available records for 1864 and 1865 provide no direct evidence, presumably a more or less decorous struggle between author and publisher occurred over the extent to which Browning would be allowed to revise. Both the cause and the resulting compromise arose directly from the kind of printing technology selected by the publisher.

Whether Chapman was provident enough to have plates made of the 1865 typesetting is not known. If he was, he never got the chance to use them, because Browning bought out Chapman's publication rights and severed relations with the firm in the summer of 1866.[1] His new publisher, George Murray Smith of Smith, Elder, and Company, sealed his contract with Browning the following year by paying him handsomely for a new collected edition, the six-volume *Poetical Works* of 1868. Browning wanted to give Smith the 1865 edition to use as printer's copy, but he had difficulty acquiring a set of the books. He wrote to his friend Isa Blagden in December of 1867: "I have arranged with Smith & Elder for a new edition of my works. . . . Smith gives me exactly five times as much for an edition,—an arrangement which is preferable. Chapman's behaviour was characteristic to the last: he apprised me "he had fifty copies on hand" (as it was stipulated he should, it being a bad thing to let a book get quite out of print) I sent for one of these copies (to reprint by)—no answer,—at last I sent a servant to bring one,—then came the avowal—all were gone."[2]

Browning did find a copy of the 1865 edition to mark up for the compositors, as shown by the repetition in the 1868 *Poetical Works* of certain literal errors that had appeared only in the 1865 typesetting. The edition appeared in the summer of 1868, the first impression comprising 1,500 copies. In a series of uncanny coincidences, this 1868 typesetting proved just as evanescent as the 1863 one had. According to Michael Meredith's research on the six-volume Smith, Elder edition, Smith wanted Browning's freshly revised text preserved, either as standing type or by stereotyping (or at least taking paper molds). But when Smith ordered a second impression in early 1870, he was informed that someone had blundered, and the types had been distributed. Once again a new typesetting of Browning's poems was required, and once again it was made to look as much like a reimpression of the preceding edition as possible. Browning performed a quick revision, making over two hundred changes in the six volumes, and this time stereos were made.

With regard to this typesetting, Browning had numerous ways to assert and maintain textual control. In his favor were (1) the existence of a recently revised and carefully proofed text to use as copy, the 1868 edition; (2) the willingness of Smith to let him revise and proof again, a solicitousness which would have been intensified by Smith's embarrassment over the confusion in the printing works; (3) sufficient time—about six months—for careful proofing (though Browning complained that Smith was slow with proofs); and (4) the awareness on all sides that this edition would be stereotyped, and should thus be as accurate as possible. Against making this a superior text stood only the fact that a fresh typesetting inevitably would contain new compositorial errors, and these could be corrected in proof. Yet this edition, of which a second impression was run in 1872, went wrong. Whether (through his fault or others') Browning's proofreading in 1870 had been inadequate, or whether the stereotype plates made then had later been damaged and faultily repaired, is not at all clear from the surviving documents. But by 1875, the poet had discovered many erroneous "changes made *since the last unstereotyped edition.*" The "last unstereotyped edition," even given the looseness with which the Victorians used the word *edition*, must mean the 1868 typesetting, which was mistakenly distributed sometime in 1869; therefore what Browning had found were either compositorial errors made in the 1870 resetting which had escaped his notice at that time or errors which had appeared in the 1870 typesetting after Browning had proofed it. His underlining and phrasing suggest to me that he suspected the latter: "New errors have appeared in the edition [i.e., 1870] which has been stereotyped, a process which is alleged to prevent such things."[3]

After suggesting to Smith that "somebody" should restore the correct readings, Browning volunteered to go through them himself, "for, I hope, the last time." Numerous corrections and restorations, as well as some further revisions, were worked into the plates, which were then used for many impressions over more than a decade. They show the predictable patterns of decay, repair, and eventual disintegration, and Meredith reports that by 1884 there were "as many as fifty lacunae in each volume." In 1887, Smith and Browning prepared what was indeed the last collected edition supervised and proofed by the poet, the sixteen-volume *Poetical Works* of 1888–89. Browning unquestionably prepared a copy of the old six-volume edition to be used as printer's copy for part of the new typesetting, but which iteration of it he revised is not now known.[4] It is, however, abundantly clear that Browning never relinquished control of even the smallest details of his texts, that he never passed up an opportunity to revise, and that his collected editions and their reimpressions stand as directly connected links in a long chain of textual evolution. In recent decades, scholars have come to agree that in Browning's case, the reprints he controlled are central to an understanding of his text and career, and are as important as his manuscripts and first editions.

Matthew Arnold

In his dealings with his two major publishers, Macmillan and Smith, Elder, Matthew Arnold experienced most aspects of Victorian reprinting. Almost every one of Arnold's works of criticism—literary, social, and biblical—first appeared in periodicals, either singly or as a series of articles. Often Arnold had arranged for the publication of a work in volume form either before or during its magazine publication, and his letters to editors and publishers show that reprinting was on his mind even as he composed. Following the familiar pattern, the magazine text was used as printer's copy for the volume publication, with the author being given time and opportunity to revise. As the textual variants recorded throughout R. H. Super's edition of the prose works make evident, Arnold was a very careful and subtle reviser, always mindful of the shades of difference between varied audiences. And the one revision—when going from periodical to book form—was seldom enough; Arnold continued to pay close attention to his texts over the years, and his publishers habitually kept him informed of reprints, invited corrections, and reassured him that he was in control.

Arnold's edition of selections from Wordsworth's poems, published by Macmillan in 1879, provides a characteristic illustration of how careful Arnold was.[5] As compositors' copy, he marked up "a recent one Volume edition" provided by Macmillan; but to preclude transmitting latter-day textual errors, Arnold wished to rely on the 1832 collected edition of Wordsworth. Macmillan complied: "Send me back the interleaved copy of Wordsworth I sent you & I could have it gone over with the 4 volume 1832 edition for collation." Two weeks later he reiterated: "The printer shall *set up* from it [i.e., Arnold's marked volume], and *read* from Craiks [*sic*] copy of the 1832 edition, so as not to destroy a copy of what you think so good an edition." Arnold, thoroughly aware of the tendencies of compositors, insisted that "Wordsworth's own punctuation, & c., is to be followed, and the Sonnets are to be printed in that close order which he always used himself—not in the open Italian order." Trying to speed the project along, Macmillan wrote: "I suppose you do not care to see proof? The printer will read from the 1832 edition & follow all the punctuation &c he finds there." But Arnold would have none of that: "Of course I don't want the trouble of proofs; still I think I had better undertake it. . . . I had better see the proofs myself. I will send them back rapidly and regularly." In letter after letter, Arnold gave instructions to the printers, complained about the proofs, and consulted about the engraved portrait of Wordsworth that served as frontispiece.

Despite his care, Arnold found faults in the volume as soon as it appeared. To his "real annoyance," his own name had appeared on the spine of the book along with Wordsworth's, and a title was wrongly given in the text; furthermore, the text was stereotyped from the outset, since Macmillan anticipated a long and steady sale. Craik apologized, guaranteed that Arnold's name would be removed, but begged that the 750 copies already bound might be simply sold off. Arnold apparently agreed to this, and in recompense Craik urged him to "make any verbal alterations you like in the plates." The mistakes were painful to Arnold, whose embarrassment was increased by the degree to which his own proofreading was responsible for errors in the works of a poet he had always venerated. Arnold detailed one instance in a letter to a friend:

> *These mis-prints or mistakes are things capable of embittering years of life. Look at the concluding Duddon sonnet entitled "After thought." For the magnificent lines*
> > "We men, who in our morn of youth defied
> >   The elements . . ."
> *the infernal printer has put—*
> > "We men, who in our morn of youth defiled
> >   The elements . . ."
> *The force of misprinting can no further go.*[6]

This was corrected in the second impression, printed before the year was out; Craik's choice of words in his letter of 21 October suggests that the errors were fairly numerous: "I think the printers can easily make all the changes you propose and I have sent them your letter."

It took Arnold a long time to get the Wordsworth selections just as he wanted them; he added poems in 1880, substituted some others in 1882, and continued to correct errors as he found them. All were worked into the existing plates, though it took some time for the alterations to appear in the books themselves. In 1884, Arnold complained to Macmillan: "I made a good many alterations last year in the little Wordsworth, and had the proofs of them from Clark [the printer]; yesterday I saw a copy brought here [to Fox How] as a new one, of which the date was 1882, and where the alterations were not made. . . . Please be sure that the alterations are made when you reprint." Craik explained that Arnold would have to wait for a new impression: "All the corrections you made last year have been put in the plates, but we have not reprinted from them yet. We have still a considerable stock of the edition printed in 1882."

The same situation had occurred ten years earlier, when Macmillan was publishing Arnold's *A Bible-Reading for Schools* (stereotyped from the first, but published in a new typesetting in 1875 as *Isaiah XL-LXVI*). Shortly after its appearance, Arnold must have found some mistakes in the first impression, and asked that changes be made before the book was reprinted. His letter does not survive, but Macmillan's response does: "The 1000 copies [of the second impression] are already struck off, but I have sent a note to the printer to correct the errors in the plates at once, so that it [*sic*] may not appear in any other edition."[7]

George Smith's approach to the reprints of another of Arnold's works on religion, *Literature and Dogma* (1873), was somewhat different. Smith may have been unsure about the probable sale, or may simply not have been as given to immediate stereotyping as Macmillan; or perhaps Arnold had warned Smith that he would probably wish to revise the work. Whatever the cause, in early 1873 the first impression of 1,500 copies of the book was printed from types, which were left standing. *Literature and Dogma* turned out to have a brisk sale. In less than three weeks, more copies were needed, and Arnold wanted to make revisions in the second impression; he wrote to Smith: "I hope [the printers] will remember to print the new 500 copies from the slightly corrected copy I left with him. This is of importance, because I have quoted in the first edition a spurious work of St. Augustine as genuine, and I should like to alter the mistake before any one discovers it."[8]

The second impression was rather more than "slightly corrected"; Arnold added over 180 words to correct his statements about St. Augustine, and inserted footnotes at various points throughout the book. Since these revisions were extensive enough to have affected pagination (and play havoc with a set of plates), the fact that Smith had them carried out in the second impression strongly suggests that the first two impressions were printed from standing type. Less than two weeks later, Smith was planning to print 1000 more copies, and this time Arnold, who was out of the country, skipped the opportunity to revise; he wrote Smith: "I want to write to you at once to answer your question about re-printing. Henceforth I shall make no more alterations for some time, though ultimately I may soften some things. . . . At all events, go on till my return, printing from the second edition without change."[9]

Arnold's reference to further alterations probably reflects a request from Smith about stereotyping; the book certainly sold well enough to justify plating it, going into its fifth impression by 1876. A further indication that plates had been made is that when this fifth "edition" was being prepared, Arnold asked to see proofs only of the pages he was altering at the time: "When you reprint let me see the pages referred to on the enclosed envelope before they go finally to press." Arnold, then, relied on the stereotyping process to preserve the rest of the text of *Literature and Dogma* against unwanted changes; but since these plates were used for many impressions, later copies undoubtedly suffered the usual corruptions caused by wear. In 1883 he carried out a final revision of the text.[10]

The later editions of Arnold's own poems illustrate the complicated path a text may follow through decades of revision.[11] Arnold and Macmillan had worked hard to produce an accurate and attractive collected edition, the two-volume *Poems* of 1869. As has been mentioned previously, Arnold was not satisfied with the arrangement of the poems, and did not want this edition stereotyped; he planned at the time to make changes in his next edition, which would then be plated.[12] It was seven years before another edition was planned; Arnold prepared printer's copy (almost certainly a copy of the 1869 edition) in December 1876 and began to read proof a month later. In response to Arnold's expression of satisfaction with his reordering of the poems, Macmillan asked: "Would you object to our stereotyping your Poems? This would enable us to print 1000 at a time, which has certain advantages." No answer is recorded, but it appears that Arnold held back his approval, as indicated by the developments of the following year.

Sometime after the appearance of the two-volume *Poems* in May of 1877, Arnold asked Macmillan to find an American publisher for the poems. Following fruitless inquiries in New York, Macmillan wrote to Arnold: "I think however that a one volume edition of the Poems would sell in the States, and if you have no objection we will get one up and publish it ourselves. . . . The poems as now arranged will go into a volume of 400 pages like that enclosed. What we should do would be to make stereotype plates at Oxford and send them out to New York to be printed from."

Arnold's reply attests to his vigilance and the preparations he had already made for revisions: "There are some misprints in the recent English edition which should not be stereotyped; and the 'Church of Brou,' an omitted poem, should be given among 'Early Poems.' . . . This will give the American edition something to distinguish it. . . . I have been correcting misprints in my copy of the Poems [i.e., the 1877 text]; shall I complete the corrections at my return and then bring the copy to you? it will serve for the next English edition too."

Now the punctuation (or lack thereof) in the first sentence of this passage leaves Arnold's meaning partially uncertain. He may mean to say "do not include the misprints in the English edition when you stereotype for the American one," or he may be saying "do not rely on, and do not stereotype, the 1877 English edition, which has errors in it." Arnold may have been under the impression that the American edition would be created by making stereotype molds from the 1877 types, mistakes and all.★ Of course the entire makeup of a one-volume edition would be so different from the two-volume 1877 edition that a new typesetting would be required, as Macmillan's response to the above letter makes plain: "It will be a great advantage to us to have your latest corrections for the American Edition of your Poems and if you will kindly let me have your marked copy at your leisure I will give it to the printers to set up from."

Arnold seems to have suspended his control over the American text after sending in the revised printer's copy. On 25 February 1878, while typesetting was going forward, Macmillan wrote: "Am I right in thinking that you said you wanted to see no proofs?" No reply from Arnold survives, and in the absence of evidence that he read proof on the American edition, the authority of this text is diminished. Even though they could not be granted priority, however, the alterations to the 1877 English edition which Arnold made for the American volume would be of great importance if this were their only appearance. However, the printer's copy he had prepared for the American edition surfaced again shortly. Macmillan's next Arnoldian project was the *Selected Poems*, which was being planned by early 1878. When it came time to assemble the selections, Arnold wrote Macmillan: "As to the poems, what arrangement do you propose? And when will they be ready? I hope they are printing them carefully from the copy I corrected for the American edition." The *Selected Poems* appeared in the summer; within a few months Arnold was again attending to textual errors, as his letter of 27 August 1878 announces: "I found a few mis-stoppings and errors of arrangement in the Selected Poems, so I thought it better to correct a copy throughout. I send it by this

---

★It is likely that these types had been distributed after paper molds had been made as a precaution, whether or not Arnold had agreed to stereotyping in 1877. Later in 1878, Macmillan took this step on his own with Arnold's edition of Johnson; Arnold may have known enough about Macmillan's practices to assume that such molds existed and would be used to make plates for America. There is not sufficient evidence to determine whether plates were in fact made and used to print any copies of the 1877 typesetting, but it appears that this was not the case. Arnold and Macmillan had contracted for "an edition of 2000 . . . whether you print the whole 2000 or not," with Arnold being paid a single sum at the outset rather than a royalty on copies sold. Whatever the number of copies actually printed, they seem to have been struck off all at once in 1877, with no later impressions to restock supplies; when more copies were needed in 1880, Arnold asserted that "this edition has actually sold itself out in a shorter time than its predecessor." The "predecessor" was the two-volume 1869 *Poems*, also apparently printed in a single impression of 2,000 copies; it had taken eight years to sell out. On such evidence as there is, my assumption would be that neither the 1869 nor the 1877 edition was stereotyped (Buckler, *Arnold's Books*, 130, 43, 37, 40, 43, 52; see also Buckler, "American Edition of Arnold's Poems").

day's post, and I hope you will see that the printers follow it when we go to press again. I think I may say that if this corrected copy is faithfully followed, no further change whatever will be required in the stereotype."

Arnold's timing was perfect, since the first impression of 1,500 copies was almost exhausted, and Macmillan had just decided to order more; the poet's promise not to make any more changes "in the stereotype" probably refers not so much to the small "corrections" he often requested as to a larger change he made at this time. For the second impression—called a "reprint" by Macmillan, but an "edition" by Arnold's bibliographers and editors—Arnold withdrew the sonnet "To George Cruikshank" and substituted "A Question: To Fausta" in its place. Because of the format of the volume, this would have necessitated the cancellation of an entire page, that is, the casting of a new plate.

This second impression of the *Selected Poems* (as revised) comprised 1,500 copies, all of which were sold within a few months; in December of 1878, Macmillan happily informed Arnold that "we are now in our third thousand," signifying that at least one further impression had been called for. When the supply again ran low, Arnold asked again for the opportunity to revise. During February 1879 the following exchanges occurred between poet and publisher. Arnold: "I must look carefully through the Selections before they are reprinted, but I think the volume is all right now, except one line where I want to change a couple of words." Macmillan: "Any slight change in the plates we would like done during the next month or so. We have under 700 out of the 3000." Arnold: "Let me have a copy of the last issue of the Selected Poems, that I may go through it carefully for the press." Arnold: "I have been most carefully through the Selected Poems. The only corrections to make are these trifling ones. Will you kindly direct that the printer makes them without fail in the next impression."

And so it went, the *Selected Poems* selling in the thousands every year. That Arnold monitored the minutiae of his texts in this evolving collection is certain, but in terms of the main line of the development of his text, the selections are either a transitional phase or a terminated branch. For when the major body of Arnold's poetic canon, the two-volume *Poems* of 1877 came to be reprinted,★ Arnold turned not to the most recent revised texts in the *Selected Poems*, but to the revisions he had made in 1878 for the one-volume American edition. In September of 1880 Macmillan wrote: "We

---

★The 1877 edition of the *Poems* seems to have been printed from types in only one impression of 2,000 copies, as noted in the previous discussion.

shall want a reprint of your two volume Poems soon. . . . Have you an interleaved copy?" Arnold's response on 3 October spells out his plan:

> *I carefully corrected the press for the American edition, and I think George [Craik] told me my corrections had been preserved. At any rate, the American edition can be followed. I think I shall restore one or two short pieces which I had excluded; I will get copies of them made and send them. They will not make, altogether, a difference of half a dozen pages. I think the* Church of Brou *has been restored in the American edition. . . . I don't think I need see proofs of the poems, except for the new pieces.*

How Arnold's alterations may have been "preserved" is not completely clear, nor is the much more important matter of what was actually used as printer's copy for the 1881 edition. On 5 October, Macmillan informed Arnold, "We have a copy of the American edition which we laid aside for the reprint. . . . kindly send the additions and restorations." Perhaps Arnold asked for a copy of the American edition to mark up as printer's copy, since Macmillan wrote on 14 October, "We had sent the only copy of the American edition of the Poems that we had down to Oxford to be printed from for the new edition." If Arnold could not make his changes to a copy of the American edition, he may have worked in 1880 with a previously unmarked copy of the two-volume English edition, which had been the basis of the typesetting for the American volume. But it is also possible that either Macmillan or Arnold discovered that the poet's 1878 corrections had indeed been preserved, in Arnold's own copy of the 1877 two-volume *Poems.* Whether he referred to a newly marked copy or to the one Arnold had corrected in 1878, Macmillan wrote on 19 October 1880, "Your copy of the "Second Edition' [i.e., 1877] is returned to you by this post." If this was in fact the copy Arnold had marked in 1878, it becomes one of the most important documents in the history of his text and its development. These volumes were definitely used in 1878 as printer's copy for the American edition and the first impression of the *Selected Poems,* and may have similarly served for the 1881 edition of the *Poems.*

But if the one-volume American *Poems* was used as printer's copy for the two-volume English edition of 1881, the American edition attains new importance. It will be remembered that Arnold did not read proof on the American edition in 1878, but if he prepared a copy of it in 1880, his revisions to his text would have unquestionable authority, an authority that would be strengthened or weakened by the degree to which the 1881 edition incorporated them. On the other hand, Arnold read proof of the

1881 *Poems* only for those pages where he had made changes; Macmillan to Arnold, 19 October 1880: "I enclose a proof of the new matter to be included in the new edition of your complete poems." Thus his control over the *rest* of the 1881 poems was rather weak, and any errors that originated in the American edition could have been carried over into the new English one without authorial scrutiny. The complexity of these central textual questions then begins to multiply. The 1881 English edition may have been stereotyped and reprinted, and it seems also to have been the basis for a two-volume American edition which definitely was stereotyped; these plates then were used in 1885 to print the first two volumes of the three-volume *English* edition—which Arnold's editors have taken as the *textus receptus.*

This is not the place to attempt a complete map of the stages and heritage of Arnold's poetic text, but one thing is certain: the economic and technical aspects of reprinting, including their limitations of revisions and corrections, had a great deal to do with the occasions, the nature, and the extent of Arnold's textual control. Arnold's may be a case where an intermediate printed text, neither the nearest to the lost manuscript nor the last one he revised, should be taken as most fully representing the author's intention.

Alfred Tennyson

Tennyson's knowledge of printing, his meticulous attention to his texts, and his penchant for laborious revision during proofing have already been illustrated in this study, and his practices regarding reprints were little different. If there is one Victorian poet that most readers would presume to be inclined by temperament toward attending to the first editions and ignoring subsequent printings, that poet is Tennyson. But the romantic image of the laureate as moody bard was a compound of defensive strategy on Tennyson's part and the baseless ruminations of Harold Nicholson, and it obscured for many years the shrewd, practical, and observant man of letters that Tennyson really was. A few instances from just one decade of his career will show how attentive he was to reprints.

If Tennyson's publishers thought that their troubles with Tennyson ended after he had revised his way slowly through trial editions, multiple revises, and first editions, they were sadly mistaken. For Tennyson proved almost as concerned with a work when it went into a new impression or edition as he had been when composing the first draft. The many subsequent editions of the 1842 *Poems*, in particular, offered him the chance to look back on his works and alter them; he often added new poems to the collection when a new edition was prepared. In 1850, when preparing a seventh edition of the *Poems*, he inserted several new works and added a stanza to the ballad "Lady Clare."* He later wrote to Moxon asking that he check and correct if necessary a spelling: "In the new stanza to Lady Clare I hope the Printers did not print the word 'dropped' I always writing 'dropt.' Correct it if there is time, if so printed."[13]

Following the usual pattern, Tennyson carried out some of his revisions by making them in a copy of the latest edition of a work, sending this to the printers to be used as compositors' copy for the next impression or edition. Like other authors, he sometimes read proof only on the pages where he had revised, as was the case with the 1852 reprint of the *Poems*. Though he aimed, he said, to make this "a perfect edition," he added, "I hope that if I am not to see the sheets except in cases of alteration yourself or your brother will be very careful in collating the proofs with the book which I sent you."[14] Edward or Charles Moxon, then, might have been responsible for the accurate transmission of the unaltered parts of the text, which were to be read against "the book," presumably a marked copy of a previous collected edition.

When he conducted lengthy revisions, Tennyson sometimes read proof more thoroughly. In 1849, while revising *The Princess* extensively for its third edition, he seems to have arranged initially for two stages of proof, just as if he were carrying a new work through the press. However, he wearied of checking revises, and begged Moxon to watch the printers closely: "I have written one or two passages twice over [on the proofs] for the greater clearness: don't let them print these twice over in their stupidity. Surely I may depend on you or your brother without having the sheets resent to me." If he was relieved of another round of revises, he also paid the predictable price. After the new edition of *The Princess* was out, he wrote to Aubrey De Vere: "I gave it up to the printer in a rage at last and left London, not having revised the last proofs and so I see there is a mistake or two."[15]

Because Tennyson continued to revise, correct, and extend the text of *The Princess*, this modified typesetting and its immediate successors almost certainly were not stereotyped, despite the poem's large and rapid

---

*As previously indicated, some basic aspects of Tennyson's textual history—such as correct, complete descriptions and discriminations of the hundreds of editions and impressions of his works—have yet to be adequately treated. Tennyson understood better than his later editors the great flexibility offered by new printing technologies, and habitually bent the printing process to his will.

sale. Moxon may have been modifying and printing from standing types throughout the poet's period of substantial revision, which lasted until the fifth "edition" in 1853; if the original 1847 typesetting was indeed kept standing, undergoing extensive alterations through the years, then all of the first five "editions" of *The Princess* would be in fact impressions of one edition. Such a history would parallel what demonstrably did occur with *In Memoriam*. As mentioned in a previous chapter, Hagen's research demonstrates that the first 8000 copies of *In Memoriam* were printed in four impressions from standing type, and further impressions may well have been struck off before the text was plated. Moxon knew his poet well enough to expect him to demand revisions, and stereotyping his poems— especially in the days of the plaster process—before he was through altering them would have been a waste of money.

The texts of Tennyson's popular early works had stabilized by the time paper-mold stereotyping became common for books, and many of his volumes appear to have been plated in the 1860s. This is the most logical explanation for the persistent availability, over many years and with different publishers, of *Maud, Enoch Arden, The Idylls of the King*, and other works in single-volume "original editions," as they were advertised.[16] The printing data for the first edition of *Enoch Arden* (Moxon, 1864) show again how stereotype plates (possibly in duplicate) and printing machines could be combined to produce astonishing results. The first *impression* of the volume (which must have been stereotyped from the first) consisted of no less than 60,000 copies, all of which were sold in four months; tens of thousands more had been struck off, in an undetermined number of impressions, before two years were up and a second edition was offered.[17]

The plates of the numerous stereotyped editions became an irritating problem for Tennyson in later years. In settling up with publishers when he left them—after Moxon, there were the firms of Alexander Strachan, Henry S. King, and Charles Kegan Paul before he fixed on Macmillan— Tennyson had to buy and sell the plates of his own works several times. Besides the inevitable squabbles about publishing rights, there was a financial danger consequent on the fact that plates could be easily duplicated. The poet's son Hallam complained in 1878 about Kegan Paul's proposal to become Tennyson's new publisher: " 'The new stereotypes' my father is 'bound to purchase at cost price' is plainly absurd—for Paul might make new stereotypes for everything *at once*—& make us pay double at the end. Judging from the outrageous amount of Editions now, there might be in fact no end to the new plates."[18]

This was hardly an exaggeration; the final agreement between the laureate and Kegan Paul[19] lists the following titles as being in stereotype:

> Cabinet Edition
> Crown Octavo Edition
> Library Edition
> Original Edition
> Miniature Edition
> Selections
> Songs
> Tennyson for the Young
> Queen Mary

But with these Kegan Paul, a master at packaging up new "editions" by using his plates with different papers, margins, and bindings, was just beginning; before a year was over, he advertised (in the last signature of the newly published *The Lover's Tale*) not only all the above editions, but also these:

> Imperial Library Edition
> Author's Edition
> Guinea Edition
> Royal Edition
> Shilling Edition

Thus there were nine simultaneous iterations of the collected works alone, not counting the special "Cabinet Edition in Case, forming an elegant ornament for the Drawing Room or Library Table," at thirty-two shillings. The intricacies of the relationships among all of these texts, as well as their predecessors and successors, have yet to be adequately explored. To what degree Tennyson attempted to control his collected editions in his later years, how carefully he continued to monitor the fine points of his text, and how many permutations and generations there were of the various stereo plates are matters which are not completely understood. In the face of our ignorance in these areas, it cannot be right to ignore the textual problems and rely on the Eversley Edition, as so many modern scholars have done.

George Eliot

Since she was the first major Victorian novelist to insist on the royalty system of payment (rather than selling her copyrights or sharing profits), George Eliot was understandably knowledgeable about and interested in reprints. For most of her works from *The Mill on the Floss* (1860) on, she received royalties of 20 to 40 percent, and her initial arrangements with Blackwood for each book usually included a planned series of ever-cheaper "editions."[20] Nowhere is it plainer than in Eliot's correspondence with her publishers how commercial prospects and technological options dictated the nature of reprints. Eliot participated in decisions about whether type would be kept standing, whether and when plates would be made, and whether the promise of sales was great enough to warrant issuing a revised text. Yet for all her attention to commercial details, Eliot's ultimate interest in her texts was more artistic than financial. She, as much as any finical Victorian poet, used reprints as opportunities to revise and correct a text. The well-documented cases of *The Spanish Gypsy* and *Middlemarch* will suffice to show how thoroughly Eliot wanted to control her texts.

The Spanish Gypsy constituted George Eliot's debut as a poet, and neither she, Lewes, nor Blackwood could predict how well her new venture might sell. Thus they agreed to print a small (for Eliot) first impression and leave the type standing, an option that was practicable once typecasting machines had been perfected. Lewes wrote to Blackwood on 30 April 1868: "I think it prudent not to print more than 2,000 at first and as I presume you will keep the type standing we shall soon see *how* it is likely to go." This approach was adopted, and to everyone's satisfaction the book sold fairly well. On 27 July Blackwood reported: "The Poem is nearly out of print. . . . We kept the type up and I think the best plan will be to print another little edition of 500 in same form and price." At the end of this letter he adds: "Inclosed is a Mem. of some corrections suggested. Have you any?" (This probably refers to Rev. William MacIlwaine's list of errata, which Eliot rather frostily acknowledged on 30 July.) Eliot's reply reveals a continuing lack of confidence in the book: "Since you have kept up the type would it not do to print 250? . . . I have always a horror of unsold copies. . . . I shall immediately look through the volume for the purpose of small corrections, and will send them to you very shortly"; a few days later she sent Blackwood "a list of corrections for the reprint." Apparently her suggestion was followed, because the actual number of copies printed in this second impression was 252.[21]

Later in 1868, demand for *The Spanish Gypsy* increased, and another run of copies was needed. About four months after the first edition was printed, the types were still standing; Eliot was informed that she might revise again. She wrote William Blackwood on 24 September: "I am now going through the poem for the sake of correction. I have read it through once and have at present found some ten or twelve *small* alterations to be added to those already made [in the second impression described above]. But I shall go through it again more than once, for I wish to be able to put 'revised' to the third edition, and to leave nothing that my conscience is not ready to swear by. I think it will be desirable for me to see proofs."[22] Here, as so often throughout her career, we see Eliot unwilling to entrust anyone with responsibility for the accuracy of her text.

Apparently it took several weeks for her to work through the poem, for on 20 October Blackwood urged: "The second edition of the Gypsy is so nearly out of print that we ought to proceed with a reprint *at once*. . . . We would propose to print a thousand and then stereotype." Eliot must have felt that her thorough revision would be adequate to her purposes because she wrote the next day: "If you stereotype, I suppose it will be easy to bring out as cheap an edition as we like, by reducing the cost of paper and binding. . . . I have gone through the Poem twice for the sake of revision, and have a crop of small corrections—only in one case extending to the insertion of a new line. But I wish to see the proof sheets, so that 'revised by the author' may be put in the advertisement and on the title-page. I will send the sheets of corrections to Mr. Simpson with the request for the transmission of proofs." The poem's sales were now steady enough to justify stereotyping, which the papier-mâché process made possible with ordinary types. Before the plates were made, a third impression of 1,055 copies was struck off; the stereos were then used over the years to produce the 1,000-copy batches which Lewes and Blackwood decided to term "editions."[23]

As has been alluded to in chapter 3, Lewes and Eliot convinced Blackwood to publish *Middlemarch* initially in the unusual format of eight parts, each costing five shillings. Sheets printed with the same stereo plates used for the part-issue were then bound up as four volumes and sold at forty-two shillings. Blackwood—who had doubted the efficacy of Lewes's unprecedented publication scheme from the first—expected the sale of this expensive impression to be slow, and pressed Eliot and Lewes to approve a cheaper version, "with thinner paper and narrower margin." He wrote on 6 January 1873: "We should as soon as possible get out a 21/- edition. We would make this one rather smaller and thinner paper than the first edition so as to look different." This impression (or impressions; the records are imprecise) sold rather better.[24]

Meanwhile, Lewes had apparently arranged on his own for a foreign reprint, whose text would also derive from the original part-issue typesetting that Eliot had proofed. In a letter to Lewes of 6 January 1873, Blackwood remarks: "Asher got casts of the stereotype plates from [the] stereotyper here and has paid us for the first four. We charged no profit upon them." The word *casts* might suggest that a plaster mold was made from the existing stereos—a process which was feasible, but hardly the method of choice in 1873; making paper molds was much easier. The matter is made more puzzling by Blackwood's reference to this transaction in an earlier letter. He wrote to Bulwer-Lytton that Lewes had arranged for Asher's "buying electroplates from us and paying the author a Lord-ship on the copies sold."[25] Though slow and costly, electroplating was certainly an excellent means of duplicating plates; the result would be an exact and durable copy of the typesetting. Since there is no casting involved in making electroplates, however, Blackwood's reference to "casts" in his letter to Lewes remains a bit mysterious. Perhaps electrotypes were originally planned, but the more expeditious papier-mâché method chosen in the event. The duplicate plates produced from paper molds could rightly be called "casts"; technically speaking, the copies printed from such duplicates constituted unsupervised impressions of an edition which had begun under the author's textual control.

After these and other versions of the first typesetting of *Middlemarch* had performed their tasks for about a year, Blackwood proposed that a new and cheaper one-volume edition be published. This new typesetting—the existing plates were designed for a four-volume format—was the true second edition of *Middlemarch*, and contained numerous revisions by Eliot. She wrote to Blackwood on 19 September 1873: "I quite assent to your proposal that there should be a new edition of 'Middlemarch' in one volume at 7/6—to be prepared at once, but not published too precipitately. . . . For one reason especially I am delighted that the book is going to be reprinted—namely, *that I can see the proof-sheets and make corrections.* Pray give orders that the sheets be sent to me. . . . It might be called a 'revised edition.'[26] About a month later she reiterated her intention to revise and control her text, using the words that serve as the epigraph to chapter 4.

Like Browning, Arnold, and Tennyson, Eliot gave equally careful attention to her collected editions. In the early and mid-1860s, Blackwood brought out a cheap edition of Eliot's works to capitalize on her growing popularity. He offered and Eliot seized upon this chance to revise the texts of her early novels and stories; she recorded in her journal: "Finished Silas Marner. I have thus corrected all my books for a new and cheaper edition and feel my mind free for other work." The corrected copies generated typesettings which Eliot carefully proofed, and these in turn were used as copy for later editions. Years later she went through all of her works again for the magnificent Cabinet Edition of 1878–79. In August of 1878 she sent Blackwood revised and corrected copies of *Deronda* and "The Legend of Jubal," and wanted to see proofs. About two months later, she submitted some additional poems to fill out a volume of the edition, and asked again for proofs of the whole volume. Lewes's death in December of 1878 destroyed her interest in any literary work for some time, and she seems not to have read the proofs she had requested. But in February of 1879 she wrote to Blackwood: "I have been looking into the last volume of the Cabinet Edition, to see if there were any errata in the poems printed from the M. S. without my correction." She wanted to make two revisions, and as usual she worried about the trouble and cost, especially since "they are on two separate leaves." She asked that either new or corrected plates be used for all subsequent copies of the volume. Blackwood assured her: "We ordered the two errata . . . to be cancelled and the stereotype plates to be altered so that the mistakes cannot recur."[27]

Like her great contemporaries, Eliot worked on her text to the end of her days. And in their weight and quantity, her revisions were also like those carried out over the years by other Victorian authors. They seldom aimed in revising to change a work from what it had been before; they habitually honored themselves as they had been when they wrote a work, and tended to tidy their texts, not renovate them, for each successive reprint. In this the Victorians were unlike both their romantic predecessors and their modernist descendants, who in several notorious cases reworked their texts so completely as to create separate versions of works. Yet the consistency and continuity of the Victorians' attentions to their texts does not mean that the last corrected impression of the final edition revised by the author is automatically the literary scholar's text of choice. For the same technology that created a sequence of opportunities for authors to revise, thus increasing for both Victorian authors and later scholars the importance of reprints, also imposed limits on the nature and extent of authorial revision.

VI

Documents, Technology,
and Evidence

*Again, printing from plates never looks so well
as that from type; and the most inexperienced eye
may instantly detect the difference, even in the
first edition.*

Thomas
Curson
Hansard
*The Art of
Printing*

THE FOREGOING chapters have shown that Victorian texts were affected, from composition through reprinted collected editions, by printing technology. In several ways, technological advances tended to multiply the stages through which a work passed during printing, with a corresponding increase in the number of documents created. The textual histories of Victorian literary works are thus fundamentally different from works produced in the days of the hand press. After handing in a manuscript, a seventeenth-century author customarily had but one further chance—author's proof—to control the text, the printers having freely altered spelling, punctuation and more; revises were not regularly sent to the author. The printer's aim in calculating the size of an edition was to print enough copies to cover immediate costs and meet probable demand for several years; the market for books was small enough, and the cost of books high enough, to render reprinting a happy but unusual circumstance.

But a Victorian writer, especially after the 1850s, could expect to have numerous chances to control a text (including the spelling and punctuation) during several stages of proof for the first edition, each step producing a set of documents. As serial publication led authors into serial writing, the very nature of composition was changed, as were the resultant manuscripts, which often did not exist as a whole until shortly before the last installment was published. When a serial work was to be published in volumes upon completion, as was usual, its author normally had another chance to revise freely for a new typesetting; a new edition would be attended by multiple proofs. Stereotyping and printing machines allowed publishers to calculate their edition quantities and printing orders in an open-ended process, every impression presenting a genuine (if limited) opportunity for authorial control and potentially creating its own set of documents.

The fact that there were so many documents—each perhaps connected in some way with an author and a long process of composition and revision—guarantees that for Victorian works, unlike most of their predecessors, large quantities of textual evidence often survive. To this quantitative element may be added historical and commercial factors: the spread of book collecting as a pastime, the Victorians' ever-increasing interest in antiquarian pursuits, and the consequent growth of a trade in literary artifacts all combined to ensure that more documents were preserved from destruction, gathered in dealers' shops, and eventually archived. Though Thomas J. Wise may have inwardly wept in 1888 as he watched Browning thrust bundle after bundle of letters, proof sheets, and other collectibles into the fire, the textual scholar who takes up any major Victorian may be forgiven for occasionally wishing that the bonfires had spread. If the Shakespearean specialist must leave some textual questions forever unresolved for lack of evidence, the Victorian specialist must face an opposite difficulty: certain textual matters verge on the insoluble because of a welter of evidence. The greater the number of documents, the more difficult it becomes to determine the importance and historical position of each one. The most elementary questions about them—in what order were the three sets of proofs before me created?—can be so difficult to answer that scholars sometimes prefer not to ask them. It may not be rigorous, but it is quite common to view all proof sheets, every manuscript, and indeed anything in an author's own hand as holding unchallengeable privileged status. The customary alternatives to this approach simply discount, through one ingenious argument or another, the importance of any document other than those which represent the earliest, or the latest, form of a text.

The values, aims, assumptions, and methods of contemporary textual scholarship both bear on and derive from interpretations of documentary evidence; it therefore seems worthwhile to try to enumerate and comprehend the forms in which such evidence comes down to us from the Victorian era. The technology that multiplied the number of documents also left its traces within them, traces that can, if recognized and understood, shed light on when, how, and how reliably a document reveals authorial intention and control. The following discussion will mimic the design of the earlier chapters, in that it will describe varieties of textual evidence in their order of creation.

Manuscripts

It would be impertinent to suggest that the present study can add more than minor footnotes to the accumulated wealth of meticulous scholarship on manuscripts. But as with all the other facets of printing, nineteenth-century technology left its own particular marks on manuscripts, and these should be noted for the sake of completeness.

Nothing, it would seem, could be more directly indicative of pure authorial intention than a holograph manuscript. Indeed, an author's manuscript that predates a work's appearance in printed form is of great interest to the textual scholar, because the wording, punctuation, spelling, and other formal aspects, as well as the content itself, had not yet been altered by anyone other than their creator. Such purity, coupled with certain beliefs about the nature of the creative process, is a cornerstone of modern textual theory and underlies the precedence accorded by scholarly editors to manuscript readings. Unquestionably, authorial manuscripts are important; but are they in fact pure? do they represent untrammeled authorial intention?

Such alleged purity cannot be absolute, of course, though a manuscript may indeed be closer to an author's original intention that the printed text that derives from it. But this original intention may not have been entirely the author's own. When a writer knows an audience, and hopes to play to its interests and its tastes, he or she may shape a work from the beginning for that readership. The rules by which a text is so shaped may not be consciously acknowledged or even recognized by an author, but those rules can be as real and binding as any alteration ordered by an editor, publisher, or printer's reader. Even in the absence of mendacious origins, the manuscript an author declares to be satisfactory—the document the author wants the printers to follow without deviation—was composed under the inescapable influence of the general conventions of language and writing, over which no individual has sway and from which any writer deviates at risk. Further, the powerful stylistic conventions of an age are absorbed unconsciously by its authors; Trollope did not have to learn to write like a Victorian novelist, and might have found it impossible to learn to write like Nabokov. And at a more mechanical level than such ineluctable influences, a manuscript may have been quite consciously and willingly conformed by its author to specific contemporary requirements; so, at least, printers and publishers hoped to compel them with authors' guides and literary instruction manuals. And with the rise of authorship as a profession, with the rapid expansion of a reading public whose views on propriety in literary subject and style were definite and well known, Victorian writers could be expected to be highly responsive to exterior, overt requirements for the marketplace.

The recognition that so many forces act to limit or alter the author's expression of intention might lead us to reduce somewhat the supremacy which manuscripts have always assumed in textual studies. We would have warrant for this in the indifferent attitude many Victorian authors took toward their manuscripts once a work was printed; it was the printed page and published form they valued, not the hand-written progenitor; and the successful authors knew that they would have chances to revise and correct for reprints anyway. Yet manuscripts do retain great importance in the Victorian period, for no matter how cruelly social and linguistic conventions may have compromised an original and pure artistic intention, it remains true that in the manuscript stage, the author was essentially in control of the words, punctuation, and form of the text. Textual control allows the expression of textual intention, even if the artistic aims have taken a beating along the way from idea to final manuscript.

Through the beginning of the Victorian era, printers held virtually complete control over punctuation, spelling, and capitalization. The study of a particular text from the 1830s or 1840s must begin with the assumption that the punctuation and other small features of a printed text are not the author's. Browning's successful retention of his own punctuation in *Paracelsus* (1835), discussed in chapter 1, was an unusual case for the time and particularly for an unknown poet. An author's punctuation might have been ingenious and meticulously systematic in manuscript, but compositors and the printer's reader would make it conform to their own standard of correctness when types were set. Many times authors protested, but often they simply accepted—grudgingly or gratefully—the punctuation they found in their proof sheets. After all, getting the work printed and published was the object, and to insist on restoring one's own punctuation would have entailed delay, expense, and irritability at both the publisher's and the printer's offices. But later in the century, having gained greater control over their texts and being presented with more numerous opportunities to alter them during proofing and reprinting, authors developed a new habit. Their tendency to punctuate lightly, very simply, or even haphazardly in their manuscripts, installing more complex and expressive punctuation during proofing, has been illustrated in chapter 2. As the technology of printing and the role of authors in the printing process changed, the proofing stages became more important than the manuscript stage in controlling the details of a text.

The composition of a literary work in manuscript and the printing of the work in its first edition became closely intertwined in the nineteenth century, especially for works that were written and published as monthly parts or quarterly magazine installments. The combination of serial composition, piecemeal proofing in sheets, and publication in parts, all influenced to some degree by printing methods, meant that an author saw a work in its complete form only at the end of an extended process. For many novels and long nonfictional prose works, there must have been only one manuscript, the compositional one, produced bit by bit and sent to the printers in batches; certainly this was common in the careers of Dickens, Thackeray, Hardy, Eliot, and Arnold. Since manuscripts were customarily not returned with proofs, an author's first comprehensive reading of a work as a whole often occurred when the entire set of installments or numbers was prepared for a new edition in volume form. The importance of this reading, and thus of the revised reprint that followed, to both author and scholar should be apparent; in my view, an author's revised copy of a part-issue (if used as printer's copy for the next edition) would have greater textual authority than the assembled segments of a compositional manuscript.

For finished works written out and perhaps even revised completely before printing began, the situation is rather different. Given enough documents, it might be quite easy to determine which of several surviving holograph manuscripts represented a stage of initial composition and which a revision, and whether one was used by compositors or another served as the author's copy. But the evidence, plentiful as it may be for Victorian authors, is usually not so clear, and manuscripts may not be what they seem. We cannot always determine with confidence how many manuscripts of a work there might have been, a matter which can be obscured by the natural tendency to treat any surviving authorial manuscript as if it were the only one (or at least the most important one) that ever existed. Of course there were any number of situations in which multiple manuscripts would have been possible or probable. If a significant amount of time elapsed between the completion of a work and its first publication, the likelihood increases that the author made a copy. Further, as we have seen, Victorian printers and publishers pressured authors to submit clean, revised fair-copy manuscripts. When this necessitated copying, a compositional manuscript might survive because it was retained by the author, while the fair copy used by the printers is lost; or a printer's-copy manuscript may have been preserved, the author having thrown away the compositional manuscript after fair-copying it. Equally, a surviving manuscript in the author's hand may have been neither the compositional manuscript nor printer's copy; the first edition may have been set up in type from another manuscript, which commonly would have been discarded or destroyed during proofing. (And this is to say nothing of authorial manuscripts deliberately produced as souvenirs, copied out or summoned from memory years after composition, having no relation to the development of a work's text. Browning, for example, was quite willing to scribble out "My Star" for favored admirers; usually he was considerate enough to date these autographed scraps.)

Then again, the actual printer's copy could have been a fair copy made by someone other than the author; Browning's remarks to his friend Isa Blagden (see chapter 1) hint that she may have copied his manuscripts, either for the printers or for the poet to keep; none of her copies is extant. We know that such seemingly nonauthorial documents were central to the publication of *In Memoriam*, which Moxon's compositors set from Emily Andrews Patmore's transcription of one of Tennyson's manuscripts.[1] Tennyson worked on *In Memoriam* for sixteen years, copying out his "elegies," as he called them, more than once, in various degrees of completeness. Thus the surviving holograph manuscripts in most cases represent stages of revision; they are not first drafts that record Tennyson's first conceptions. These manuscripts undoubtedly shed invaluable light on Tennyson's creative processes, but their textual significance may not be as great as the Patmore transcription, which apparently (and predictably, since it served as printer's copy) has not survived. It was the latter document—copied perhaps from one of the surviving holographs, perhaps from some other lost manuscript—which directly gave rise to the proofs that Tennyson revised for the first edition of *In Memoriam*. From this text in turn, through various modes of reprinting over the years, descended the entire sequence of revised editions. Though it was not in the poet's hand, though it may have varied extensively from any of the surviving holographs, and though it undoubtedly contained scribal errors, Emily Patmore's fair copy of *In Memoriam* might legitimately be considered the most important manuscript of all.

Employment as printer's copy confers great textual authority on documents. Unfortunately, several aspects of nineteenth-century printing practice made the preservation of printer's copy anything but automatic. Furthermore, the survival of manuscripts of uncertain purpose or status can be as troublesome as a complete absence of manuscripts. When we find that a manuscript in an author's hand varies only slightly from the text of the first edition, we tend to assume that we have the printer's copy before us. Yet there are only two ways to be certain about this matter: the author's own contemporaneous testimony must establish that only one complete manuscript existed (as with many of George Eliot's works, for example), or the signs of use in the printing-house must appear on the manuscript itself.

Passing through the stages of composition and in-house proofing left two kinds of marks on a manuscript, those which communicated instructions and information among the people who handled the copy and those which are the result of the processes themselves. Fairly common examples in the first category are: "casting-off" marks, usually penciled lines at the edges of or entirely across the text, which divided the copy into page-length segments for estimating quantities; "take" lines, similar in appearance to the preceding but dividing the whole of the copy into batches for individual compositors; other take marks, such as a sequence of numbers corresponding to neither the sheets of manuscript nor the page-sized segments; the names of compositors assigned to the takes; notations of typeface and size; a reader's copyediting symbols, unusual until late in the century; a reader's signature and folio marks, associating the copy with a specific proof sheet; and directions to the printers in the author's hand. Among the artifacts of the processes are: smudges and blots of ink different from that used by the author, not uncommonly in the form of fingerprints; the residue of paste used to attach paper "tickets" to the copy, the compositors and readers making their marks on these slips; manuscript leaves that have been cut up (and perhaps reassembled) when the copy was divided into takes.

If these or similar reliable signs can be seen, the manuscript at hand was certainly used as printer's copy at some time. Other kinds of marks, made by auctioneers, dealers, binders, collectors, librarians, and even bibliographers will often be found in manuscripts and must not be taken as evidence of use in printing. The absence of such marks on a manuscript, however, does not completely preclude its having served as printer's copy. Manuscripts might be handled very carefully in the printing works, and marked as little as possible—as, for example, Eliot's might have been after Lewes and Blackwood gave orders to preserve them. When compositors and readers made their marks on paper slips rather than on a manuscript itself, the tickets could be removed and any remaining glue scraped off. Penciled numbers and lines could be erased thoroughly enough to make their former presence very difficult to detect, especially on rough-finished paper.

First Edition Proofs

The several stages of proof offered Victorian authors prime opportunities to exert textual control, a control that increased through the century as the role of authors in printing and publishing changed. As has been shown in earlier chapters, the appearance of a work in printed form often had powerful effects on authors, sometimes evoking more intense concentration on textual accuracy during proofing than during original composition or even copying. If the compositors scrupulously followed copy and made few errors, a complaisant author might make very few changes in proof; another author, in the same circumstances, might find that seeing the work in print prompted an overwhelming urge to revise. In short, proofs usually contain information and material of great textual interest, particularly for those authors who viewed proofing as part of the composition process. Revised and corrected proofs may offer unique forms of evidence about an author's textual intentions.

Of the numerous varieties of proof, those which survive are almost inevitably one or another form of author's proof. The earlier forms of proof—the in-house first proofs and revises—were normally discarded when their brief usefulness had passed. This is less of a loss to textual research than it might seem at first. First proofs or rough galleys were indeed closest to the author's manuscript (which may well no longer exist), and the altering hand of the printer's reader was not laid on the text until the next stage of the process; but first proofs also contained all the compositors' initial errors, and despite what he may have done about punctuation and capitalization, the reader strove, for the most part, to move the printed text toward conformity with the manuscript copy. Printers took an indifferent view of "dead" copy (that is, previous documents from which readings are no longer to be taken) and made little effort to preserve it; authors, on the other hand, were more likely to keep the versions of a work as they developed. For these and other reasons, including the monetary value dealers and collectors place on anything associated with a famous author, it is author's proofs that we usually find today, ranging from first author's proof, with many corrections, to the final revise, which should conform almost exactly to the first edition.

All of these are very valuable, and scholars who study writers whose proofs survive in quantity can count themselves lucky. But a warning must be sounded immediately: the very fact that a set of proofs does survive may mean that it was not used in the printing house. Duplicate proofs were commonly sent to authors in the Victorian era, especially in later decades when technology made proofing faster, easier, and cheaper. When a work was not being rushed through serialization but was to be published only when the author was satisfied, multiple copies of proofs could assist the author in the process of revision. George Eliot's letter to Blackwood about her first proofs of *The Spanish Gypsy* provides a clear example; she asked that he send extra sets so that she and Lewes could both work on the poem: "3 or 4 will be enough—one for him, one for me, and one for the resolution of our differences." Lewes independently asked for (and got) six copies of each set,[2] and of the six the most likely to survive would be those which they read, worked over, and kept as a record, not the set that went back to the printers. In a parallel to the situation with manuscripts, the documents that most completely and validly recorded the author's intention at this stage were the proof sheets that were revised and corrected for use by the printers: the very proofs most vulnerable to being discarded when they became dead copy.

Thus surviving proof sheets filled with revisions in the author's hand can give us definitive evidence of the author's attempts at textual control; but if these were duplicate proofs, not used by the printers, they may be able only to direct us toward the author's exact textual intention. The proofs that went back to the printers may have contained any number of further or differing alterations, and there may have been additional sets of revises and still further authorial changes before the text of the first edition was approved. On the other hand, proofs can indicate what must have been present in a lost manuscript, either by accurately preserving a reading which exists in no later text of the work, or by the very nature of an error in typesetting. The scholar who is thoroughly familiar with an author's handwriting can make plausible conjectures about the words or punctuation in a missing manuscript, based on the way in which a compositor misread and mis-set the text.

Except in the most bizarre circumstances, proofs as found today represent a text in a state either earlier than or identical to the published edition that immediately derives from them.* But by their nature, most proofs present an imperfect version of a text; one of their chief purposes is,

---

*Or occasionally less bizarre ones, as when a dealer or collector assembles fragmentary proofs from different impressions or editions into a single set. Precisely this was done with a set of proofs of Browning's *The Ring and the Book* now in the Beinecke Library at Yale.

after all, the detection and subsequent correction of errors. Given the proclivities of compositors and printers' readers, "earlier" does not necessarily mean "purer," or closer to what the author intended; furthermore, early proofs are more likely than later ones to include both authorial slips and compositorial mistakes, and it is extremely difficult (in the absence of a manuscript) to distinguish one from the other. Textual scholars, who normally like and admire the authors they work on, have to resist the understandable tendency to attribute the correct and sensible parts of a text to the author, and the mistakes and nonsense to the printers. When we find identity across an authorial manuscript, a set of proofs, and the first edition, we can conclude that a reading is authorial in origin; but when texts vary on a given point, it may be impossible to determine who is responsible for a printed reading, whether it be apparently correct or an obvious blunder. If the author made an alteration on a set of proofs, and the replacement reading is printed in the first and later editions, we again know where, when, and with whom the reading originated. But proof sheets that contain no alterations in the author's hand do not so plainly declare their purpose, use, and position in the development of the text.

In unmarked proofs, printed readings which vary from a preceding manuscript, earlier proofs, or the following first edition may be authorial or not, erroneous or correct. If the proofing process worked normally (and the author was not repeatedly moved to extensive alterations), later proofs should contain fewer marks than earlier ones. The scholar is placed in the ironic position of hoping that the compositors made at least a few errors; if there were none, there would be no need for corrections. Without corrections or instructions in the author's hand, it cannot be known whether the author actually read the surviving set of proofs. An unaltered set of apparently early proofs might at least reveal something about a lost manuscript, while an unmarked set of final revises identical to the first edition can at most confirm that an author approved a text in its first-edition state. Final author's revises frequently survive, since authors would naturally save themselves the trouble and expense of returning proofs on which they had made no alterations. A letter to the publisher was sufficient to authorize printing, and the final revises stayed in the author's possession, with the resulting increased chance of preservation.

Such a set of proofs would have been duplicates of the set retained by the printers, who denominated their set as press proofs upon receiving authorial approval. The importance of a set of final revises consists in their identity to the press proofs, which very rarely survive; once the subsequent foundry or machine proofs had been read against them, press proofs were retained in the printer's office only until the job was done. Since they were then discarded, a set of unaltered duplicates provides a replica of what the author approved for printing. The very lack of alterations may silently testify that this text represented the author's intention at the time. For press proofs (and their duplicates), taken from imposed pages of revised type and approved by the author after one last reading, represent a freezing (however brief!) of the author's intention at a special moment. Authorial control over the text as a whole has been exercised as completely as intention and circumstance allow; none of the processes of textual change—revision, correction, decay, or restoration—has yet begun.

The scholar of nineteenth-century texts may also encounter an iteration of a text which was slightly subsequent to press proofs: the complete examples of first editions which some dealers and bibliographers call "proof copies." These stitched (and often bound) volumes had several purposes; they might be retained as records by publishers, presented as mementos to authors, or sent to reviewers as advance copies. Intended by printer and publisher to be typographically identical with the published copies that followed, these were made up from extra copies of machine proofs, and are proofs only in that they preceded publication and were printed on cheap paper. Certainly the author had no expectation of using this as a normal stage of proofing in which textual changes could be freely made. These documents have importance to textual scholarship in those rare instances where they vary from the published copies of the first edition, thus pointing to the possibility of deliberate or accidental alterations in the types or plates after press proofs had been approved.

Unmarked and unaltered proofs of a first edition, then, can be of real importance even if the author never read them. And the converse can also be true: a set of first-edition proofs bearing extensive alterations in the author's own hand may be of lesser scholarly significance than might be presumed. Though any kind of autograph markings on a document increase its interest and value to a collector or curator, the textual scholar must consider the date, purpose, and use of an author's changes to proof sheets. The paramount matters are always when, how, and with what aim the author made the alterations. Were the changes made during the proofing process or later? Did they arise from a concentrated reconsideration of the text, or were these alternative readings mechanically transferred to the existing proofs from some other document? Were they seriously intended as modifications to appear in the published form of the work, or were they trial readings, no more than artistic doodlings? As printing technology both accelerated and multiplied the stages of proofing, and as the pulling of multiple sets of proofs at each stage became common, more and more interim versions of a printed text came to exist; and once they were at hand, these convenient documents were put to many uses.

We have not far to look for examples of first-edition proofs which would bear authentic, but problematic, changes in the author's hand. G. H. Lewes, it will be recalled, obtained six copies of the first author's proofs of George Eliot's *The Spanish Gypsy*; some of these were to be read and marked by Lewes, some by Eliot, and some would be reserved for, in Eliot's phrase, "the resolution of our differences." Since Eliot had originally asked Blackwood to provide three or four copies, her intentions appear to have been to compare and reconcile the two sets as each had altered them, working out the "resolution" on the third set, and copying the final readings onto the fourth set, which would then be returned to Blackwood. The printed readings in these proofs would be of obvious textual importance as a compositional step between manuscript and first edition, but what of the various revisions, Eliot's, Lewes's, and the jointly approved results? Is it possible to make a legitimate and inherent distinction in importance between readings suggested by Lewes and revisions originating with Eliot? Indeed, the very fact that these were initial revisions to galley proofs, removed several times from the published first edition of *The Spanish Gypsy*, somewhat diminishes their authority. Eliot understood printing practices quite well, well enough to know that she had several more stages of proof available in which to make her text read as she wanted. In my view, the proofs that went to Blackwood's printers, or later revises, or the first edition itself would have increasingly greater textual authority than any initial autograph revisions, because these subsequent documents unquestionably manifest the intention to publish.

Still less clear, though no less intriguing, is the case of the one surviving set of proofs of Chapman and Hall's first edition of Robert Browning's *Men and Women* (1855). These proofs in pages, now in the Huntington Library, are probably first author's proofs, closely reflecting the lost printer's-copy manuscript; they contain at several points the kinds of compositorial errors that often resulted from indistinctness in Browning's handwriting. The provenance, the early textual state, and the general condition of these proofs establish that these are not the set of revises that Browning sold to the publisher James T. Fields for the American first edition (of which Browning read no proof). There was at least one further stage of revision and proofing of the text of *Men and Women*, as shown by the extensive differences between the printed readings of these proofs and the English first edition. As the earliest representation of most of the text of *Men and Women*, these proofs have great interest, and they also contain a fair number of alterations in Browning's hand. But Browning's changes do not clearly belong to a definable stage of revision during proofing; the altered readings do not correspond with the first edition, nor can they always plausibly be taken as an intermediate state between the printed reading of the proofs and that of the first edition. Though many of the manuscript alterations seem to be rather tentative trial readings, a substantial number correlate closely to the revised text of the 1863 *Poetical Works*. It may be that the Huntington proofs were duplicate first author's proofs, a set on which Browning made some initial attempts at revision; a more heavily altered set would have gone back to the printers to become a step on the way to the first edition. The duplicates, whether marked or not, might have remained in Browning's possession for some time, possibly being used as work sheets when the poet prepared copy for the collected edition of 1863. It is even remotely possible that Browning inserted some of the manuscript readings still later than this, transferring them back into the Huntington proofs from the 1863 edition. The point is that in this set of proofs the printed readings are of greater and more certain textual significance than the revisions in the author's hand; the history and purpose of these can only be guessed at.

On the evidence of printers' manuals and the histories of individual publications, it was generally true that until the middle of the nineteenth century authors accomplished their proofing and revising in one or perhaps two somewhat protracted stages of serial page proofs (Tennyson being a distinct exception). Due to their purpose and employment in the printing house, authors' proofs from this earlier period do not often survive, but when they do—whether marked or not—they are likely to represent a significant, definable stage of composition and revision. Later in the century, as technology and custom expanded the stages of proofing, authors had more and different opportunities to alter their texts before publication. Galley or page proofs of entire works could be provided as complete sets, and multiple copies became commonplace. The number of documents produced between manuscript and first edition multiplied, and with this increased both the frequency of revision and the likelihood of preservation of textual evidence. But in place of a single, comprehensive stage of revision there developed a more incremental process of alteration, perhaps diminishing the importance of each individual step and of the documents that represent it.★

First Editions with Authorial Changes

It is not uncommon to come across copies of first editions of Victorian works bearing manuscript alterations by their authors. While highly valued by collectors, such marked copies—often presentation copies signed by the author—do not have automatic textual authority. Though the revisions in them may be interesting in themselves, their appearance in such a document is not evidence of an intention to incorporate them into the text; nor do they necessarily represent a stage of serious reconsideration of the text by its creator. A subsequent edition of a work, if it has undergone proofreading and revision by the author, would have much superior inherent authority. On the other hand, a copy of a first edition which was prepared by an author as printer's copy for a later edition would have great importance, being the result of an author's determined effort to control the text of a work. As reprinting in small impressions became a common mode of publication, the likelihood that authors went over their existing texts increased.

When paper-mold stereotyping and mechanized typecasting made it possible for publishers to adopt a marketing approach dependent on cheap reprints, authors had more chances to revise. The usual pattern, as revealed in the careers of numerous Victorian authors, was straightforward: when stocks of a work ran low, the publisher informed the author of a need to reprint and invited textual changes or corrections. The author then obtained a copy of the most recent edition (or other preferred text, as with

---

★In 1864, for example, Browning appears to have received four sets of what were to be the final revises of *Dramatis Personae*—and then proceeded to revise again. Two sets, bearing almost identical manuscript revisions, are extant: one is in the Berg Collection of the New York Public Library, and the other is part of the Tinker Collection at Yale. Browning may have copied the revisions (occasionally inaccurately) as a record of what he actually returned to his printers on another copy of the proofs, not surviving. An essentially unmarked fourth set must have gone to James T. Fields for the American first edition of *Dramatis Personae*, which closely follows the unrevised printed readings of the Berg and Yale proofs. It should be remembered that in the 1860s proof sheets would have come to Browning and been returned to the printers a few at a time; one would thus expect to find noticeable variations in ink, penpoint, and handwriting among the corrections in an entire set of proofs. The lack of such variation in Browning's alterations in the two sets of surviving proofs strongly suggests that all the changes were worked in on a single occasion at the end of the proofing process, when complete sets of proofs could have been accumulated.

Matthew Arnold's use of the American edition of his poems) and worked the revisions into it. In other words, the author acted rather like a modern scholarly editor, selecting a suitable copy-text containing an accumulation of authorial revisions and emending it—with a rather freer hand than any scholar would assume. This copy was then sent to the printers, who were expected to follow it exactly as the author had marked it. Such printer's copy constitutes a very important class of documents: an existing edition—let us say the first—that had already been supervised and proofed by its author was subjected to as thorough a rereading and revision as the author cared to give it, with the direct purpose of immediate publication. By building on an existing edition, previous revisions were preserved; canceled passages could be restored; and compositors made far fewer errors when setting from printed copy.

An author preparing such printer's copy worked in circumstances that provided both the freedom to revise and control a text and the guarantee of great accuracy in printing; the resulting documents, when extant, would have very great textual authority. Examples of copies marked for a subsequent reprint are not common, but they do survive. A copy of the first edition of *Dramatis Personae* (1864), completely revised by Browning and containing his instructions to the printers for the second edition, is today in the Tinker Collection at Yale University. It would not be surprising to find the copies of the various editions of Arnold's poems which the poet marked for use in reprinting, since he specifically asked his publisher to return them. And given the habits of G. H. Lewes and George Eliot, it seems possible that somewhere there may exist some of the volumes they prepared for the various collected editions of Eliot's works.

But because we are entranced by the human side of literary texts and their creators, because any manuscript seems to carry an inherent significance, it is easy to confer excessive importance on documents bearing the marks of an author's hand. Tinker and Lowry, in their Oxford edition of the poetical works of Arnold, include among their selection of variant readings every alteration that the poet made in one copy of the 1854 *Poems* and in a set of the collected edition of 1881. It is by no means certain—or even likely—that either of these copies was used in the preparation of a subsequent edition, nor is there any clue as to when and to what purpose Arnold marked the books up. These manuscript changes might have been no more than very tentative trial readings, or the volumes may have been marked in preparation for a reprint. The editors' choice of a late copy-text automatically diminishes the importance of all earlier alterations, especially when they have no demonstrable position in the lineage of the text as revised and published by the poet. Yet Arnold's manuscripts are so scarce that his editors felt compelled to include these autograph changes, granting them a textual importance equal, for instance, to the carefully considered revisions Arnold made in the collected editions of 1869 and 1877. Similarly, though we might find great human interest in the copy (now at Harvard) of the first edition of *Dramatis Personae* that Browning revised and gave to George Eliot, Yale's marked copy—the one sent to the printers—is of far greater textual importance; indeed, Browning almost certainly transcribed his alterations and additions from the printer's copy into the volume he presented to Eliot.

Later Editions

As printing technology, publishing practices, and the nature of authorship itself all changed, it became commonplace for Victorian authors to revise their works through a series of reprints. Second and later editions—particularly collected editions viewed by their authors as destined to stand for some time—thus attain major textual importance. Yet for the last hundred years, descriptive bibliography has dwelt so intensely on first, special, and rare editions that the later textual history of many nineteenth-century authors remains underexplored territory. It has been all too usual for even the soundest and most reputable scholars to dismiss later editions as "mere reprints." Fifty years ago, even E. K. Brown could characterize the freshly composed editions of Arnold's prose works produced in the 1880s as merely "page-for-page, word-for-word reprints"[3] of previous editions.* Today most textual scholars would grant much more potential significance to any edition produced during an author's lifetime, if there is a chance that the author prepared copy for, read proof on, or otherwise supervised a reprint. As I have already urged and attempted to demonstrate, even a small intermediate impression of a given edition can form an essential link in a chain of textual transmission; somewhere along this chain will be the printed version that most fully represents the text as the author intended it to be read. Since the most common process by which reprints were generated was regarded by Victorian authors as one which accumulated approved revisions and drove out errors, their later collected editions are often candidates for privileged textual standing.

For any edition under scrutiny, and particularly for works which

---

*Yet Brown not only knew that Arnold had read proofs on some of these, but also recognized the importance of Arnold's numerous revisions to punctuation, as his comments on style make plain.

went through many editions and impressions during their author's lifetime, we must try to establish what was used as printer's copy for the
typesetting at hand.★ Whether an author prepared copy for a given edition, and what printed text was used as the basis for the new typesetting,
may be indicated in an author's correspondence with printer or publisher;
by the presence or absence of specific corrections and alterations appearing
in later editions that are known to have been revised and controlled by the
author; or even by the persistence of errors that originated in earlier
editions. Indeed, the nature of errors carried over from one typesetting to
another may establish both what was used as printer's copy and what kind
of supervision, if any, the author exercised on the reprint. The relations
among various iterations of a text are often extremely subtle, particularly
when stereotype plates were used and reused, in ever-altering states, for
multiple impressions and so-called editions.

Stereotyped Editions and Impressions

In an earlier chapter on printing, I argued that—despite the assertions and
beliefs of most Victorian printers, publishers, and authors—stereotyping
did not absolutely fix and stabilize a text. Because printing with stereotype
plates typically went on in numerous small impressions over a substantial
period, both deliberate alterations (some of which may be errors) and
unintentional changes (all of which can be classed as inaccuracies) accumulated within one long-preserved typesetting. And since any impression
may have contained authorial revisions as well as new inaccuracies, it is
incumbent on the textual scholar to detect the use of stereo plates and to
identify discrete impressions of a stereotyped edition.

　　Despite Hansard's pronouncement, cited at the beginning of this
chapter, it is not immediately apparent whether a Victorian book was
printed from types or plates. The detection of stereotyping is occasionally
made simpler by external evidence, such as authors' correspondence.†
Publishers' records, especially for those houses that had their own printing
works, can provide irrefutable and perhaps unique evidence of the existence and number of stereo impressions. In the halcyon days of the paper

---

★It is discouraging to observe how often this essential matter is ignored, even in excellent
scholarly editions and expert discussion.

†It should be remembered, however, that a publisher might have paper molds made of a
typesetting but never actually have stereo plates cast. And no matter what the method by
which they were made, a set of plates might well be melted down without ever having been
used to print a single copy. Neither planning to stereotype nor even making the plates
guarantees that a stereotyped edition or impression was printed.

process, some printers announced in their colophons that they had "set up and stereotyped" a volume. Collected or standard editions containing no direct statement about plating were sometimes listed in publishers' advertisements as one of "Messers So-and-So's Stereotype Editions." A publisher's offering of multiple "editions" of the same work simultaneously, in different sizes and bindings and with attendant adjustments in price, strongly suggests that plates (perhaps in duplicate sets) were being used on papers of differing dimensions and weights. Similarly, the continued availability of an edition over a long period—several decades, for instance—almost certainly depended on stereotyping.

But confirming evidence and actual proof must be sought through the examination of books themselves. Direct internal evidence of stereotyping is not easy to find, but it does exist, even though the entire process was designed to make the stereotyped page indistinguishable from one printed from types. The reader is referred back to chapter 3 for discussions of the signs of repair and decay in plates; these form the most important and readily visible class of evidence of plating. The use of stereos for an edition or impression can sometimes be tentatively deduced after examining a single copy of a book, if it presents numerous instances of the methods of alteration practiced with plates but not with types. Those portions of a text which are known to have undergone revision are the first places to seek signs of how changes were accomplished in the composing room or foundry. Misaligned letters and words, uneven inking, and slight differences in the sizes of letters can constitute strong indications of the insertion of revised matter into an existing plate. Usually, however, close examination of numerous copies of an edition is necessary before it can be confidently labeled as printed from types or from plates. Some of what can be learned from comparisons across multiple copies is evident to the unaided eye, while other information is detectable only with an optical comparator such as a Hinman or Lindstrand collator.

We have seen that the longer an edition was in print, the greater the likelihood that stereotype plates (or, later, electrotypes) were used. A long-lived edition may both gain and lose accuracy; it may accumulate legitimate corrections and revisions, and it may suffer the decay of the printing surface which results in lost or changed words, letters, and punctuation. If the title-page dates of various copies of an edition clearly show that impressions were taken over a substantial span of years, we may line them up from early to late and view the alterations of the plates in correct historical sequence. Unfortunately, while some Victorian publishers regularly updated their title pages to trumpet the number of impressions a book had achieved, others obscured the fact that they were reprinting—either deliberately or through indifference—by never changing a title-page date. It is perfectly possible for several identical-appearing copies of an edition, all bearing the same date on their title pages, to have been printed decades apart, thus presenting their text in distinctly different states. To date such examples exactly may prove impossible, but there may be clues as to their sequence of production.[4]

The first is the overall condition of the typesetting. Only marginally successful or downright disreputable printers and publishers produced books from utterly worn-out types or plates, but since much of the commercial advantage of stereotyping depended on printing a large number of copies, even the major houses issued volumes that show the wear and tear of repeated impressions. Batters, scratches, and a general bluntness of letters and punctuation are often found in later copies.* After some experience at examining volumes in this light, it is often not too difficult to line up a half-dozen copies of the same edition in the order in which they were produced; one can then add chronological considerations to the process of evaluating any textual variations among the copies.

The advertisements with which Victorian publishers commonly filled any empty pages in the last sheet of a book can also provide hints about when a volume was produced. These advertisements were often updated to reflect the latest offerings, and by determining the publication dates of the advertised titles one may establish a date after which a given volume must have been manufactured. It is not unusual to find that advertisement pages contain references to books that first appeared years after the date on a volume's title page. One must not overinterpret such evidence; the latest work mentioned in an advertisement (sometimes the advertisements themselves bear a date) tells us, strictly speaking, only when the volume was gathered and bound. The advertisements must have been printed, at the earliest, around the time of the latest title they mention; but the part of the last sheet bearing the final pages of the text itself might have been struck off much earlier. A sheet of octavo might, for

---

*Of course "later" here means later in sequence of impressions, not necessarily much later in time. With the rates of production achieved by the 1870s, it did not take very long to run off numerous impressions or to wear out a set of plates. Plate decay and the resultant inaccuracies accumulate as the number of impressions mounts, no matter how much or how little time passes. The deliberate and repeated processes of correction and revision, on the other hand, would seem to be more time-dependent, and an author might be presumed to make an increasing number of alterations as months and years went by, no matter how many or how few copies are printed.

instance, have contained the last three pages of a novel, a colophon, and twelve empty pages. A thousand, say, of these final sheets would be run off, five hundred to make up the first batch of copies, and five hundred to be stored in quires until sales warranted binding them up. The first five hundred sheets would then be put through the press again to print on them the current advertisement. Later on, when the second five hundred sheets were to be used, they would be printed with a newer advertisement. Though the resulting copies would differ in the advertisements, and were produced some time apart, they are components of the same edition and impression. However, with paper-mold stereotype technology, it is equally likely that different advertisements do indeed indicate separate impressions, which may contain any number of variant readings.

Mechanical aids such as the Hinman collator can reveal physical evidence of printing processes and thus aid in determining whether an edition was produced from types or plates. The most important form of evidence occurs when a part of a text has been reset or repaired. Resetting types results in slight relocations of letters and spaces, no matter how painstaking and expert the compositor. The shifts are visible with the Hinman machine when a page printed before the resetting is compared with one printed afterward, and some kinds of alteration are indicative of types rather than plates. For instance, a compositor fixing or altering a typeset text can adjust the spaces along an entire line to get a good appearance. The methods employed to alter or repair stereotype plates, however, make it likely that the compositor will leave unadjusted as much as possible of the adjacent matter. Thus the soldered-in slug will show itself, and prove that plates were being used. When used on multiple copies of the same edition, the Hinman collator will also reveal the incremental processes of plate decay; both the design of plates and the metal they were made from result in the gradual breaking away of small features of the printing surface. These fragments often print as distinct, migrating flecks, and they strongly indicate that plates were in use; the position of such flecks on a page can also provide the determining evidence for the exact sequence in which a group of copies were printed.

Even beyond the area of printed text on a given page, evidence of the use of plates may be discerned with optical comparators or collators. As a consequence of the way plates were mounted, the size of the margins could change, and correct register be lost, with no disturbance of the printing surface itself. This was unlikely with matter set in types, because each page was firmly positioned with metal or wooden "furniture"; the entire forme was clamped all the way around in a chase, and the shifting of one page relative to the others was effectively prevented. A single-page plate, however, was mounted on blocks or risers and locked in place with one or two mounting clamps per side. The plate was liable to shifting on its riser, and the riser might move in the clamps during a run of the machine. Southward, quoting the *Printer's Every-Day Book*,[5] urges the pressman to check repeatedly for this persistent problem when making-ready a machine; and Wilson and Grey observed in 1888: "When the forme is sent to the machine room, it is generally carefully gauged; but it will be found that several plates will have to be slightly moved and readjusted, in order that their impressions may exactly back each other when registering. . . . If the work is half-sheet work, i.e., perfecting on itself—each copy when backed forming a duplicate of the entire forme—one half must be registered to the other. . . . The whole of the foregoing relates, of course, simply to plates."[6]

If a page of types had to be moved within its forme, the surrounding furniture would have to be loosened, adjusted, and retightened. Registration could be maintained, but the distance between the pages is measurably different, and almost inevitably individual types shift slightly in the process. The consequent shifting of printed letters between one copy and another is a sure sign that types were used, and is easily detected with a Hinman collator. In contrast, printers could unlock a forme of plates, move individual plates as necessary to attain correct registration, and relock the forme, all without moving a single letter of text. When collation and measurement show that margins have changed while the printed area of a page remains completely unaffected, the scholar may confidently hypothesize that the books under examination were printed from plates.[7]

Another measurement which ought to supply evidence of plating is the overall size of the printed area of the page. Since both the mold and the metal plate itself contracted during manufacturing, a stereotype plate was slightly smaller in every respect than the typeset page from which it derived (see chapter 3). Two typographically identical impressions—one printed from types and the other from plates—might be distinguishable on this basis alone, because the image produced from a plate should be of discernibly smaller dimensions than its counterpart from types. Though such differences have been noticeable in my experience, they are sometimes submerged by other aspects of the printing process. It was, for instance, standard practice in the nineteenth century to dampen the paper before it was printed.[8] As they dried, the printed sheets shrank, at a rate which increased with the thickness of the paper; the printed image could shrink so much as to overwhelm any dimensional changes caused solely by plate making.

In one case I have investigated, the difference between two impressions in the size of their printed images was so profoundly affected by paper shrinkage that a demonstrably false conclusion about plating could have been reached. The circumstances of production were not unusual for the later nineteenth century. The author having approved a final set of proofs of a new edition, paper matrices were taken from the typesetting. The types were not immediately distributed, but instead were imposed in a hand press and used to print a limited number of special copies; these were printed on heavy, hand-laid paper that was thoroughly dampened. Meanwhile, plates were cast from the paper molds and used in printing machines to produce standard trade copies of the edition, printed on thinner, hard-finish paper that needed only slight dampening.

Because the trade copies were printed from plates, their printed areas should have been from 1 to 3 percent smaller than those of the corresponding pages of the special copies. Indeed, fresh from the press and machine, the sheets might well have borne such traces of their respective printing surfaces. But when I examined surviving copies of the two varieties (one is not quite sure whether to define them as separate impressions or as differing issues), the printed area of the standard trade copies was not a few percent smaller, but 7 to 8 percent *larger* than that of the special copies. The dampened heavy paper had shrunk so much that any dimensional difference caused by molding and casting had vanished. If shrinkage of the printed image alone had been taken as sufficient evidence that plates were used, an erroneous judgment would have been made as to which copies were printed from which surface. But it should be noted that if the trade copies could have been compared with page proofs, rather than with the special-issue copies, plate shrinkage might have been detectable. In the later nineteenth century, page proofs were printed from the types on thin, hard-finish paper that was not dampened at all, and thus did not shrink. Even allowing that the slightly dampened sheets of the standard trade copies would have shrunk a bit, a significant reduction in the overall size of the printed image—say 3 percent or more—would most likely be a visible sign of stereotyping.

These matters—whether plates or types were used, in what sequence copies of an impression were printed, at what date a given copy was produced, and so forth—are important because they shed, at various removes, some light on the central issues of textual variation, revision, and authorial control. The more we know about the printing history of a work and the technology used to produce various iterations of it, the better will be our scholarly judgments about when, to what extent, and with what degree of diligence the author strove to make a printed text represent his or her intentions. A consideration of all the available evidence that can be extracted from the textually significant surviving documents must underlie an adequate understanding of authorial control in the Victorian era.

VII

Authorial Control

I was aware that an artist should keep in his hand
the power of fitting the beginning of his work to
the end. No doubt it is his first duty to fit the end
to the beginning, and he will endeavour to do so.
But he should still keep in his hands the power of
remedying any defect in this respect.

Anthony
Trollope,
*Autobiog-
raphy*, on
his dislike
of serial
composi-
tion

BECAUSE TROLLOPE so often characterized himself as an artisan rather than
an artist, as a workman employing his skill rather than serving his genius,
his vehemence about retaining control of his texts is somewhat surprising.
Despite the prevalence of serialization of novels and the consequent potential for greater profits, Trollope did not wish to succumb to "this hurried
publication of incompleted work." He held that "the rushing mode of
publication to which the system of serial stories had given rise, and by
which small parts as they were written were sent hot to the press, was
injurious to the work done."[1] To Trollope's eyes, the serial system, when it
came to affect not only the publication but also the initial composition of a
work, resulted in a loss of artistic control. His customary protection
against pressure that might have led to hasty publication was to complete a
novel and revise it thoroughly before sending any of it to a publisher. If
serial issue was planned, he then metered out manuscript to the printers
while he went to work on his next book. Whenever possible, he liked to be
at least one book ahead of himself, and boasted that he would have several
finished novels in reserve to be published after his death.

Trollope's strategy reminds us how deeply printing practices had
influenced publishing, authorship, and literature itself. The serial system

whose artistic consequences Dickens exploited and Trollope excoriated had been both created and rendered obsolete by technology and its changing limits. For by the time Trollope achieved his greatest success, there was no technical necessity for serial publication, whether in sequential volumes or monthly parts. The mechanical typecaster and efficient stereotype foundry guaranteed an adequate supply of type, and printers, who in earlier times had had to recycle their fonts from one portion of a work to the next, could from the 1860s quickly produce tens of thousands of copies of complete large volumes at once. In the early decades of the rise of the English novel, the necessity of printing serially had spawned the practice of serial publication; authors responded to publishing in parts by composing in parts. And long after the original necessity had vanished, authors and publishers wrote and sold by "the rushing mode of publication" deprecated by Trollope.

Trollope exercised authority over his texts at a time when his control would be complete and unchallenged: before he sent it in. He would have been a paragon of virtue in the eyes of the old printers, for he aimed to perfect his manuscript: "The writer for the press is rarely called upon—a writer of books should never be called upon—to send his manuscript hot from his hand to the printer. It has been my practice to read everything four times at least—thrice in manuscript and once in print [i.e., in proof]. Very much of my work I have read twice in print. In spite of this I know that inaccuracies have crept through."[2]

Such inaccuracies could be remedied in later impressions or editions, and we have already seen in earlier chapters how authors whose writing ran just ahead of the compositors' demands used "reprints" to revise and correct their works. For Trollope, artistic concentration and textual control were probably at their peak when he produced the printer's-copy manuscript upon his third reading of his work. For an author who customarily responded to first seeing a work in types by carefully revising author's proofs, press proofs or the first edition would achieve a greater textual authority. For writers who exerted more control over their texts later in the process, when subsequent printed versions were created, one revised edition or another would be of paramount importance. The scholar must gauge textual control according to several variables: the ability (and power) of an author to assume it, the desire and intention of an author to use it, and the thoroughness and care with which an author exercised it. No single rule or textual principle can establish which version of a text should stand as authoritative, but some historical generalizations may be attempted. In the framework of the present study, there are two pertinent questions. How much did Victorian authors want to control their texts down to the last detail? How far could they exercise such control?

I believe it to be axiomatic that authorial control of a text seldom if ever matches authorial intention toward that text. An author's ability to control a text—that is, to execute or prevent changes to it—varies widely over numerous occasions, according to personal circumstances and to the technical possibilities of the moment. The complete freedom an author has to make changes in a manuscript becomes, upon submission, subject to limitations of taste, style, and competence imposed by publishers, print-ers' readers, and compositors. Later occasions for exerting control may be limited in other ways: a writer must be aware of the existence of a typesetting in order to correct it, and be able to communicate with printers in order to direct them. An author may propose textual changes too sweeping to be made in a new impression from existing stereo plates. On the other hand, an author may be granted absolute freedom to alter a text for a new edition and yet have no real interest in conducting a careful revision.

Furthermore, authors' desires or intentions to control their texts fluctuate over time. While an author lives, intention may be considered limitless, since an author may freely consider and propose any reading at any time; the forcefulness and the very nature of such intentions, of course, will vary. An author's manuscript alterations in a presentation copy of a book may have been very seriously meant at the moment of their inscription, but they will have less significance (for the textual critic) than the changes the author made in the proofs for the next edition of the work. When making changes in a presentation copy, an author is in complete, free control, but is not giving orders to a printer. If our author enters these same changes into the printer's copy for the next edition, the textual intention has been ratified and intensified. But now, to demonstrate the axiom again, the author's serious textual intention is not accompanied by complete power: commercial, personal, and technical circumstances will limit what can be accomplished. When aiming at publication, the author will find textual control inhibited by insistent practicalities.

It must also be remembered that the degree to which textual control was granted to an author might vary considerably according to his or her public standing. This study has delineated a pattern of technological development through which Victorian authors progressively gained greater control over their printed texts at the cost of greater responsibility for accuracy in printing. True as this generalization may be over the nineteenth century, each author's career inevitably contains a unique variable: reputation. Reputation—which in this case means not so much personal or artistic standing as a solid record of commercial success—is an enormously influential factor in establishing authorial control; any sensible publisher will try to please an author who is a popular success and gains a great sale. Authors at the beginning of their careers may find adequate textual control impossible beyond the manuscript stage, because publishers and printers owe them no favors. Earlier chapters of this work have mentioned the experiences of Richard Blackmore when first attempting to become a novelist; until he earned his publishers a substantial sum with *Lorna Doone*, his works were routinely and freely censored, cut, rewritten, and even expanded, most often without notice or explanation. And this was definitely a matter of reputation, or of what twentieth-century politicians call "clout," for Blackmore complained specifically to his publisher that Dickens was allowed a latitude of language and situation denied to others.[3]

In compensation, authors could eventually achieve a great degree of control over their printed texts, if fame and success conferred sufficient power on them. Some came to dictate not only in matters of substance and style but also on edition quantities, binding details, and marketing. George Eliot, for example, strengthened her grip on various aspects of publishing and printing as her growing reputation allowed. On the sole strength of her genuine but quite minor initial success with two tales from *Scenes of Clerical Life*, she got an unauthorized textual change in "Janet's Repentance" reversed, as mentioned in an earlier chapter.

On a much more substantial aspect of "Janet's Repentance," Blackwood wanted to override the author but did not; he wrote to G. H. Lewes after the story was published: "I wish I had pressed George Eliot more to curtail or to indicate more delicately the Delirium Tremens scene." Later, during the composition of *The Mill on the Floss*, Blackwood did object and prevail: he didn't like "lymphatic" as an adjective for Mrs. Tulliver, and it was cut. He objected to the description of Mrs. Moss as "a patient, loosely-hung, child-producing woman," and Eliot altered it to "a patient, prolific, loving-hearted woman."[4] Of course these were instances not of censorship or unauthorized alteration, but of suggestion and cooperation between the parties in a remarkably harmonious author-publisher relationship, and from the time of *Silas Marner* (1861) on, George Eliot had complete control over the printed editions of her texts.

The long career of Thomas Hardy presents perhaps the most famous example of how a growing reputation—and changing public taste—

conferred textual control on an author. In his early days, Hardy substantially altered his novels in response to the objections of editors and printers for the sake of getting published and getting paid. By the 1920s, when he had achieved an unassailable position as a living literary institution, he was free to restore his texts to their once-shocking original state.

With or without the aid of reputation, nineteenth-century authors exercised close textual control wherever they could, and on occasion tried to command it where they couldn't. At the height of his fame, Byron, for example, made great efforts from a great distance. He wrote to his London publisher John Murray from Ravenna in August 1821 to complain vehemently about numerous errors in the first five cantos of *Don Juan*. The poet demanded that the printed text "be carefully gone over with the MS," which in his view could not have been the source of inaccuracies: "I copied the *Cantos* out carefully, so that there is *no* excuse." Byron has repeatedly been taxed with accusations that he was an indifferent or incompetent proofreader, and that he paid little attention to the punctuation of his poems. But Jerome McGann insists in his authoritative edition that "the many extant proofs show quite clearly that he cared a great deal about accurate punctuation and that he corrected punctuation in proof after proof." The degree to which Byron's wishes were finally carried out was less consistent than his desire to control his text and his understanding of how to do it, through "proof after proof." In Byron's day, many matters of punctuation and spelling were still decided by compositors and printers' readers, who had direct, final control over the types, especially when an author went traipsing off to the Continent. It was with Byron's experience in mind that the veteran who wrote *The Perils of Authorship* urged "the necessity of his *remaining in town, and in the printing office* ALL NIGHT."[5]

Even when publisher and printer sincerely set out to guarantee an accurately printed representation of the author's considered intention, authorial control could be inhibited by the same technological advances that normally increased it. In 1855 Robert Browning sent a set of proofs of Chapman and Hall's two-volume first edition of *Men and Women* to J. T. Fields in Boston for Ticknor and Fields's first American edition. Browning sent the sheets, for which he got sixty pounds, on 12 October, expecting them to arrive in Boston in ten days. Even in the unlikely event that the proofs arrived considerably sooner, Ticknor set up the new edition with remarkable rapidity. Just how remarkable is open to some doubt: on one hand, it was customary for printing houses to order paper for a job after composition was completed (in this case Houghton & Co. set the type and made stereo plates); this was done for *Men and Women* on

24 October. On the other hand, having a set of proofs, rather than a manuscript, would immediately allow a very accurate estimate of the number of pages in the work and thus the amount of paper required. The entry in Ticknor and Fields's accounts for the composition costs is not dated, and the work may have been done at a more ordinary rate during late October and early November.

Types were certainly set and plates cast within two weeks of the proofs' arrival in Boston, as shown by ensuing events. On 26 October, Browning sent Fields a list of changes to be made in his poems; this letter would have reached Fields by about 5 November at best, and it was too late. Though Fields was in every way eager to please Browning, and though Browning clearly intended to control the American text as much as he could without actually reading proof on it, the alterations he wanted were not made. They could not be made, and the printing—whether from the types or the plates is not clear—was completed and paid for by 21 November. The first American edition of *Men and Women* does not read exactly as Browning intended, but the cause was neither indifference or incompetence of the publisher nor any lack of will or attention on the author's part. The admirable speed with which composition and printing went forward simply meant there was no time for last-minute changes by the poet. And if, as seems probable, the American edition was printed from stereo plates, we can àdd the impediments of time and cost required for altering plates. Once Browning had sent his English proof sheets, the advanced printing technology available to Boston publishers took over, and his text was out of his control.[6]

But Browning, like other successful Victorian authors, would have further opportunities to get his works printed as he wanted them. In his case, Browning closely supervised collected editions of his poems in 1863, 1865, 1868, 1870, and 1888–89; these editions form a continuous record of his corrections and revisions and demonstrate his habitual meticulous, detailed monitoring of his texts. For other authors the documents may be less exhaustive, but the situation was the same: collected editions presented excellent opportunities to revise and restore the texts of earlier works. With the enhanced reputation implicit in the very need for a new edition, a Victorian author gained not only the power but also the leisure to alter and correct numerous proofs carefully, making additions and driving out both great and small errors that appeared in previous editions. As mentioned above, Thomas Hardy had been forced to bowdlerize his novels to get them in print; when a remedy presented itself in 1894–95, he seized it, as Robert Gittings reports: "*Tess* had quickened public interest in all his previous novels. Since the beginning of the year, he had been revising these for collected publication in a uniform edition by Osgood, McIlvaine, to which *Jude* was added as the latest title. He had used his reputation over *Tess* to make some of the sexual expressions in these other novels more frank."[7]

Hardy did more than insert frank language and restore censored passages; he also paid close attention to punctuation and attended to the details of layout. The Osgood, McIlvaine edition, called the Wessex Novels, continued in print for many years; Hardy signed with Macmillan and Co. in 1902, but his new publishers simply reused the plates of the Osgood edition through numerous reimpressions. When in 1911 Macmillan finally proposed to produce its own edition, Hardy revised his texts thoroughly and carefully; the result was the great Wessex Edition of 1912. Given that *Jude the Obscure* (1895) was Hardy's last novel, and that he had been thereafter almost completely occupied with poetry, it would be logical to assume that this edition settled the texts of his novels. But he did not ignore still later opportunities: the Wessex Edition was followed in 1919 by the lavish Mellstock Edition, for which Hardy prepared numerous changes. These alterations and more were worked into the original plates of the Wessex Edition when it was reimpressed in 1920.[8]

Many similar examples could be adduced to reinforce the point that for Victorian authors, collected and reprinted editions can be of the greatest textual importance. Changes in attitudes toward authorship, changing customs in the printing and publishing worlds, different marketing strategies, and advancing technology combined to make it likely that authors—successful authors, at least—would have repeated chances to control their printed texts. Almost every aspect of the nineteenth-century revolution in printing was aimed at increasing the speed with which books could be produced in large numbers. In two ways the drive for speed aided authors: typecasting machines allowed rapid composition, so that complete sets of proofs and the copy for them could be sent to the author; and fast printing machines made it possible to issue an edition from stereo plates in numerous small impressions, each of which presented an opportunity for revision and correction. The more that successful authors came to understand and expect this, the less the inherent textual authority of the first appearance of a work. If haste, censorship, imperious printers, a lack of reputation, or other circumstance limited an author's control of a text and allowed errors to appear in the first printing of a work, the problems could be rectified in the reprint.

The confidence that there would soon be the opportunity and the leisure to rework his text as he chose probably contributed to Matthew Arnold's readiness to skip a stage of proof and get on with the publication of his essay on Marcus Aurelius. A few weeks before the piece first appeared in the *Victoria Magazine* for November 1863, Arnold returned proofs to the editor. He wrote: "I return you the enclosed: it was very correctly printed, and I shall not want a revise, but I daresay you will kindly see that my corrections are attended to." Arnold may have been rushed, and he may have trusted his editor, but it is also very likely that he was already thinking of collecting his critical essays into a book. A new edition would allow him to alter and correct as necessary this and his other pieces, each of which first appeared in a magazine. By the following summer, he and Macmillan were preparing *Essays in Criticism*, which appeared in early 1865. Arnold made a number of small changes in the text for this edition and continued to revise his diction and punctuation through several later appearances of "Marcus Aurelius"; about one-fourth of all the verbal and punctuational alterations he made over the years were made for the first book edition.[9]

Arnold was usually a diligent and meticulous proofreader, but when circumstances dictated, he sometimes surrendered opportunities for alteration and control that he normally exploited. As briefly mentioned earlier, Arnold read first proofs of *Higher Schools and Universities in Germany* (a republication of part of his *Schools and Universities on the Continent* [1868]) in February of 1873. Alexander Macmillan collected a complete set of proofs of the book and sent them to Nice; the parcel missed Arnold there but caught up to him at Mentone. On 6 March he returned the corrected sheets, saying "I need not see them again." He also was ready to forego seeing any proofs at all of his new preface, which he promised to send immediately (in fact, it was some months before he finished the preface). There was only a slight chance that this topical work would go into further editions and allow its author later corrections or revisions, but Arnold had sufficient reasons for waiving proofs. First, the text of *Higher Schools* had been set up from the previously published book, and thus few compositorial errors would be expected; second, the author trusted Macmillan's printers to set the alterations correctly. Further, Arnold was on an extended business journey on the Continent, so that the usual exchanges of proofs might have been difficult and would have slowed down the publication, which was being undertaken specifically because higher education was in the news. Finally, since he received a complete set of proofs, Arnold was able to exercise adequate control by reading and revising the whole work in one concentrated effort.[10]

But when it came to his poems, Arnold's idea of adequate control was total control, and his willingness to attend to the minutiae of his text was nearly unlimited. The partial history of editions given in chapter 5 not only suggests a complicated sequence of alterations in multiple stages but also shows that Arnold's conception of textual control and of the relative authority of various documents was similar to our own. Though he never intended that the 1877 American edition of his poems should be his final text, he certainly recognized the edition's importance and utility in maintaining his control over later editions. Having corrected very carefully for the American "reprint," Arnold asserted its textual primacy by ordering that it be used as printer's copy for two important subsequent English editions. Thus what Arnold and the modern textual critic would normally treat as a dead-end branch of the textual tree was grafted back into the main English stem by the author, in order to preserve his substantial "corrections."

Like Browning, Eliot, and other great contemporaries, Arnold thought of the development of his text as an accretive process, one which he could control by altering, extending, amending, and perfecting a central body of work. Each later impression of the latest edition afforded new opportunities for getting the text right, for including improvements and driving out errors. To the Victorian mind, accustomed to thinking in terms of progressive development, the stereotyping of a text represented both a plateau of perfection achieved and a platform on which to build. The more an author knew about this and other printing processes, the greater the textual control. Tennyson, as has been shown, was knowledgeable enough to exploit every one of his publishers and printers in matters of proofs or private printings. Lewis Carroll, often misrepresented as detached or indifferent to the details of everyday life, was very well informed about printing with plates and understood the effects of printing on dampened paper. He gave very specific orders to Macmillan about how he wanted the illustrations for *Through the Looking-Glass* to be printed and dried.[11]

All of this, of course, prompts a question. Granted that Victorian authors usually wanted, and often were able, to control their printed texts, what aspects and features of those texts did they bother to control, and to what end? The possible answers to that question vary across the range of individual authors and situations and have serious consequences for textual criticism and scholarly editing. I mention the plurality of answers because for Victorian authors and texts, no single rule can apply. The power to govern every detail of an edition which George Eliot or Robert

Browning eventually had was not theirs when they were unknowns, no matter how they may have desired it. Conversely, the intense attention to minutiae which a budding author will give to the manuscript and proofs of his or her first published work may not be matched when preparing a later collected edition, though the writer's ability to exercise command over the printer's reader may have increased.

At the beginning of a career, an unknown author without influence or experience, desperate for publication, may be quite willing not only to revise and delete whole passages, but also to defer to a publisher's or printer's house-style in spelling, capitalization, and punctuation. Even an established author may be unaware of errors that accumulate over the repeated impressions of an edition. Precisely for this reason, the prevailing theory of textual criticism enunciated by W. W. Greg and Fredson Bowers makes a fundamental distinction between those features of a text which the theory deems "substantive" (affecting the words of a text) and "accidental" (having to do with spelling, punctuation, capitalization, spacing, typography, and page layout). After closely comparing all editions of a work which may have been to some degree controlled by the author, the scholarly editor will produce a critical edition by employing this distinction. The printed "substantive" readings of the edited text will include proven or probable authorial revisions appearing in any edition chosen for collation, but the "accidentals" will be those of either the manuscript or first edition.

The aim of this procedure is to recover authorial intentions about the text by separating, through a process of subtraction, an author's own original text from the formalities and regularizings that the publisher and printer may have imposed on it. It is important to note that the Greg-Bowers theory was developed to deal with literary works from the English Renaissance, and to acknowledge that it has served admirably for those often-problematic documents. But what suits the texts of the seventeenth century does not always work for those of later epochs. If it was once normal for an author to surrender all control over a text upon sending it to a printer, if it was once commonplace for compositors and printers to reword and repunctuate as they saw fit, authorship and publication were very different by Victorian times. In the nineteenth century, the corruption of texts through inaccurate transmission over time still occurred, and printers' conventions did sometimes override authors' desires, but there were certain built-in remedies for authors who worked at maintaining textual control.

In light of the surviving evidence and the known practices of the nineteenth century, I believe that a rigid distinction in kind between the verbal content and all the other features of a printed text ignores or at least inaccurately characterizes the subtler interactions of authors, publishers, and printers. Suppose we find that the chapter divisions of a Victorian novel vary significantly, from its first appearance as a serial, to its three-volume form, and in the later one-volume format it had as part of a collected edition. This aspect of a text would be taken in the standard view as accidental, and the original arrangement of the manuscript (if it survived) would prevail in a critical edition. But if we know, or can confidently guess, that the author calculated the length of chapters to meet the strict requirements of publication in monthly parts, and adjusted dialogue and incident accordingly during composition, does this imposed and accidental textual feature become substantive? What standing and authority should be granted to alterations to chapter divisions in the later, more ample publishing formats? If these might be adopted for a modern critical edition, what about punctuation changes in these later editions? To some degree, solutions to such problems must be as subject to the idiosyncrasies of individual authors as is the matter of authorial control itself. What is "accidental" in one author's practice may be taken as "substantive" by another, and what writers take casually at one stage of their careers may strike them as very important at another.*

The deeper problem is how to arrange variant texts along a scale of authority. This will best be done by establishing as certainly as we can the nature and extent of authorial control over each text, according to the three criteria stated earlier: the power of an author to exert textual control, the intention of an author to use that power, and the thoroughness with which the control was applied. The extent of authorial control increased so

---

*As an interesting and not particularly eccentric example, we may consider the various readings of line 267 of Browning's "Bishop Blougram's Apology." From the earliest text, a set of proofs of the first edition, through the collected edition of 1863, the line read

That's the first cabin-comfort I secure—

In 1865, the line was altered to

That's the first-cabin comfort I secure:

and the line remained this way through three more collected editions supervised by the poet. The alterations are certainly Browning's, and without entering on the questions of which reading is better or more authoritative, we can see that the shift of the hyphen constitutes a shift in idiom—a substantive shift by any standard. Yet were we to take our "accidentals" from the earliest printed version of the poem, we would have to override this meaningful revision to the text (*Complete Works*, 5:302).

much in Victorian times that in the cases of authors with firm intentions, established reputations, and strong wills, a textual scholar might do well to assume that a given reading is authorial until shown otherwise. Authors gained control in part because the business of making books expanded so far that the participants had to specialize more and more. Gone were the days of the printer–publisher of Samuel Johnson's time, who had served as reader, corrector, designer, promoter, and benign despot over the printed word. In the nineteenth century, publishers were responsible for sales and profits, printers were responsible for manufacturing books as rapidly and inexpensively as possible, and authors became, to some extent by default, responsible for texts themselves, even to the last detail. Authorial control expanded at the same time as changes in technology and marketing practices multiplied the number of editions of a successful work and invented the reprint business. Consequently, the scholar working with Victorian texts must be ready to consider and examine a wider range of documents than has usually been defined by modern textual criticism as essential and authoritative.

VIII

Textual Change and
Textual Criticism

But by the time youth slips a stage or two
While reading prose in that tough book he wrote   Browning,
(Collating and emendating the same   "Transcen-
And settling on the sense most to our mind),   dentalism"
We shut the clasps and find life's summer past.

BROWNING'S MAIN point about reading Jacob Boehme's "tough book" has
to do with the relentlessness of life's changes, but he shrewdly suggests in
his parenthesis that texts also change and vary, requiring subsequent
"collating"; that they undergo alteration and will need "emendating." The
matter of what a text may signify seems to be variable too, a matter of
consensus or of individual critical judgment as to the sense most agreeable
to our notions. Twentieth-century textual critics have come to recognize
this situation as clearly as the nineteenth-century poet, and where the
former aim of scholars was to produce a relatively pristine, authoritative,
single text of a given work, textual editors are now interested in representing the growth, the life, the history of a text. Thus the scholarly study of
texts has become more than ever a study of differences and variations,
attended by broader, more flexible ideas of authority.

Much of this study has dealt, directly or by implication, with the
identifiable stages of textual change, and the picture that emerges is of a
discontinuous process, not a smoothly graded development. Such discon-
tinuities are the obvious norm in the hand-press period, when the entire
history of a text might have consisted of a single manuscript (now lost), a
single set of page proofs (also lost), a first edition, and perhaps a much later
collected edition. The era of machine printing and stereotyped reprints
certainly multiplied the number of discrete stages a text went through
during a span of time (the author's life, perhaps, or the use of a set of
plates), but it did not enforce any particular model of textual change.
Nineteenth-century texts do not necessarily change a bit at a time over

many editions and impressions, nor do they always show a steadily increasing or decreasing number of alterations over a given period. What they do show, and show more clearly than earlier texts simply because there are more stages and more surviving evidence, is subtly differing kinds of changes which appear and are dealt with on various occasions. To discuss these and suggest their implications for textual criticism, I must attempt some definitions.

Kinds of Textual Change

VARIANT READINGS

A *textual variant*, or *variant reading*, is simply a reading that differs from one text to another. The degree of difference may be very small (the spelling of a word, the placement of a hyphen, the use of a colon rather than a semicolon) or quite large (the insertion, deletion, or rearrangement of passages or entire chapters). Scholars disagree to some extent about the minimum amount of difference required to define a variant, and to a great extent about the amount of difference necessary to make a variant significant or meaningful. Texts from the Victorian era tend to display large numbers of small variants, occurring over numerous sequential iterations; over a span of editions and impressions, these variants may accumulate until they constitute a pattern of revision (or decay and corruption, for that matter). Questions about the origin—and thus the authority—of variant readings are never far from the textual critic's mind, because declaring a reading an error, a correction, or a revision requires deciding how the variant came to exist. A variant may be characterized as a *substitution* (*had* in one text for *has* in another), an *insertion* (a punctuation mark, a word, a phrase, a sentence, or much more added to a preexisting text), or a *deletion* (textual material, small or vast, removed from a preexisting text). When a variant reading occurs, the scholar customarily assigns a human origin to it by calling it an author's slip of the pen, a compositor's error, a reader's change, an author's revision, an editor's imposition, or some other human act. The study of Victorian texts makes it plainly apparent that variant readings can and repeatedly do appear as the result of the mechanical processes of printing, having no origin in any human choice, and arising in spite of a uniform desire that there be no change to a text.

ERRORS

When we scrutinize a printed work with an eye toward determining its accuracy, all sorts of things may strike us as wrong in one way or another.

From the mechanics of book manufacturing to the subtleties of rhetoric and intricacies of subordination, faults often abound. Sheets get gathered out of sequence, inadequate inking or uneven plates cause portions of pages to disappear; even if the work is complete and coherent, we may encounter strange spellings, odd punctuation, confused references, even misstatements of basic matters of fact. All of these are errors, and all may have their interest, but some of them fall beyond the realm of textual scholarship and belong to the biographer or historian. A detailed history of every aspect of the text of *Pippa Passes* cannot determine for us whether Browning—who knew his Chaucer—truly thought that a *twat* was part of a nun's attire or whether he might have been attributing this confusion to the utterly innocent Pippa. All the record shows is that on at least eight occasions over forty-eight years Browning chose not to change the word, which can hardly be a misspelling of some other word. If this was an error from first to last, it was not a *textual* error. On the other hand, where Browning's Bishop Blougram asked for decades, "You criticize the soil? it reared this tree—" in the authoritative edition of 1888–89, *soil* is replaced by *soul*.[1] A compositor's error, surely—yet Browning passed up several chances to correct it; and despite the arboreal metaphor, "Bishop Blougram's Apology" is about the soul, not soil; and thus what initially appears to be a simple typographical mistake can become so problematic as to lose the name of error.

Of course, some kinds of textual errors—those, for instance, which the printers term "literals"—are so obvious that they defy worthwhile definition (*waht* for *what*), but in more interesting cases things are usually not so clear. Certainly, to identify an error is to point out a difference between a faulty reading and a correct one, but the correct reading may be only putative or virtual, not actual. This would be the case when an author misspells a common word in a compositional manuscript: when the juvenile Jane Austen repeatedly wrote *freind* and *freindship*, the correct spellings existed in the realm of linguistic convention, if not in Austen's lexicon, and her error does not represent a deviation on her part from a prior state of correctness. The nature of a textual error becomes less ethereal when a written work enters the process of development and comes to exist in more than one stage. A fair copy may contain errors that are readily identifiable as inaccurate transcriptions of the preceding compositional manuscript. A set of proofs will almost inevitably manifest errors that arise with the compositor and exist as deviations from his copy. These the author or printer's reader will mark for correction, and indeed even the most cautious scholar would have to admit that an erroneous reading—even one that makes sense, such as *soul* for *soil* or *human* for *humane*—is proved to be an error if the author corrected it. This most common sort of *textual error*, then, is a species of undesired variant reading: a reading that does not conform to the intentions of the person having authority over the text. Such intentions can be represented by a previously-approved iteration of the text (a manuscript or other printer's copy, a set of prior proofs, corrections on proofs, an earlier edition, etc.) or by one subsequent to the erroneous text (a list of errata, a later edition, etc.).

Since our ordinary understanding of erroneousness carries with it an implication of human agency, it would be natural to think that behind every error lies a slip, a mistake, a misunderstanding. But some kinds of variants (textual differences) that quite rightly get called errors do not necessarily arise from human actions. Pick up one copy of the fourth volume of Browning's 1888–89 *Poetical Works*, and it appears that someone has removed the word *but* from line 837 of "Bishop Blougram's Apology," creating a rhythmic, if not syntactic error. Collate four or five more examples, and you may see how *but* disappeared piece by piece as the stereo plate of page 271 disintegrated.

Textual errors are not always confined to the level of the individual word or punctuation mark; if a sentence or a paragraph has been marked by the author for deletion, but reappears in the next iteration of the text, the passage's continued presence is a textual error. (To decide to remove it was probably an act of revision, as discussed below.) The well-known reversal of chapters 28 and 29 of James's *The Ambassadors* was an enormous but straightforward textual error, irrespective of any aesthetic or critical consequences. What the offending words or passages actually say is largely unimportant to this definition of the erroneous. True textual errors inhabit a category quite separate from an author's mistake in wording or error of fact, such as writing "Cortez" when you mean "Balboa," or believing that Cortez was the first European to see the Pacific.

CORRECTIONS

From this narrowed concept of error, we may draw more than one definition of *correction*. At the simplest functional level, a correction is a variant that consists of a restoration, replacing an erroneous reading with the approved prior reading from which the error deviated. When a printer's reader or an author makes a set of proofs conform to copy, he or she performs this sort of routine correction. Seemingly little more than this is involved in a second kind of correction, that which occurs when a printer's reader or an editor makes a text conform to the basic elements of common spelling and usage; but difficulties and uncertainties can arise as the functional slides toward the conceptual. An apparent error may actually have some artistic purpose. For example, it seems obvious that the spelling in Austen's "Love and Freindship," should be corrected. Yet one might also argue that such changes could be counter to the author's possible intention: what better way to represent the hilarious silliness of the inexperienced young lovers who are the butt of the story's comedy than by suggesting that they can hardly understand what they cannot even spell.★

Out of such possibilities grew the compositor's maxim "Follow your copy," and it is tempting to limit the term *correction* to those variant readings which witness an effort to make a text conform to its approved immediate predecessor. However, since it is a primary characteristic of language that it must make literal sense before it can become ironic or figurative, we may still rightly describe many of an author's insertions, deletions, and substitutions as corrections. To replace the period in "When did you leave." with a question mark is to correct; so is to insert *his* after *tried* in "After he tried grey suit on," or to cancel *on* in "He later went on into the house." But when a change does more than restore the preceding approved reading, or involves more than the basic rules of grammar or the requirements of simple idioms, it goes beyond correction and verges into revision.

Revisions

If many a publisher has trumpeted a somewhat corrected impression as a "thoroughly revised edition," so too has many an author characterized a detailed revision as "minor corrections of the press." The publisher's motive is to persuade the buyer that the book is something new and improved; the author aims to assure the publisher that the book will not have to be redesigned, or perhaps hopes to avoid paying for the alter-

---

★To the detriment of this ingenious proposition, Austen frequently spelled the word *freind* in letters and in other circumstances where no potential irony is likely. But within the text of this one juvenile work, the seeming error can readily be taken as deliberate. Authors from Plato to Joyce have employed deliberate errors, but often at their peril. Thousands of readers have ignored the dramatic framework of Browning's "The Bishop Orders His Tomb at St. Praxed's Church" and pointed out the poet's supposed blunder in line 95, "Saint Praxed at his sermon on the mount." George Eliot once received from an assiduous and admiring reader, William MacIlwaine, a list of the errors he found in *The Spanish Gypsy*; Eliot gently replied to MacIlwaine: "Some of the passages marked by Mr MacIlwaine for revision were deliberately-chosen irregularities" (Browning, *Complete Works*, 4:192; Eliot, *Letters*, 4:463).

ations. The printer traditionally bore the cost of "corrections"—changes made to conform to copy—while the author or publisher paid for any other insertions, deletions, or substitutions. While modern textual experts can hardly accept a distinction between correction and revision based on who pays the bill, another kind of quantitative notion still prevails. A revision, as usually imagined, comprises a significant number of variant readings between two texts, not just a few; furthermore, revision involves something fairly substantial, and correction by restoration would not qualify. Most scholars would probably agree, however, that a large number of corrections—particularly of the kind described at the end of the preceding section—eventually add up to a revision. Enough revisions and you might find yourself with a new version of a work.

The advantage of these notions is that they allow certain kinds of intellectual problems to be solved by counting, but clearly an arithmetical grasp of the evidence of textual change is only the merest beginning for a valid approach to revision. A purely quantitative approach fails to take adequate recognition of three highly important aspects of revision: the possible sources of a textual change, the nature of the change, and the intention behind it.

Of all the sources and agents of change to a text—author, copyist, compositor, reader, editor, publisher, printing machine, stereotype process, plate damage or decay—only an author can truly revise. This does not mean that readings which *look* like revisions always come from or through the author of a text. I have before me a volume of Browning's 1888–89 *Poetical Works* in which lines 60–61 of "Fra Lippo Lippi" read (in part): "And a face that looked up . . zooks, sir, flesh and blood. / That's all I'm made of!" Collations show that in every typesetting supervised by Browning, including this last one, *blood* was followed by a comma; the period was created when the tail of the comma loosened from the stereo plate, curled around, and ultimately disappeared. This textual change, created entirely by the mechanical processes of printing, would surely have the standing of a revision (rather than an error) if its origin were not known. The change from comma to full stop makes a distinct change in the syntactical coordination and the rhetoric of the lines, thus qualifying as a revision in substance.

Other persons may suggest revisions, and mechanical processes and technological faults may prompt them by creating new opportunities for alteration, but a textual variant earns status as a genuine revision by virtue of a particularly authorial activity. Other agents of change may correct, rearrange, censor, corrupt, or mutilate, but authors alone can create or sanction a revision. To select but one of the hundreds of examples of the composite nature of some revision, consider George Eliot's response to her publisher's evaluation of one of her poems. She sent the manuscript of "How Lisa Loved the King" to Blackwood in February of 1869, characterizing the draft as "*absolutely* unrevised"; Blackwood apparently had it set in type immediately and sent her a proof bearing his suggestions for alterations. She wrote on 19 February: "I do not return the proof as you requested; though I have read it and made every correction that I see my way to now, except those lines about which you are doubtful and which I will reconsider." A few days later she announced: "I have made various verbal corrections of importance, and have rewritten the passage you had marked." However closely Eliot did or did not follow Blackwood's suggestions, the changes she made for the succeeding printed text were, in my view, her own revisions.[2]

I have already used the phrase "correction by restoration" for the act of replacing an erroneous reading with a reading from an immediately prior approved text (such as printer's copy or marked proofs). Another kind of restoration, involving more than two iterations of a text, constitutes a fairly common kind of revision, likely to be encountered in authors who superintended numerous editions of their works. The pattern can be easily illustrated by the following imaginary variants:

1. Printer's copy MS in author's hand:
   Since thou didst hold thy father in thy heart,
2. Author's proof of first edition, printed reading:
   Since thou didst hold thy fahter in thy heart,
3. Author's MS alterations on proof:
   If thou didst ever thy dear father love—
4. Revised proof of first edition, printed reading:
   If thou didst ever thy dear father in love—
5. Author's MS alteration to revises:
   If thou didst ever held thy father dear:
6. First edition:
   If thou didst ever hold thy father dear:
7. Collected edition, set from copy of first edition as revised by author:
   If thou didst ever thy dear father love—

Variant 7, the author's final version of the line, is identical to variant 3; what the author performed in preparing the collected edition was a restoration, even though variant 3 was not previously published. Having revised reading 2 into 3, the author discovered a new error in 4; on the occasion of correcting this, the author tried out a further revision, which was faithfully reproduced in the first edition as published. A literal error in variant 2 is corrected in 3, and someone has corrected the verb tense between 5 and 6.

Few would disagree that variant 3 represents a significant authorial revision of a preexisting text. But what kind of difference between the two underlies our recognition of revision? The substitution of one or more words for others cannot be the key, since such an act may constitute no more than a correction. A new line added to a passage or five lines marked by the author for deletion certainly must be revisions, but even tiny changes may have substantial weight. In the instance from "Bishop Blougram's Apology" cited in chapter 7,[3] Browning's alteration of line 267 from "That's the first cabin-comfort I secure—" to "That's the first-cabin comfort I secure:" in 1865 accomplishes with the movement of a mere hyphen a shift from one scale of value (acquiring something immediately) to another (acquiring something of the highest quality). We might say that this is a revision because it seems to involves a change of meaning, but the very term *meaning* is too broad and controvertible to be of much use. Besides, is there any genuine difference in meaning consequent on this change? Blougram is still characterized as greedy for his comforts, despite the emphasis on taste in the revised version. To revert to the earlier fabricated example, the alteration from "Since" to "If" in variant 3 represents a falling-off from confident presumption to uncertain hope, yet our essential understanding of the line is not deeply affected.

I believe that what we recognize as different, as revised, is not just words or punctuation, and not some generalized thing called "meaning"; it is the rhetoric of the passage. The nature of revision is that it changes the expression of an idea, not the idea itself. A revision, no matter how small, always involves a rhetorical shift, not a shift in underlying conception. Since only an author can claim a full grasp of the ideas and conceptions behind his or her work, only an author can *revise*, changing expression without betraying his or her broader intention.

A particular kind of authorial intention manifests itself in revision, one that goes beyond striving to conform an iteration of a text to an existing standard (i.e., correcting) but does not aim at making a new iteration say something quite different from its predecessors. Thackeray's revisions of *Vanity Fair* in 1848 and 1853 offer a clear example of how an author can make numerous changes throughout a text with no intention of changing a work into something other than what it had been. Thackeray made the novel more fully expressive, a more complete manifestation of his conception, without altering the novel's direction, tone, or balance.[4] On a similar scale, the thousands of changes Browning made over the years to *The Ring and the Book* constituted an elaborate, careful finishing and polishing of the poem as it was, a vast and extended process of revision.

REVISIONS AND VERSIONS

Whitman's changes to *Song of Myself,* James's reworkings for the New York Edition of his works, and Wordsworth's modifications to *The Prelude* represent something more than finishing or completing a text. The authorial process of revision has in these cases given way to wholesale rewriting. Such works come to exist in two or more versions containing numerous variant readings, but the crucial degree of difference between one version and another does not result solely from numerous corrections and revisions. A new version is the work of an author who has changed his or her intentions toward the work. When an author's view of a work's statements, ideas, structures, and themes has shifted significantly, and this author sets out to alter the text of that work in accordance with the shift, what occurs will be not so much revision as re-creation. The re-created text is intended by the author not to improve the existing work as it has been but to replace it with a version which has been altered in an essential way.

Authors usually create substitute versions in the belief that they are offering the public a better product, or are being truer to their own talents. If pressed, most authors would assert a proprietary control over their works which entitles them to rewrite however they like, though few would offer a completely different work under the old title. The balance of old and new in the case of James's multiple versions has been neatly described by Robert Bamberg: "Although there is only one novel by Henry James called *The Portrait of a Lady*, we have what amounts to two separate 'Portraits.' The first appeared in 1880–81, and the other, with extensive retouching, was unveiled over a quarter century later in 1908."[5] Ultimately, one must conclude that to denominate a text as a new version, rather than a revision, of another involves an informed critical judgment, not just counting or calculating percentages.

AUTHORIAL CONTROL OF TEXTUAL CHANGES

Textual scholars struggle to detect precise distinctions between correction and revision or revision and re-creation, but authors seem to recognize the differences instinctively, despite the occasional inexactitude of their terms.

When trying in 1847 to convince Moxon to put out a collected edition of his earlier works, Browning wanted to claim the right to revise without alarming the publisher with the possibility of major changes: "But the point which decided me to wish to get printed over again was the real good I thought I could do to *Paracelsus*, *Pippa*, and some others; good, not obtained by cutting them up and reconstructing them, but by affording just the proper revision they ought to have had before they were printed at all. This, and no more, I fancy, is due to them."[6]

Many years later, when preparing the collected edition of 1888–89, Browning sent his printers a set of proofs on which the poet had extensively revised his first published poem. The sheer number of changes must have made it appear that Browning wanted to print a new *Pauline* in place of the old embarrassing one, but the poet insisted—correctly, in my view—that he had not in fact created a new version of the work. His letter to his publisher, which defensively employs the word *correcting* for what was in anyone's definition a concentrated revising, reveals Browning's sense of the outer limit of revision and his presumption of textual control:

> *My dear Smith,—When I received the Proofs of the 1st. vol. [in which Pauline was to appear] on Friday evening, I made sure of returning them next day—so accurately are they printed. But on looking at that unlucky Pauline, which I have not touched for half a century, a sudden impulse came over me to take the opportunity of just correcting the most obvious faults of expression, versification and construction,—letting the thoughts—such as they are—remain exactly as at first: I have only treated the imperfect expression of these just as I have now and then done for an amateur friend, if he asked me and I liked him enough to do so. Not a line is displaced, none added, none taken away. I have just sent it to the printer's with an explanatory word: and told him that he will have less trouble with all the rest of the volumes put together than with this little portion.*[7]

This letter and the record of Browning's revisions to *Pauline* make explicit the hierarchy of levels of thought and expression on which this discussion has depended.[8] To a considerable extent, the distinctions between various levels are based on the degree to which a competent user of language consciously attends to them. Thus the basic features of written language, such as grammatical necessities, spelling, and capitalization, are automatically observed by a competent writer unless his or her aim is to be deliberately unconventional. Punctuation, particularly if it is complex and unorthodox, is often more consciously selected. Above this is the level of rhetoric, which includes diction, rhythm, and sound as well as sentence length and structure, patterns of coordination and subordination, and figurative language. At the highest level of conscious direction stands what Browning calls "thoughts," that which the author wants us to grasp more than anything else: the cluster of ideas, statements, judgments, and structures we call meaning. All the lower levels serve to forward the writer's aim to get something across, to stimulate and then control the reader's emotions and thoughts.

No author can completely control a reader's associations and interpretations, but the most effective means of trying is to control the printed text that reader encounters. Controlling the fundamental, compulsory elements of written language often involves the correction of textual errors, though when artfully used, these basic features may become part of rhetoric, and changes to them then become revisions. Clearing up a minor confusion at the rhetorical level—by rearranging word order, for example—may be called correction, but most changes in rhetoric must be seen as revisions, because they result from the author's conscious attention and intention. Deeply considered revision, of a kind which manifests a substantial change in what a work has to say, usually attends the re-creation of a work into a new version; the substitution of a new version for an older one testifies most powerfully to an author's control of a text.

Three Views of Textual Change

I would hope that by now it is abundantly clear that nineteenth-century printing technology shaped texts, and that it did this in two fundamental ways. First, technology dictated the processes by which texts were transmitted and books were made, and had the potential to alter, create, and destroy readings by itself. Second, the ingenious employment of this technology by printers and publishers multiplied the number of occasions on which textual changes—errors, corrections, and revisions—could occur. The corresponding increase in documents at every stage of a text's history often provides ample evidence of a Victorian author's efforts to alter and control how a work read. With careful research and great labor, the scholar of texts can determine which documents and iterations of a work must be scrutinized (all of those, surely, over which the author exercised any degree of control). Collation will then yield a list of all textual variants, and from these variants the scholar must decipher a pattern of textual change and detect within it the best evidence of authorial intention.

All textual critics, no matter what their theoretical stances and axioms, are committed to the effort to identify and recover authors' intentions, variable though they may be, toward their texts. But rueful experience teaches us that intentions, whether of authors or scholars, are neither uniform, nor consistent, nor particularly stable. Intentions may be uncon-scious or conscious; impulsive or considered; fleeting or fixed; initial, interim, or final. The tasks of textual criticism include deciding what kinds of intention must be taken most seriously, determining which iterations of a text best represent a work as the author intended it to read, and attaining a grasp of what the history of a work's text signifies. As twenty years and more of intense scholarly discussion has shown, these are anything but settled questions.*

INITIAL INTENTIONS

The best-known mode of textual criticism goes by several names: the "Greg-Bowers" school, from the names of two of its founders; the "Anglo-American" school, so called because both basic theoretical work and landmark applications were done in England and America around the middle of the twentieth century; and the "first-edition" school, reflecting the emphasis these critics put on the early stages of a text's history. Critics in this camp confer the highest textual authority on the manuscript or, if a complete manuscript is lacking, to the first edition of a work. They locate the apex of authorial control in these early stages of a text's history and see later phases as occasions for the intrusion of unauthorized readings and textual corruptions. The success of this approach to scholarly editing, especially for literary works from the sixteenth through eighteenth cen-turies, is widely acknowledged; its rationales and methods are succinctly described by Philip Gaskell in his *New Introduction to Bibliography*. Schol-arly editors working on these principles have cleared great literary works of gross inaccuracies and restored unauthorized cuts.

Textual critics of this school aim to recover an author's initial inten-tions about a text, which they grant privileged status because it stands closest in time to the creation of the work. The Anglo-American school developed as a means to establish texts for the great works of the English literary Renaissance, a period during which an author typically exercised

---

*For a fascinating overview and discussion of various concepts of authorial intention, see G. Thomas Tanselle's essay in *Studies in Bibliography* and the first two chapters of Hershel Parker's recent book, both cited in the Bibliography. Since I have neither the desire nor the ability to undertake here a comprehensive review of the intensely argued positions of the contending schools of textual criticism of recent decades, I will forgo any attempt to integrate this chapter's generalizations into current textual theory. Anyone likely to read this work has his or her own views, and scarcely needs to be told of the important work of dozens of critics, theoreticians, editors, and other textual scholars. I hope to sketch just enough about textual criticism to establish a background against which the critical effects of the nineteenth-century revolution in printing technology may stand out.

very limited control over a text once the manuscript was handed in. Under such circumstances, authorial intention often will be best represented by the earliest text, on the grounds that it will bear the smallest number of nonauthorial readings (though this may still be quite substantial). Of course the earliest text may not derive directly from any authorial document, and some later text may better reflect what the author intended, as in the case of the first and second quartos of *Hamlet*. This famous example alone points up one problem inherent in any view of textual authority that depends exclusively on chronology.

As printing technology, the book trade, and the nature of authorship all changed during the ensuing centuries, authors increased their command over their printed works. By the nineteenth century, as we have seen, authorial control often increased over a writer's career, so that the history of a text is one of increasing accuracy, not spreading corruption. Leading scholars trained in the Greg-Bowers school have been reluctant to alter their theoretical framework to incorporate these historical changes. Even when dealing with nineteenth-century texts that were carefully revised by their authors for later editions, some textual critics strongly assert the primacy of the manuscript or first edition. They take a view of textual development which rests, I think, on the romantic concept of inspiration, in which it is posited that the unconscious (or preconscious) artistic impulse can never be adequately realized in words. The image of the inspired artist, feverishly working to grasp the fragments of a vision before it fades, has been very powerful indeed in recent centuries. If art begins in transcendent visions, if a work of art is whole and radiant only as a dream, inspiration, or other phenomenon of the mental realm, then no text can truly represent what the artist originally intended. With this premise, we will come closest to the original artistic intention by hewing to the earliest complete manuscript or printed text; earlier is always better, whether we are considering revisions of unknown origin or a genuine authorial second version. An extreme version of this theory, proposed by a few scholars, sees *all* revision—by anyone, including the author—as corruption, a falling away from the pristine original.

FINAL INTENTIONS

The rival position seeks to recover an author's final intentions about a text, not the original inspiration. Textual critics of this school, which has no agreed-upon name, elevate to the position of greatest importance, not the first edition of a work, but the last edition seen through the press by the author. To these scholars, an author's revisions, especially when spread over many years and editions, are part of a creative process which ends

only with the author's death. They grant privileged standing to the revising author, who becomes a specially qualified editor in a lifelong attempt
to bulwark a text against agencies of corruption.

Taking their cue from Tennyson, Browning, George Eliot, and other
Victorian authors who prepared their own collected editions, a few modern textual critics and editors have applied this approach to nineteenth-century authors. A very late or even final edition is taken as the copy-text to be
followed, and earlier editions provide variant readings, which inevitably
contain numerous compositorial errors and other nonauthorial material.
But where the adherent of Greg–Bowers sees corruption, the "final intention" critic sees development—perhaps even, to misapply an Arnoldian
tag only slightly, "the pursuit of perfection." (Certainly Arnold himself
saw his meticulous revisions to the many editions of his poems in these
terms.) To trace this development, however, this critic must pay close
attention to many documents which the Greg–Bowers critic would see as
secondary in importance. The proliferation of evidence about nineteenth-
century authors, printers, and publishers almost guarantees that the modern scholar will find that a text exists in a substantial number of incremental
stages. The exact sequential order, as well as the textual significance, of
intermediate proofs and editions may be anything but obvious.

This kind of textual critic needs more than the basic notion that a
succession of revised editions constitutes a developing text, rather than a
disintegrating one. The choice of a late copy-text must repose on historical
and biographical evidence about the habits of the author under study and
on an informed judgment about how fully this author sought and achieved
textual control. The scholar who enshrines an author's final intentions
must have confidence that the process preserved in the particular textual
history represents an accumulation of authorial revisions and a diminution
of textual errors. That is, it should be demonstrable that the author's desire
and ability to control the text of a work increased through the series of
editions that culminates in a final edition. Indications of an author's desire
to control a text are often plentiful; many writers have fulminated against
publishers' or printers' alterations to even the most minute aspects of their
works, and many a writer has averred that every particular in a set of
proofs has been attended to.* But such claims and desires are not neces-

---

*Equally, some authors have been—or were said by others to have been, or have themselves
claimed to be—indifferent to their writings once the manuscripts had left their hands.
Despite the careful proofreading she always did, George Eliot once denied any interest in
revision: "I could no more live through one of my books a second time than I can live through
last year again" (*Letters*, 4:396).

sarily commensurate with ability, and a high degree of both is required for a textual process to be rightly described as driving out, rather than accumulating, textual errors and nonauthorial readings. Certainly the technological advances of nineteenth-century printing increased the author's chances of doing just that, if the author was willing to work assiduously and swiftly. In turn, as technology gave authors opportunities to revise repeatedly through multiple stages of proof, and to make still further revisions in later impressions, their desire to do so may have increased.

Maximum Authorial Control

Experience and vigorous scholarly argument have shown that neither of these approaches is satisfactory for all authors. Each carries within it propositions about the nature of artistic creation, the manifestation of authorial intention, and the processes of book production which cannot fit every case. Indeed, some of these propositions are subject to shifts in literary taste, as seen in the recent changes in attitude toward the "bad" quartos of Shakespeare. Scholars have not arrived at, and may never agree upon, a single critical system that will give adequate status and proper importance to an author's initial artistic intentions, while recognizing and respecting that author's developing textual intentions and proprietary right to revise unto death.

Nevertheless, I want to propose a third view, one that takes into account the effects of changing printing technology and the expanded body of evidence that are encountered with nineteenth-century works and authors. This proposal sanctifies neither original intention nor final intention and does not dictate a uniform choice of preferred text. The Greg-Bowers approach, it seems to me, often depends too much on chronology and on a belief in inspiration. It also tends to elevate the textual critic's judgment over the author's in matters of revision, and I am never completely at ease with the notion that an accomplished, talented author didn't know what he or she was doing in this case or that. On the other hand, the critical scheme seeking and emphasizing final intention depends just as heavily on chronology and on a belief in textual progress, and consequently may overvalue revisions that any sensitive reader will see as tantamount to distortions. We should not grant privileged standing to one stage of a text solely because it is the first or the last in a historical sequence, because history alone does not govern the expression of intention.

The fullest, most important, most valuable expression of authorial intention toward the text of a work occurs—if indeed it occurs on a single occasion at all—when: (1) the author is working at maximum concentration on the accurate preparation of a written or printed text; (2) the author is most interested in and capable of governing the presentational features of the work, such as spelling, punctuation, chapter arrangement and length, stanza indentation, and so on; (3) the author is most free from external compulsion or limitation as to how the work will read; (4) the author is bent on perfecting and finishing the work at hand, not on changing it into another work; (5) the author has the maximum control over the outcome of the labor, the text which will be produced. An alert and imaginative scholar, given sufficient surviving documents, diligent research, and sound bibliographical knowledge, will be able to see these conditions when they obtain. In most cases, this full and intense effort will be signaled by numerous textual variants.

A given iteration of a text may well meet some of these criteria and not others; most manuscripts, for instance, rate high in terms of authorial freedom, but proofs and revises will be worked over before the first printed edition is produced. An intermediate revised edition may represent an author's most concentrated review of a particular work as a whole, but the degree of alteration possible may have been constrained by printing and publishing limitations. At the time of a final collected edition, an author may have absolute command over what the works will say, but lack the stamina for an exhaustive revision. The situation will vary from author to author and from age to age, but the object of the scholar's labors does not vary. The textual critic seeks that text which most fully embodies the author's best, most complete, most successful effort to get the work right, even if that effort occurred years after the work was created; even if the author's taste and judgment differ from ours; even when the author revised further (if less successfully) in later editions.

To a scholar working on these lines, all iterations of a text on which an author worked are of primary interest, and any one of them may emerge as the representation of the author's maximum concentration and control. This approach properly respects an author's proprietary rights over a text, while not necessarily taking all authorial revisions as improvements. Instead of beginning with a model of textual change as disintegrative corruption or evolutionary progress, this last view emphasizes the recoverable and inferential history of the individual text and author; it does not employ an a priori notion about which text ought to be superior. Perhaps, since textual criticism depends on textual history, we should accept gracefully some of the axioms and limitations of the historian, and dispense with this kind of judgment. No competent historian is likely to argue seriously that the events of one year or decade are superior to another, or that one era is preferable to an earlier one; such terms are practically nonsensical.

In the study of the arts, of course, we make a little more room for pleasure, taste, and systematic aesthetic judgment. An art historian might find the finished version of Turner's *Rain, Steam, and Speed* indeed superior to the sketches that preceded it, and by this would mean not so much that the sketches were faulty but that the finished painting manifests the artist's most concentrated attempt to get the thing right, to control every brush stroke and swipe of the knife, to leave nothing undone that lay within his power to execute his idea. Turner "published," as it were, his finished painting in 1844; he did not publish his sketches, interesting though they might be. I think that multiple, revised texts of a literary work can be sorted out on such bases as these. Presented with the whole intricate textual history of a work and all its revisions and alterations, we can, with diligent enough research, answer the essential questions: Which texts did the author publish? Which of these did the author concentrate on the most? Which one did the author control most completely? Was the author attentive and meticulous at the time? Was the author revising freely, without compulsion or limitation? Was the aim to finish and perfect the work, not to turn it into another work? We can find that text which most fully embodies the author's best and most successful effort to make the work come out right, and that text we can fairly declare superior. But it may be neither the earliest text nor the final one, and it may not always be the one endorsing "the sense most to our mind," in Browning's phrase.

Because nineteenth-century printing technology multiplied the stages of textual development and expanded opportunities for authorial control, it also increased the burdens of the modern textual scholar. The longer the history of a work's text, and the more successful the career of its author, the more editions and documents there are to be collated and sifted for variants. Concealed impressions are the rule with stereotyped editions, and any impression may contain important authorial changes to the text. Careful scholars have long taken each individual impression (whether acknowledged or concealed) as a discrete stage in the history of a typesetting. Within an impression an editor must be alert for stop-press corrections, but it has been a conventional belief that the rest of the text remained fixed. This assumption, or hope, has been clung to with quiet fervor by past authors and publishers, as well as the scholars who study them. In light of what we know about printing techniques in the age of mechanized typefounding, stereotype plating, and machine printing, this belief must be abandoned. Every time the bed of a printing machine passes under the cylinders, an opportunity for textual alteration occurs: letters and words disappear; punctuation transforms itself; in consequence, grammar, rhetoric, and meaning can be changed. With luck, the Victorian pressman saw the edge of a plate collapse, stopped his machine, and called for a replacement to be cast from the matrix. The next sheet printed off will offer the scholar a text in which the pages printed from the fresh plates revert to the level of press proof and reflect closely what the author approved, while others have decayed away from the intended readings.

Fortunately, twentieth-century technology offers powerful means of dealing with the multiplicity of documents and the subtlety of textual changes. The Hinman and Lindstrand collating machines use simple principles of optical comparison to highlight any differences between one exemplar of a typesetting and another; these devices have assisted in proving the use of stereotype plates, detecting concealed impressions from them, and tracking decay and repair of the plates. The combination of optical character recognition systems ("reading machines") with moderately powerful computers has made possible the electronic collation of different typesettings, the output being a highly reliable list of variants culled from multiple editions.

The late twentieth century is proving to be a great age of preservation and restoration in Europe and North America, as a visit to any major city shows. People everywhere strive to preserve old buildings; no sizable art museum is without its conservation expert; the market in antiques expands yearly; the Sistine chapel is renovated; millions of public dollars are spent to stop the disintegration of our library collections, rendered fragile by Victorian papermaking practices. Textual scholarship, with its roots reaching back to the Fathers of the Christian church, is one of the oldest and noblest forms of preservation and restoration, and like its kindred enterprises of later date, it has turned to technology to accomplish its task. As with the crumbling of nineteenth-century paper, modern technology can provide a solution only when we understand the previous technology that caused the problem. Our optical scanners and computers will enable us to restore and preserve nineteenth-century texts when we have come to a thorough understanding of how the technology that reproduced them also shaped them.

Notes

Bibliography

Index

Notes

Introduction

1. Gaskell, *New Introduction*, 289–96.
2. Trollope, *Autobiography*, 127.

I. Composition

1. Hansard, *Typographia*, 745.
2. Timperley, *Manual*, 4.
3. Beadnell, *Guide*, 1:242.
4. Saunders, *Assistant*, 21–22.
5. Bull, *Hints*, 11.
6. Eliot, *Letters*, 3:462; see also 2:480, 3:250–51, 5:185.
7. Browning, *Dearest Isa*, 134, 142; idem, *Letters*, 180. The composition and history of the manuscript are treated at length in Browning, *Complete Works*, 7:261–62.
8. Hagen, *Tennyson and His Publishers*, 83.
9. Hardy, *Letters*, 1:48, 1:46; see also the articles by Kramer, Weber, and Winfield listed in the Bibliography.
10. Hansard, *Typographia*, 741–42.
11. Timperley, *Manual*, 4; Savage, *Dictionary*, 672; Bull, *Hints*, 20.
12. Arnold to J. W. Parker, 20 Mar. 1855. Letters of Arnold which are cited only by date are quoted from Cecil Y. Lang's forthcoming edition of the Arnold letters.
13. Beadnell, *Guide*, 1:242. The range of nineteenth-century printers' views is surveyed by John Bush Jones in a 1977 article in *PBSA*, cited in the Bibliography.
14. Gould, *Letter-Press Printer*, 22; Nowell-Smith, *Letters to Macmillan*, 62.
15. Buckler, *Arnold's Books*, 113; Arnold to J. T. Knowles, 14 Sept. 1874.
16. Russell, *Literary Manual*, 64–65; *Comprehensive Guide*, 16–17.
17. Gaskell, *New Introduction*, 191–94.
18. Dickens, *Bleak House*, 805.
19. Southward, *Practical Printing*, 148.
20. Gaskell, *New Introduction*, 163, 207–8.
21. Bull, *Hints*, 17.
22. Saunders, *Assistant*, 4n.
23. Eliot, *Letters* 4:265; Saunders, *Assistant*, 5n.
24. Austen-Leigh, *Story of a Printing House*, 37; Bull, *Hints*, 50; Saunders, *Assistant*, 5n.
25. Eliot, *Letters* 2:361, 386, 394, 3:258–59.
26. Hardy, *Letters* 1:49–57; F. E. Hardy, *Early Life*, 154.
27. Arnold, *Poetical Works*, v.
28. Eliot, *Letters* 3:250, 4:405, 5:326.
29. *Comprehensive Guide*, 18.
30. Gaskell, *New Introduction*, 207–8; Eliot, *Letters* 2:506n., 507.
31. Charles Tennyson, *Tennyson*, 241; Hagen, *Tennyson and His Publishers*, 30–36; Tennyson, *Letters*, 1:80–81, 84 and n.

32. Eliot, *Letters* 4:396, 406, 445; see additional discussion in chapter 2.
33. Buckler, *Arnold's Books*, 123–24.

II. Proofing

1. Stevenson, *Victorian Fiction*, 158; T. H., *Perils*, 15; Clowes, *Family Business*, 53; Newman, *Author's Guide*, 15.
2. This description combines information from Beadnell, *Guide*, 2:234, Fisher, *Letterpress Printing*, 334, and Hansard, *Typographia*, 412–13.
3. Beadnell, *Guide*, 2:234.
4. Timperley, *Encyclopaedia*, 103; Dodd, *Factories*, 333; Noble, *Machine Printing*, 1.
5. Dodd, *Factories*, 341.
6. Bull, *Hints*, 17; Southward, *Dictionary*, 110.
7. *Comprehensive Guide*, 18; Neill & Co., *Guide*, 8.
8. *Comprehensive Guide*, 18; Southward, *Practical Printing*, 153.
9. Saunders, *Assistant*, 3.
10. Southward, *Practical Printing*, 153; idem, *Dictionary*, 109.
11. Southward, *Practical Printing*, 154.
12. Southward, *Dictionary*, s.v. "Galley"; Gaskell, *New Introduction*, 195; Hargreaves, "Correcting in the Slip," 305–10; Beadnell, *Guide*, 2:234.
13. The two kinds of galley presses are described and illustrated in Hargreaves, "Correcting in the Slip," 300–301.
14. Southward, *Dictionary*, 42.
15. Southward, *Practical Printing*, 154–55; Hargreaves, "Correcting in the Slip," 302.
16. Southward, *Practical Printing*, 154.
17. Southward, *Dictionary*, 40, 129; Dodd, *Factories*, 343; Southward, *Practical Printing*, 560.
18. Hansard, *Typographia*, 746.
19. Ibid., 747.
20. Timperley, *Manual*, 53.
21. Hansard, *Typographia*, 753.
22. Saunders, *Assistant*, 34.
23. Bull, *Hints*, 45.
24. Ibid., 23.
25. Saunders, *Assistant*, 29.
26. Eliot, *Letters*, 2:296–97; Arnold to Smith, 12 Jan. 1866.
27. Eliot, *Letters*, 3:253–59, 265; Tennyson, *Letters*, 1:84n.; Buckler, *Arnold's Books*, 33; Arnold to Macmillan, 23 July 1867; Nowell-Smith, *Letters to Macmillan*, 96.
28. Eliot, *Letters*, 2:499–509 and nn.
29. Buckler, *Arnold's Books*, 42.
30. Hansard, *Typographia*, 413, 752–53; idem, *Art*, 94; Saunders, *Assistant*, 3.
31. *Comprehensive Guide*, 18; Neill & Co., *Guide*, 8; Southward, *Dictionary*, 109; idem, *Authorship and Publication*, 29; idem, *Practical Printing*, 153.
32. Eliot, *Letters*, 3:390; idem, *Mill on the Floss*, 236, 17; idem, *Letters*, 4:422.
33. For a discussion of the composition and proofing of *Vanity Fair*, see Geoffrey and Kathleen Tillotson's introduction and appendices to their edition of the novel, and Peter Shillingsburg's two essays on the first edition, all cited in the Bibliography.
34. Dickens, *Bleak House*, 806.
35. Hagen, *Tennyson and His Publishers*, 60–61; Browning, *Letters*, 180.
36. Southward, *Authorship*, 30.
37. Tennyson, *Letters*, 1:80; Eliot, *Letters*, 2:159, 3:253; Buckler, *Arnold's Books*, 33.
38. Buckler, *Arnold's Books*, 112–13, 120.
39. Eliot, *Letters*, 7:93, 88, 93, 94.

40. Hardy, *Letters*, 2:91.
41. Ibid., 2:63, 91; Eliot, *Letters*, 7:107, 110–11.
42. Eliot, *Letters*, 4:407–8, 411, 421–22, 426, 427.
43. Southward, *Dictionary*, 110.
44. Eliot, *Letters*, 4:433, 435.
45. Ibid., 5:198–99, 224, 308–9.
46. Ibid., 3:383, 4:422; Dickens, *Bleak House*, 887: letter of 18 Mar. 1852.
47. Arnold to Mary Penrose Arnold, 5 June 1869.
48. Hagen, *Tennyson and His Publishers*, 50–51.
49. Dickens, *Bleak House*, 805.
50. Eliot, *Letters*, 4:422; Buckler, *Arnold's Books*, 123.
51. Arnold to Smith, 10 Feb. 1865; Arnold to Mary Penrose Arnold, 4 Dec. 1865 and 1 Nov. 1871; Arnold to Smith, 5 Nov. 1871; Arnold to C. E. Norton, 21 Nov. 1883. The manuscript and one of the sets of proofs of Arnold's "Emerson" are preserved in the Houghton Library at Harvard.
52. Hagen, *Tennyson and His Publishers*, 31–36; Tennyson, *Letters*, 1:80–84; Hagen, *Tennyson and His Publishers*, 61, 124–25.
53. Tennyson, *Letters*, 1:321–22.

III. Printing

1. Nowell-Smith, *Letters to Macmillan*, 63; Eliot, *Letters*, 2:361–62.
2. Of the numerous works about stereotyping and its history, Hodgson's *Stereotype Printing* (1820) and Wilson's *Stereotyping and Electrotyping* (1880) together offer a comprehensive view from within the nineteenth century.
3. Hansard's most comprehensive work was *Typographia*, which first appeared in 1825 and was republished several times thereafter. A book entitled *The Art of Printing* was published under Hansard's name by Adam and Charles Black of Edinburgh in 1851; this was years after Hansard's death, but the volume is in fact a revised, rearranged, and augmented version of *Typographia*. Whether it was Hansard himself or others who undertook the revision is unknown, but it seems acceptable to call it "Hansard's *Art of Printing*"; the book reflects in detail the state of printing technology and practice at mid-century.
4. Hansard, *Art*, 130.
5. Hansard, *Typographia*, 834; Wilson, *Stereotyping*, 48; Hansard, *Typographia*, 834–35.
6. Hansard, *Art*, 133.
7. Ibid.; Howe, *London Compositor*, 217.
8. Saunders, *Assistant*, 17.
9. T. H., *Perils*, 19; Russell, *Literary Manual*, 129.
10. Hansard, *Art*, 130; Merriam, *Moxon*, 100.
11. Spedding, *Publishers and Authors*, 51; Gaskill, *Practical Handbook*, 75.
12. Cited from Howe, *London Compositor*, 260; Beadnell, *Guide*, 2:118.
13. Hansard, *Art*, 129–30.
14. Ibid., 127–28.
15. My calculation is based on the estimates given in Wilson, *Stereotyping*, 83; the figures are confirmed in Smart, "Electrotyping and Stereotyping," ix.
16. Smart, "Electrotyping and Stereotyping," 32; a full description of the techniques and difficulties of altering plates is found in Wilson, *Stereotyping*, chapters 12 and 13.
17. Gaskell, *New Introduction*, 203; Wilson, *Stereotyping*, 20; Beadnell, *Guide*, 2:118.
18. Southward, *Progress in Printing*, 67–68 (drawing on Wilson, *Stereotyping*, 21); ibid., 26; Hodgson, *Stereotype Printing*.
19. Southward, *Dictionary*, 129.

20. Eliot, *Letters*, 2:393, 399.
21. Buckler, *Arnold's Books*, 130.
22. Southward, *Practical Printing*, 561.
23. Wilson and Grey, *Modern Printing Machinery*, 276–78, 283; Howe, *London Compositor*, 260; Southward, *Practical Printing*, 495.
24. Noble, *Machine Printing*, 10–17; Wilson and Grey, *Modern Printing Machinery*, 281–89.
25. Savage, *Dictionary*, 783.
26. Hansard, *Typographia*, 835, 868.
27. Dodd, *Factories*, 358.
28. Russell, *Literary Manual*, 128.
29. Hansard, *Typographia*, 834; idem, *Art*, 133.
30. Buckler, *Arnold's Books*, 139–40.
31. The printing of this edition is discussed at length in Dooley, "Browning's *Poetical Works* of 1888–89."
32. Russell, *Literary Manual*, 129.
33. Eliot, *Letters*, 4:320, 3:392.
34. Ibid., 5:366; see also 5:347–49.
35. Ibid., 5:439.
36. Hansard, *Art*, 130; Partridge, *Stereotyping*, 113; Russell, *Literary Manual*, 129.
37. Buckler, *Arnold's Books*, 123.
38. Arnold to Mary Penrose Arnold, 5 June 1869.
39. Gaskell, *New Introduction*, 118–41, 251–65.
40. Wilson and Grey, *Modern Printing Machinery*, 270; Gaskill, *Practical Handbook*, 11; Southward, *Printing Machinery*, 43–46.
41. Plomer, *English Printing*, 253.
42. DeVinne, *Printing in the Nineteenth Century*, 7; Eliot, *Letters*, 3:283–84; Noble, *Machine Printing*, 1.
43. Noble, *Machine Printing*, 1; Wilson and Grey, *Modern Printing Machinery*, 268–69.
44. A good synthesis is given by Noble, *Machine Printing*, chapters 1–4.
45. Saunders, *Assistant*, 5; Bull, *Hints*, 50–51; Austen-Leigh, *Story of a Printing House*, 37.
46. Eliot, *Letters*, 4:257–65.
47. Southward, *Practical Printing*, 440 ff.
48. Wilson and Grey, *Modern Printing Machinery*, 271–72.

IV. Reprinting

1. Buckler, *Arnold's Books*, 48–49, 59.
2. Eliot, *Letters*, 2:387–88.
3. I have traced the history of these editions more fully in "The Textual Significance of Robert Browning's 1865 *Poetical Works*."
4. Eliot, *Letters*, 4:495.
5. Ibid., 4:434, 460n., 479n., 498; there is a slight inconsistency in the figures about the size of the first impression.
6. Ibid., 4:497 and n.
7. Arnold to Herbert Hill, 5 Nov. 1852.
8. Dodd, *Factories*, 358–59.
9. Arnold to Longman, 29 Sept. 1853.
10. Hagen, *Tennyson and His Publishers*, 84–85, 203n.
11. Merriam, *Moxon*, 100.
12. Southward, *Practical Printing*, 560.
13. Southward, *Authorship*, 54.
14. Eliot, *Letters*, 4:73–74.
15. Buckler, *Arnold's Books*, 121.

16. Ibid., 34.
17. Sutherland, *Victorian Novelists*, 56.
18. Trollope, *Autobiography*, 307.
19. Tennyson, *Letters*, 2:52; Thackeray, *Vanity Fair*, xxiv.
20. Partridge, *Stereotyping*, 113–20.
21. Craik to Arnold, 7 and 9 Sept. 1879; Buckler, *Arnold's Books*, 143; Eliot, *Letters*, 2:388.
22. Tennyson, *Letters*, 2:1.
23. Hagen, *Tennyson and His Publishers*, 189.
24. Southward, *Authorship*, 55.
25. Hansard, *Art*, 133; Gaskill, *Practical Handbook*, 8.

V. Some Victorian Authors and Their Reprints

1. A detailed account is given in Browning, *New Letters*, Appendix C.
2. Browning, *Dearest Isa*, 286–87.
3. Meredith, "Learning's Crabbed Text," 101.
4. Ibid., 101, 102; see also Dooley, "Browning's *Poetical Works* of 1888–89."
5. Unless otherwise noted, the materials in this and the following two paragraphs derive from Buckler, *Arnold's Books*, 132–46.
6. Arnold to George Venables, 22 Sept. 1879.
7. Buckler, *Arnold's Books*, 121.
8. Arnold, *Prose Works*, 6:451–53; Arnold to Smith, 2 Mar. 1873.
9. Arnold, *Prose Works*, 6:533–81; Arnold to Smith, 15 Mar. 1873.
10. Arnold to Aitcheson, 23 Dec. 1875; Arnold, *Prose Works*, 6:453.
11. If not otherwise documented, the correspondence in this discussion of Arnold's poems is quoted from Buckler, *Arnold's Books*, 33–61.
12. Arnold to Mary Penrose Arnold, 5 June 1869.
13. Tennyson, *Letters*, 2:1.
14. Ibid., 2:52.
15. Ibid., 1:318, 320.
16. See, for instance, the catalogues bound into the first editions of *Harold* (Henry S. King, 1877) and *The Lover's Tale* (Kegan Paul, 1879).
17. Hagen, *Tennyson and His Publishers*, 112–13.
18. Ibid., 152.
19. The contract is quoted in part in chapter 4 above and is given in its entirety in Hagen, *Tennyson and His Publishers*, Appendix C.
20. Sutherland, "Fiction Earning Patterns," 84–85, 90–91.
21. Eliot, *Letters*, 4:434, 460–63, 460n.
22. Ibid., 4:474–75.
23. Ibid., 4:479 and n., 480–81, 495, 497–98; see also chapter 4 above.
24. Eliot, *Letters*, 5:347–48, 363, 386, 438.
25. Ibid., 5:365 and n. By "Lordship" is meant a royalty.
26. Ibid., 5:441.
27. Ibid., 3:462n., 7:55, 51, 58, 58n., 70, 109, 112.

VI. Documents, Technology, and Evidence

1. Hagen, *Tennyson and His Publishers*, 83; see also chapter 1 above.
2. Eliot, *Letters*, 4:404–6.
3. Brown, *Arnold's Prose Works*, 1, 87.
4. For an application of some of these dating techniques to a specific long-lived edition, see my "Browning's *Poetical Works* of 1888–89."
5. Southward, *Dictionary*, 89.

6. Wilson and Grey, *Modern Printing Machinery*, 287–89.
7. See Shillingsburg, "Register Measurement."
8. See Saunders, *Assistant*, 5, and Noble, *Machine Printing*, 8, for comments on this from 1839 and 1881.

VII. Authorial Control

1. Trollope, *Autobiography*, 127–28.
2. Ibid., 163.
3. Nowell-Smith, *Letters to Macmillan*, 67–68.
4. Eliot, *Letters*, 2:361–62, 394, 3:256 and n., 259 and n.; idem, *Mill on the Floss*, 71.
5. T. H., *Perils*, 16–18; Byron, *Works*, 1:xxxvii; T. H., *Perils*, 15.
6. Tryon and Charvat, *Ticknor and Fields*, 336–49.
7. Gittings, *Hardy's Later Years*, 79.
8. Gaskell, *New Introduction*, 342; Hardy, *Letters*, 2:63, 91; Gittings, *Hardy's Later Years*, 145; Laird, *Shaping of "Tess,"* 3.
9. Arnold to S. E. Davies, 19 Oct. 1863; Arnold, *Prose Works* 3:399–402, 520–22.
10. Buckler, *Arnold's Books*, 112–13; Arnold, *Prose Works*, 7:423 ff.
11. Nowell-Smith, *Letters to Macmillan*, 74–75.

VIII. Textual Change and Textual Criticism

1. Browning, *Complete Works*, 3:82, l. 96; 3:351; 5:315, l. 608; 5:356.
2. Eliot, *Letters*, 5:16–17.
3. Browning, *Complete Works*, 5:302.
4. See Thackeray, *Vanity Fair*, xxiii–xxvii; Shillingsburg, "Final Touches and Patches in *Vanity Fair*" and "The Printing of *Vanity Fair*."
5. James, *Portrait of a Lady*, vii.
6. Browning, *Letters*, 14.
7. Orr, *Life of Browning*, 403–4.
8. In Browning, *Complete Works*, 1:9–52.

Bibliography

Arnold, Matthew. *The Arnold Letters*. Ed. Cecil Y. Lang. Cambridge: Harvard Univ. Press, forthcoming.

———. *The Complete Prose Works of Matthew Arnold*. Ed. R. H. Super. 11 vols. Ann Arbor: Univ. of Michigan Press, 1960–77.

———. *Poetical Works*. Ed. C. B. Tinker and H. F. Lowry. London: Oxford Univ. Press, 1950.

[Austen-Leigh, Richard Arthur]. *The Story of a Printing House*. London: Spottiswoode, 1912.

Bastien, Alfred J. *Practical Typography*. London: Bastien, 1947.

Beadnell, Henry. *A Guide to Typography*. 2 vols. London: Bowring, 1859–61.

Billing and Sons. *The Foundry*. London: Billing, 1949.

Brown, E. K. *Studies in the Text of Matthew Arnold's Prose Works*. Paris: Pierre André, 1935.

Browning, Robert. *The Complete Works of Robert Browning*. Ed. Roma A. King et al. 8 vols. to date. Athens, Ohio, and Waco, Tex.: Ohio Univ. Press and Baylor Univ., 1969–.

———. *Dearest Isa: Robert Browning's Letters to Isabella Blagden*. Ed. Edward C. McAleer. Austin: Univ. of Texas Press, 1951.

———. *Letters of Robert Browning*. Ed. Thurman L. Hood. London: John Murray, 1933.

———. *New Letters of Robert Browning*. Ed. William Clyde DeVane and Kenneth Leslie Knickerbocker. New Haven: Yale Univ. Press, 1950.

Buckler, William E. "An American Edition of Matthew Arnolds's *Poems*." *PMLA* 69 (1954): 678–80.

———. *Matthew Arnold's Books: Toward a Publishing Diary*. Geneva and Paris: Droz and Minard, 1958.

Bull, Edward. *Hints and Directions for Authors*. London: Bull, 1842.

Byron, George Gordon. *Complete Poetical Works*. Ed. Jerome J. McGann. 3 vols. Oxford: Clarendon Press, 1980–81.

Clowes, William B. *Family Business, 1803–1953*. London: Clowes, [1955].

The Comprehensive Guide to Printing and Publishing. London: Collingridge, 1869.

DeVinne, Theodore Low. *Printing in the Nineteenth Century*. New York: Lead Mould Electrotype Foundry, 1924.

Dickens, Charles. *Bleak House*. Ed. George Ford and Sylvère Monod. New York: Norton, 1977.

Dodd, George. *Days at the Factories*. London: Knight, 1843.

Dooley, Allan C. "Browning's *Poetical Works* of 1888–89." *Studies in Browning and His Circle* 7 (1979): 43–69.

———. "The Textual Significance of Robert Browning's 1865 *Poetical Works*." *Papers of the Bibliographical Society of America* 71 (1977): 212–18.

Eliot, George. *The George Eliot Letters*. Ed. Gordon S. Haight. 7 vols. New Haven and London: Yale Univ. Press and Oxford Univ. Press, 1954–55.

———. *The Mill on the Floss*. Ed. Gordon S. Haight. Boston: Houghton Mifflin, 1961.

Fisher, T. *The Elements of Letterpress Printing*. Madras: Higginbotham, 1906.

Gaskell, Philip. *From Writer to Reader*. Oxford: Clarendon Press, 1978.

———. *A New Introduction to Bibliography*. New York and Oxford: Oxford Univ. Press, 1972.

Gaskill, Jackson. *The Printing-Machine Manager's Complete Practical Handbook*. London: Haddon, 1877.

Gittings, Robert. *Thomas Hardy's Later Years*. Boston: Little, Brown, 1978.

Gould, Joseph. *The Compositor's Guide and Pocket Book*. London: Farrington, 1878.

———. *The Letter-Press Printer*. London: Farrington, 1876.

Greg, W. W. "The Rationale of Copy-Text." *Studies in Bibliography* 3 (1950–51): 19–36.

H., T. *The Perils of Authorship*. London: Ingham, [c. 1840].

Hagen, June Steffensen. *Tennyson and His Publishers*. University Park and London: Pennsylvania State Univ. Press, 1979.

Hancher, Michael. "Browning and the *Poetical Works* of 1888–1889." *Browning Newsletter* 6 (1971): 25–27.

Hansard, Thomas Curson. *The Art of Printing*. Edinburgh: Black, 1851.

———. *Typographia*. London: Baldwin, Cradock, and Joy, 1825.

Hardy, Florence Emily. *The Early Life of Thomas Hardy*. New York: Macmillan, 1928.

Hardy, Thomas. *The Collected Letters of Thomas Hardy*. Ed. Richard L. Purdy and Michael Millgate. 5 vols. to date. Oxford: Clarendon Press, 1978–.

Hargreaves, Geoffrey D. " 'Correcting in the Slip': The Development of Galley Proofs." *The Library* 26 (1971): 295–311.

Hodgson, Thomas. *An Essay on the Origin and Progress of Stereotype Printing*. Newcastle: Hodgson, 1820.

Howe, Ellic, ed. *The London Compositor*. London: Bibliographical Society, 1947.

James, Henry. *The Portrait of a Lady*. Ed. Robert D. Bamberg. New York: Norton, 1975.

Jones, John Bush. "British Printers on Galley Proofs: A Chronological Reconsideration." *The Library* 31 (1976): 105–17.

———. "Victorian 'Readers' and Modern Editors: Attitudes and Accidentals Revisited." *Papers of the Bibliographical Society of America* 71 (1977): 49–59.

Kramer, Dale. "A Query concerning Handwriting in Hardy's Manuscripts." *Papers of the Bibliographical Society of America* 57 (1963): 357–60.

Laird, J. T. *The Shaping of "Tess of the d'Urbervilles."* London: Oxford Univ. Press, 1975.

McGann, Jerome J. *A Critique of Modern Textual Criticism.* Chicago: Univ. of Chicago Press, 1983.

Meredith, Michael. "Learning's Crabbed Text: A Reconsideration of the 1868 edition of Browning's *Poetical Works.*" *Studies in Browning and His Circle* 13 (1985): 97–107.

Merriam, Harold G. *Edward Moxon, Publisher of Poets.* New York: Columbia Univ. Press, 1939.

Neill & Co. *Guide to Authors.* Edinburgh: Neill, 1897.

Newman, Edward. *The Author's Guide for Printing.* London: N.p., 1876.

Noble, Frederick. *Difficulties in Machine Printing, and How to Overcome Them.* London: Printers' Register, 1883.

Nowell-Smith, Simon, ed. *Letters to Macmillan.* London: Macmillan, 1967.

Oliphant, Margaret. *Annals of a Publishing House: William Blackwood and His Sons.* 2 vols. Edinburgh: Blackwood, 1897–98.

Orr, Mrs. Alexandra [Leighton] Sutherland. *Life and Letters of Robert Browning.* 2d ed. London: Smith, Elder, 1891.

Padwick, E. W. *Bibliographical Method.* Cambridge and London: James Clarke, 1983.

Parker, Hershel. *Flawed Texts and Verbal Icons.* Evanston: Northwestern Univ. Press, 1984.

Partridge, C. S. *Stereotyping.* Chicago and New York: Inland Printer, 1909.

Plomer, Henry. *A Short History of English Printing.* New York: Empire State, 1927.

Porter, Mrs. Gerald. *Annals of a Publishing House: William Blackwood and His Sons.* Edinburgh: Blackwood, 1898.

Russell, Percy. *The Literary Manual; or, a Complete Guide to Authorship.* London: London Literary Society, 1886.

Saunders, Frederic. *The Author's Printing and Publishing Assistant.* 2d ed. London: Saunders and Otley, 1839.

Savage, William. *A Dictionary of the Art of Printing.* London: Longman, 1841.

The Search for a Publisher: or, Counsels for a Young Author. 3d ed. London: Cash, 1856.

Shillingsburg, Peter L. "Final Touches and Patches in *Vanity Fair*: The First Edition." *Studies in the Novel* 13 (1981): 40–50.

———. "The Printing, Proof-Reading, and Publishing of Thackeray's *Vanity Fair*: The First Edition." *Studies in Bibliography* 34 (1981): 118–45.

———. "Register Measurement as a Method of Detecting Hidden Printings." *Papers of the Bibliographical Society of America* 73 (1979) 484–88.

Smart, Herbert G. "Electrotyping and Stereotyping: A Record of Effort and Achievement Spread over the Generations." 1984. St. Bride Printing Library, London.

Songs of the Press and Other Poems Relative to the Art of Printing. London: Simpkin and Marshall, 1833.

Southward, John. *Authorship and Publication: A Concise Guide for Authors*. London: Wyman, 1884.

———. *A Dictionary of Typography*. London: Powell, 1875.

———. *Practical Printing*. London: Powell, 1884.

———. *The Principles and Progress of Printing Machinery*. London: Menken, 1888.

———. *Progress in Printing and the Graphic Arts during the Victorian Era*. London: Simpkin, Marshall, 1897.

Spedding, James. *Publishers and Authors*. London: Smith, 1867.

Stevenson, Lionel, ed. *Victorian Fiction: A Guide to Research*. Cambridge: Harvard Univ. Press, 1964.

Sutherland, John A. "The Fiction Earning Patterns of Thackeray, Dickens, George Eliot, and Trollope." *Browning Institute Studies* 7 (1979): 71–92.

———. *Victorian Novelists and Publishers*. Chicago: Univ. of Chicago Press, 1976.

Tanselle, G. Thomas. "The Editorial Problem of Final Authorial Intention." *Studies in Bibliography* 29 (1976): 167–211.

Tennyson, Alfred. *The Letters of Alfred Lord Tennyson*. Ed. Cecil Y. Lang and Edgar F. Shannon. 3 vols. to date. Cambridge: Belknap Press of Harvard Univ. Press, 1981–.

Tennyson, Charles. *Alfred Tennyson*. London: Macmillan, 1950.

Thackeray, William Makepeace. *Vanity Fair*. Ed. Geoffrey and Kathleen Tillotson. Boston: Houghton Mifflin, 1963.

Timperley, C. H. *Encyclopaedia of Literary and Typographical Anecdote*. London: Bohn, 1842.

———. *The Printers' Manual*. London: Johnson, 1838.

Trollope, Anthony. *An Autobiography*. London: Oxford Univ. Press, 1947.

Tryon, Warren S., and William Charvat, eds. *The Cost Books of Ticknor and Fields*. New York: Bibliographical Society of America, 1949.

Weber, Carl J. "The Manuscript of Hardy's *Two on a Tower*." *Papers of the Bibliographical Society of America* 40 (1946): 1–21.

Wilson, Frederick J. F. *Stereotyping and Electrotyping*. London: Wyman, [1880].

———, and Douglas Grey. *A Practical Treatise upon Modern Printing Machinery and Letterpress Printing*. London: Cassell, 1888.

Winfield, Christine. "The Manuscript of Hardy's *Mayor of Casterbridge*." *Papers of the Bibliographical Society of America* 67 (1973): 33–58.

Index